Heinrich Graetz

THE STRUCTURE
OF JEWISH
HISTORY

and Other Essays

Translated, edited and
introduced by
ISMAR SCHORSCH

Heinrich Graetz

THE STRUCTURE
OF JEWISH
HISTORY

and Other Essays

Volume III in the **Moreshet** Series, Studies in
Jewish History, Literature and Thought

Heinrich Graetz

THE STRUCTURE
OF JEWISH
HISTORY

and Other Essays

Translated, edited and introduced by

ISMAR SCHORSCH

THE JEWISH THEOLOGICAL SEMINARY OF AMERICA

NEW YORK, 1975

Library of Congress Cataloging in Publication Data

Graetz, Heinrich Hirsch, 1817-1891.
  The structure of Jewish history, and other essays.

  (Moreshet; v. 3)
  Translation of Die Konstruktion der jüdischen Geschichte, and other works.
  "Selected bibliography on Graetz's work": p.
  Includes index.
  CONTENTS: Schorsch, I. Ideology and history in the Age of Emancipation.—The structure of Jewish history. —Introduction to volume four of the History of the Jews. [etc.]
    1. Jews—History—Philosophy—Addresses, essays, lectures. 2. Messiah. 3. Judaism—Apologetic works—Addresses, essays, lectures. 4. Graetz, Heinrich Hirsch, 1817-1891. I. Schorsch, Ismar. II. Title. III. Series: Moreshet (New York); v. 3.
DS115.5.G713   909'.04'924   75-9609
ISBN 0-87068-466-3

Distributed by KTAV Publishing House, Inc.
New York, New York 10002

Manufactured in the United States of America

To the memory of
CALVIN HAHN
1925-1974

Published by
The Jewish Theological Seminary of America
through the generosity
of the Bar Ephraim Fund

Contents

Abbreviations

AZJ	*Allgemeine Zeitung des Judentums*
BLBI	*Bulletin des Leo Baeck Instituts*
INJ	*Der Israelit des neunzehnten Jahrhunderts*
JJGL	*Jahrbuch für jüdische Geschichte und Literatur*
JSS	*Jewish Social Studies*
JZWL	*Judische Zeitschrift für Wissenschaft und Leben*
LBIYB	*Leo Baeck Institute Year Book*
MGWJ	*Monatsschrift für Geschichte und Wissenschaft des Judentums*
PAZR	*Protokolle und Aktenstücke der zweiten Rabbiner-Versammlung* (Frankfurt a.M., 1845)
WZJT	*Wissenschaftliche Zeitschrift für jüdische Theologie*
ZGJD	*Zeitschrift für Geschichte der Juden in Deutschland*
ZRIJ	*Zeitschrift für die religiösen Interessen des Judenthums*
ZWJ	*Zeitschrift für die Wissenschaft des Judenthums*

Preface

Timing is at least one of the keys to success. In the euphoric days following the completion of my doctoral dissertation at Columbia University, my teacher and sponsor, Professor Gerson D. Cohen, urged me to consider translating Heinrich Graetz's important German essay "The Structure of Jewish History." I was in the proper state of mind to find the suggestion appealing, and the present volume represents the ultimate harvest of that distant planting. However, the prolonged delay in effecting the idea, caused by the heavy demands which attend the first years in academic life, is not to be regretted. In the interval, my understanding of the man and of the movement with which he was so closely identified has steadily matured. The result, I hope, will not merely diminish somewhat the paucity of Graetz's work available in English, but will also contribute to a fresh appreciation of the forces which gave rise to the *Wissenschaft* movement in Germany and influenced Graetz in staking out his position in it.

In the execution of this work, I received help from several sides. A few months after I had begun, Professor Shmuel Ettinger of the Hebrew University published a similar volume in Hebrew, though marked by a somewhat broader focus than the one I envisioned for my volume.[1] The excellent

1. Shmuel Ettinger, editor, *Heinrich Graetz: Darkhe ha-Historiah ha-Yehudit* (Jerusalem: 1969).

Hebrew translation by Yeruḥam Tolqas often helped me to unravel an opaque passage of Graetz's frequently purple prose. On other occasions, it was the wise and witty counsel of my colleague and friend Professor Fritz A. Rothschild that bailed me out. For the gaffes that remain I take full credit. I should also like to record my debt to Mr. Shaye Cohen for providing me with the English translation from the Loeb Classical Library for the Greek passages of Philo cited by Graetz.

Above all, I want to express my gratitude to Professor Cohen, who in the meantime had assumed the Office of Chancellor of the Jewish Theological Seminary of America, for finding the time to read a draft of my introductory essay and to enrich it with his still unfailing critical touch.

In translating, I have taken the liberty of introducing several minor changes in the text. These essays are replete with biblical quotations. Since Graetz never bothered to cite his source, I have inserted it into the text in brackets. Graetz was an enthusiastic and independent student of the Bible and usually rendered his translations quite freely. In my own translation I have always followed his rendition of the original. These essays are also replete with phrases, proverbs, and quotations in Latin, Greek, and French. By rendering nearly all of them into English I have admittedly altered the façade of learning which the original text sports by virtue of its polyglot appearance. But my overriding concern throughout the translation was always to produce a readable English text. Finally, regarding the notes, I have marked those belonging to Graetz with the letter "G" in brackets to distinguish them from those which I have added to illuminate the text.

Ismar Schorsch

The Jewish Theological
Seminary of America
November 1973

Ideology and History
in the Age of Emancipation

Heinrich Graetz was the most energetic, versatile, and durable practitioner of *Wissenschaft des Judentums* in the nineteenth century. His comprehensive eleven-volume *History of the Jews,* published from 1853 to 1876, at the torrid pace of approximately a book every two years along with numerous other monographs and several revised editions of earlier volumes, still remains, a century later, the best single introduction to the totality of Jewish history. That is no mean achievement in a field where the discovery of new sources, the development of different tools and perspectives, the proliferation of original monographs, and the construction of new syntheses have continued unabated. And yet the extraordinary combination of narrative skill and basic research which was the hallmark of Graetz's work has never been matched.

Historians may be read in several ways: simply for information on a given subject, or in terms of the advance which their work represents in our understanding of that subject, and finally as part of the social and intellectual history of the period in which they wrote. For this essay, our reading of Graetz will be limited primarily to the interplay between his conceptualization of the Jewish past and the issues agitating his own generation. No man can be understood fully outside the context of his time; in the case of Graetz, a tempestuous personality deeply involved in the crises of a transitional age, even a partial glimpse is denied those who ignore the contemporary scene.

1

I

Graetz was part of a radically new intellectual movement in Jewish life, whose thoroughly German character was already adumbrated by its awesome-sounding name. *Wissenschaft des Judentums* as name, program, and ideology was born out of the debates in the Verein für Kultur und Wissenschaft der Juden, an association founded in 1819 by several young Jewish intellectuals who had been driven to explore the nature of Judaism by the resurgence of anti-Semitism in post-Napoleonic Germany.[1] For the next century, German Jewish scholars, nurtured on the vocabulary of German idealism and trained in the critical philological methods of the German universities, continued to be the major purveyors of the scientific study of the Jewish past.

The complex phenomenon of nineteenth-century German Jewish *Wissenschaft* comprised several key aspects. Most obvious was the design to undertake a critical study of the Jewish past. Both parts of this intention were decisively new. Since the Sephardic and Renaissance historians of the sixteenth and early seventeenth centuries, Jewish savants had not displayed any particular interest in the convolutions of Jewish history. Moses Mendelssohn, who differed in so many respects from the vast majority of his Jewish contemporaries, still shared fully their antipathy toward an historical understanding of Judaism.[2] In contrast, David Friedländer's

---

1. Sinai Ucko, "Geistesgeschichtliche Grundlagen der Wissenschaft des Judentums," reprinted in *Wissenschaft des Judentums im deutschen Sprachbereich*, edited by Kurt Wilhelm, 2 vols. (Tübingen, 1967), I, pp. 315–352.

2. Heinrich Graetz, *Geschichte der Juden*, 11 vols. (Berlin & Leipzig, 1853–1876), XI, 2nd ed., p. 13. On precisely this passage, the library of the Jewish Theological Seminary has an unpublished letter, dated July 19, 1872, by Graetz to a an unknown correspondent defending his criticism of Mendelssohn, whom he otherwise revered, for his aversion to the study of history.
   Dear Sir:
   In regard to your letter of the 14th [of July], I have the honor to answer you that my presentation in the text [of volume XI] is beyond

realization of the usefulness of historical arguments on behalf of religious reform clearly anticipated later developments and marked only one of several crucial areas in which the disciple departed from the master.[3]

Equally audacious was the willingness to subject the normative sacred texts of the Jewish past to critical analysis. Long-accepted versions of the origins of religious texts, practices, and institutions were now thoroughly reexamined using the new techniques and perspectives of historical research. The right to such independent analysis had already been contested successfully toward the end of the sixteenth century when exercised by Azariah de' Rossi, the most important forerunner of nineteenth-century *Wissenschaft*. In a collection of critical essays published in 1573 and informed by an astounding amalgam of rabbinic, classical, and contemporary learning, de' Rossi offered an impressive array of original historical interpretations. For example, to counter the penchant for messianic speculation which constituted one of the major Sephardic responses to the catastrophe of 1492, de' Rossi undertook an exhaustive study of the Jewish method of computation, *anno mundi*, in which he proved its mathematical inaccuracy and relatively late introduction (fourth century C.E.). But de' Rossi's critical stance was

---

doubt. Mendelssohn practically did not know the events of Jewish history. He openly admitted that he had no understanding for history. Thus, he did not know that since Maimuni's death excommunication had inflicted many wounds. In Spain and France the spokesmen of both parties excommunicated each other in the thirteenth century. Later, excommunication drove apostates into the camp of the Christians and they became accusers of the Jews and Judaism. That continued down to Uriel Acosta and Spinoza. At the end of the seventeenth century, the Amsterdam authorities revoked the Jewish community's right to excommunicate. These were the harmful effects and they were unknown to Mendelssohn.

Respectfully,
Prof. Graetz

3. David Friedländer, *Sendschreiben an seine Hochwürden Herrn Oberconsistorialrath und Probst Teller zu Berlin* (Berlin, 1799), pp. 29–42.

repudiated immediately by the leading rabbinic authorities both inside and outside Italy. In Renaissance Italy his work could be read only with the written permission of the local rabbi.[4]

Yet the entire venture of *Wissenschaft des Judentums* was premised on freeing the critical method from the shackles of belief. Launched by laymen steeped in rabbinics but deeply distressed by its present state and spokesmen, *Wissenschaft* battled to emancipate the historian from the authority of the theologian. The objective was articulated with disarming candor by Isaac Jost, whose comprehensive *Geschichte der Israeliten* (1820–1828) rightly deserves to be regarded as the first major product of the nascent *Wissenschaft* movement.

> No prejudice should blind the historian; no universally held dogma should darken his views; no apprehension should intimidate him from revealing the truth as he sees it. He must be able to look around freely, to examine clearly the subjects of his field, to illumine the dark, to bring out what is hidden. Anyone who might take offense at this should retreat into the darkness and refresh himself in indolent slumber.[5]

Sacred texts were now to be combed as historical documents for information about their origins and times. Jost's own critical analysis of the Pentateuch was but an extreme instance of the new spirit. Because of the explosive nature of the subject, later generations of *Wissenschaft* made no effort to match the radical quality of his conclusions. Appropriating the methods and views of earlier and contemporary Christian scholars, Jost contended that the Pentateuch consists of numerous fragments. In Genesis alone he tried to identify twenty-five different fragments on the basis of style,

---

4. Salo W. Baron, *History and Jewish Historians* (Philadelphia, 1964), pp. 171–172, 233–237. Regarding Azariah de' Rossi's anti-messianic intent, see his *Me'or 'Einayim*, edited by David Cassel (Vilna, 1866), pp. 276, 376, 382.

5. Isaac M. Jost, *Geschichte der Israeliten*, 9 vols. (Berlin, 1820–1828), IV, Vorwort, p. iii.

content, ideology, geographical designations, and divine names. Early in the Second Commonwealth, these diverse human documents were collected as a monument to the past and an honor to God. But they were quickly surrounded by an impenetrable nimbus of sanctity. The legend of Mosaic authorship obliterated all contradictions. The divinity and centrality associated with this new text eventually transformed the nation of Israelites into a religious community of Jews, a metamorphosis which amounted to a break in historical continuity. Despite the misleading title of the book, Jost was writing a history of the Jews, a story which dated from the period of the Hasmoneans when the canon was completed and the break with the past effected.[6]

The program to study the past critically implied a second major aspect of *Wissenschaft des Judentums*. The sacred history of the Jews was now to be secularized. It was to be rewritten in terms of the naturalistic idiom which had become the common property of European intellectuals. During the preceding three centuries, theology, the queen of the sciences, had been reduced to a constitutional monarch. Providence no longer governed the fields of politics, economics, science, and history. Each one had achieved autonomy under its own laws. Immanuel Kant summed up the nature of this intellectual revolution with his definition of enlightenment as "man's release from his self-incurred tutelage" from the "inability to make use of his understanding without direction from another."[7]

---

6. Ibid., III, "Anhang zum zehnten Buche," pp. 120–136, "Excurs," pp. 198–218. Jost weakly justified his use of the term Israelites by a twofold argument: first, that his work would encompass Israelites still in exile from the destruction of the Northern Kingdom in 722; and second, that before the destruction of the Second Temple Jews in Palestine were still known as Israelites (Ibid., I, p. xii). Indeed, the title bespeaks the widespread embarrassment of emancipated Jews with the word *Juden*, which had become a pejorative term. (See Ismar Schorsch, *Jewish Reactions to German Anti-Semitism, 1870–1914* [New York, 1972], pp. 157–158.)

7. Immanuel Kant, "What is Enlightenment?" translated along with his *Foundations of the Metaphysics of Morals* by Lewis W. Beck (The

In 1818, the young Leopold Zunz, still a student at the recently founded University of Berlin, heralded the shift from sacred to profane history in the Jewish world with a bold programmatic essay entitled "Etwas über die rabbinische Litteratur." With vision and conviction, he espoused the startling proposal that rabbinic literature be defined as comprising all of post-biblical Hebrew literature. He fully rejected the religiously inspired and universally accepted definition which restricted the subject to the legal literature of the Jews. Like every living people, the Jews had created a literature that touched every area of human concern. With an amazing degree of expertise, he classified and surveyed the unknown treasures of Hebrew literature. The unmistakable thrust of the essay was toward transferring the study of Hebrew literature from the synagogue to the university, the only proper forum for pursuing the history of mankind.[8]

The impact of the secular spirit is even more evident in the comprehensive history by Jost. A former schoolmate and friend of Zunz, Jost had spent three decisive semesters in 1813–1814 at the Hanoverian University of Göttingen, the academic center of the German *Aufklärung*. Göttingen became the scene of his own intellectual and social emancipation. The university carried into the nineteenth century also a reputation as the German pacesetter in scientific history, and it is entirely plausible that the orientation of Göttingen first inspired Jost to conceive his history, an idea which received the warm support of Friedländer and Lazarus Bendavid when Jost settled in Berlin in 1814.[9] Not only was the end result permeated by the

---

Library of Liberal Arts, Indianapolis, 1959), p. 85. On the process of secularization, see Ernst Cassirer, *The Philosophy of the Enlightenment* (A Beacon Paperback, Boston, 1961) and Franklin L. Baumer, *Religion and the Rise of Scepticism* (A Harbinger Book, New York, 1960).

8. Leopold Zunz, *Gesammelte Schriften*, 3 vols. (Berlin, 1875–1876), I, pp. 1–31.

9. Reuwen Michael, "I.M. Jost und sein Werk," *BLBI*, 1960, no. 12, pp. 242–243. My conjecture that the idea for the history was born in Göttingen is based on the following evidence: In his foreword to the first

anti-religious animus of the *philosophes,* but it also revealed the extent to which Jost had internalized the negative critique of Judaism leveled by the Enlightenment.[10] Rabbinism (his term) was a near fatal malignancy spawned by a disintegrating Jewish society. Furthermore, it represented a complete departure from the Mosaism of the First Commonwealth. The product of a power hungry, arrogant, and narrow-minded clerical elite, rabbinism rested on fabrications and fed on superstitions. By deceit and manipulations, the rabbis gained control over the masses. The totalitarian demands of rabbinism crushed the freedom of the spirit and the right to secular learning, forced the Jews into commerce, where more time was available for religious concerns, and finally incarcerated them behind a wall of separatistic injunctions.[11] Jost's assessment of rabbinism thus fully paralleled the *philosophes'* furious assault on medieval Christianity, though he never matched his mentors in wit, sarcasm, passion, and eloquence.[12]

---

volume, Jost stated that he had been gathering the sources for his history for six years, that is since 1814 (*Geschichte der Israeliten,* I, p. ix). In his last work, nearly forty years later, Jost revealed in a note that Friedländer and Bendavid had influenced his decision decisively. But that remark, I think, ought not to be construed to mean that they planted the idea in his head (*Geschichte des Judenthums und seiner Sekten,* 3 vols. [Leipzig, 1857–1859], III, p. 319). Given the time sequence, the character of Göttingen, and its general impact on Jost's development, the conjecture is not implausible.

10. On the nature of this critique, see Shmuel Ettinger, "Jews and Judaism as Seen by the English Deists of the 18th Century" (Hebrew), *Zion,* XXIX (1964), pp. 182–207; Arthur Hertzberg, *The French Enlightenment and the Jews* (New York, 1968), pp. 268–313; and especially Arnold Ages, *French Enlightenment and Rabbinic Tradition,* Analecta Romanica, no. 26 (Frankfurt a.M., 1970).

11. The above summary is a distillation of volumes three and four of Jost's *Geschichte der Israeliten,* which purport to offer a cultural history of the Greco-Roman period. Critical remarks about the Pharisees and rabbinism abound. See, for example, I, pp. 55–57; III, pp. 18–28, 120–126, 128, 132–133, 145–146, Anhang, pp. 158–159; IV, pp. 18, 114–115, 117–119, 131–143.

12. Peter Gay, *The Enlightenment: An Interpretation,* 2 vols. (New York, 1966–1969), I, 207–255.

In addition to their critical method and secular mood, the founders of *Wissenschaft des Judentums* also operated with a specific concept of history. While the first two aspects of the movement were not particularly German, the third derives directly from German idealism. Hegel had transformed history from the utterly chaotic "slaughter-bench at which the happiness of peoples, the wisdom of states, and the virtue of individuals were sacrificed," into "the rationally necessary course of the World Spirit" or, more precisely, "the exhibition of spirit striving to attain knowledge of its own nature." In Hegel's monistic universe, the rational and the real were identical and Spirit was the true motive force behind the passions of men. The dialectic unfolding of Spirit in the multiplicity of historical forms culminated in self-understanding, and *Wissenschaft* became the instrument by which Spirit knows itself. In the words of Hegel:

> The highest point of a people's development is the rational consciousness of its life and conditions, the scientific understanding of its laws, its system of justice, its morality. For in this unity (of subjective and objective) lies the most intimate unity of which Spirit can be with itself.[13]

The mandate of the age, therefore, was the attainment of consciousness, and it served to inspire the fledgling Verein für Kultur. According to its gifted president Eduard Gans who was later to edit Hegel's posthumously published *Lectures on the Philosophy of History,* the age

> wants to acquire self-consciousness; it does not merely want to be but also to know itself. No life should be lived of whose necessity it is not convinced, no phenomenon should manifest itself without the conviction that it could not appear otherwise.[14]

---

13. Perhaps the best introduction to Hegel's concept of history is his own lengthy introduction to his *Philosophy of History.* The above quotations are taken from the edition of that introduction translated by Robert S. Hartman, *Reason in History* (The Library of Liberal Arts, Indianapolis, 1953), pp. 27, 12, 23, 92.

14. Ucko, p. 344.

Wissenschaft des Judentums became the medium through which Judaism would come to know itself. In 1870, in light of the self-discovery achieved by two generations of *Wissenschaft*, Graetz confidently designated the final period, from Mendelssohn to the middle of the nineteenth century, which was covered by his *Geschichte der Juden* as "the age of growing self-consciousness." The scientific study of the Jewish past heralded the dawn of a new era in Jewish history.[15]

Nevertheless, despite its professed comprehensive scope, the ultimate and often primary interest of the proponents of *Wissenschaft* was restricted to the quintessence of Judaism. Equipped with the idealistic conceptual apparatus of Hegel, they tended to reduce the tortuous history of the Jews to the progressive unfolding of the idea of Judaism. Long before the necessary research had even been conceived, they were ready to identify the ruling idea of Jewish history. One immediate and much-needed benefit which they derived from this shortcut was the chance to link Judaism with the unfolding of the universal World Spirit.[16]

II

Even a brief attempt at a conceptual analysis of the nature of *Wissenschaft des Judentums* is enough to suggest that it was never intended as an end in itself. On the contrary, it was forged and employed by the intellectuals of an embattled minority as the most effective instrument for handling the formidable challenge of emancipation. Recourse to the critical study of the past was taken to serve the overwhelming needs of the present, with the inevitable result that ideology dominated the writing of scientific history.

Emancipation, its prospect, the arduous and extended effort

15. Graetz, *Geschichte*, XI, 2nd ed., p. ix.

16. See, for example, the programmatic essay by Immanuel Wolf, "Ueber den Begriff einer Wissenschaft des Judenthums," *ZWJ*, I (1822), pp. 1–24. An English translation of this important essay was published in *LBIYB*, II (1957), pp. 194–204.

required to win it, and the partial and tenuous quality of its achievement, constituted the overriding concern of German Jewry in the nineteenth century. As in earlier periods of Jewish history, a fundamental change in the legal status of the Jews dictated substantial modifications in the practice of Judaism. The varied legal conditions under which Jews lived in the Babylonian exile, the Second Commonwealth, the Baghdad caliphate, medieval Christian Europe, and seventeenth-century England inevitably effected communal and religious adjustments. But very few shifts in legal status were as far-reaching and as bitterly contested as the emancipation of German Jewry.

The major instrument for altering the structure and image of Judaism so as to accord with the legal status eagerly sought by certain sectors of the Jewish community and grudgingly held out by a deeply ambivalent Christian society was *Wissenschaft des Judentums.* In nineteenth-century Germany the study of Jewish history functioned as both authority and medium. Construed as authority, a proper reading of Jewish history could yield the indispensable guidelines and validating principles to determine the future shape of Judaism. Invoked as medium, Jewish history could readily provide an interpretation of Judaism in terms of the idealistic idiom of the century. In the Middle Ages these two functions were fulfilled by different disciplines: a rich and flexible legal tradition generally served as sole authority for changes within the Jewish community, while philosophy offered the common idiom in which Judaism could be expounded for Jew and non-Jew alike. In the wake of emancipation, with the repudiation of Jewish law and the historicization of philosophy, history assumed the role of both. It became the functional equivalent of halakhah and philosophy in the medieval world. Scientific history alone transcended the passions and partisanship of a turbulent age, and it alone had access to the truth that would accord a revamped Judaism its rightful place in the century of self-cognition.

Invested with such power, *Wissenschaft des Judentums* soon became the most potent intellectual force on the German Jewish scene. Its devoted band of practitioners steadily increased, and the accumulated results of their investigations revolutionized the understanding of Judaism and the self-image of the Jew. Very few were able to resist the compelling appeal of the historical approach. Perhaps the most notable exception was Graetz's former teacher, Samson Raphael Hirsch, whose highly personal brand of allegory was far closer to the medieval than the modern idiom. When Esriel Hildesheimer, his Neo-Orthodox associate, finally opened a modern rabbinical seminary in Berlin in 1873 where *Wissenschaft* would be practiced no less assiduously than at Breslau or the Hochschule, Hirsch refused to extend the slightest support.[17]

However, the near universal use of *Wissenschaft* produced no universal agreement as to the nature of Judaism. Like most instruments, *Wissenschaft,* too, could be used in different ways. It could be wielded radically or conservatively, to reshape traditional Judaism or to defend it, to legitimize religious reform or to resist it. The intellectual leadership of the nascent Reform movement perceived the study of Jewish history as a liberating force, the means by which to bury the burdensome legacy of an insufferable past. By the 1840s, the exclusive and often reckless use of history in the cause of religious reform provoked a spontaneous counter-attack by a cluster of historians, appalled at the price of emancipation, who began to wield *Wissenschaft* in defense of traditional Judaism. Both sides shared a common idiom. The dilemmas posed by the emancipation struggle were to be resolved by a proper reading of Jewish history. The bitter disagreement over that reading derived not from differences in method but from prior religious positions that were deeply antagonistic. *Wissenschaft* history was programmatic history.

III

The first program in the field came in the guise of a full-blown theory of Jewish history which marked as sharp a

---

17. Mordechai Eliav, *Rabbiner Esriel Hildesheimer Briefe* (Jerusalem, 1965), pp. 207–216.

departure in self-perception as did the emancipation in legal status. Long before Abraham Geiger's brilliant summation of this Reform theory of Jewish history in the 1860s in his *Das Judenthum und seine Geschichte,* it had become the regnant interpretation of the Jewish past. In the name of this novel theory, the spokesmen for religious reform advocated overhauling the major institutions and beliefs of Judaism. Graetz detested the program and formulated his own philosophy of Jewish history to challenge that prevailing in Reform circles.

The revision of Jewish history by the intellectuals of the Reform movement rested on two conceptual assumptions which often merged into substantive conclusions. Like every living phenomenon, Judaism was subject to the law of development. Its ideas and forms were part of a historical continuum, emerging gradually and constantly changing. The Talmud itself offered the most convincing proof of this, for it amounted to a vast reworking of biblical Judaism. The spirit of Judaism had always appropriated new forms, since old ones condemned to the rubbish heap of history could never be revived. This vitality of growth in the past was the guarantee that Judaism could also meet the dictates of the present.[18]

What saved Jewish history from the fate of pure historicism was the concept of essence. Behind the panorama of events existed and operated the essence of Judaism. It was this unchanging though ever unfolding idea which provided the continuity as well as the motive power of Jewish history. Present from the very outset, the idea was locked in combat with its materialistic adversaries. With each round it managed to assume a higher form more appropriate to its nature. But every resolution was merely temporary, for the very assumption of material form marked a compromise of the idea.[19]

On the basis of these assumptions, the architects of Reform

---

18. Abraham Geiger, *WZJT,* I (1835), p. 2; idem, *Nachgelassene Schriften,* 5 vols. (Berlin, 1875–1878), V, pp. 181–182; Sigismund Stern, *Zur Judenfrage in Deutschland,* I (1843), p. 154 and II (1844), pp. 26–41; idem, *INJ,* VIII (1847), pp. 377–379.

19. Geiger, *WZJT,* V (1844), pp. 56–57.

designed a comprehensive reinterpretation of Jewish history whose general outline had been sketched as early as 1822 by Immanuel Wolf on behalf of the ephemeral Verein für Kultur. Its point of departure was the a priori identification of the essence of Judaism, and later ideologues felt no need to repudiate Wolf's bold formulation.

> What is this idea that has existed throughout so much of world history and has so successfully influenced the culture of the human race? It is of the most simple kind and its content can be expressed in a few words. It is the idea of unlimited unity in the all. It is contained in the one word יהוה which signifies indeed the living unity of all being in eternity, the absolute being outside defined time and space. This concept is revealed to the Jewish people, i.e., posited as a datum.[20]

Monotheism thus constituted and exhausted the idea of Judaism. To be sure, men like Geiger and Samuel Holdheim later acknowledged the centrality of ethics, though even for them the irreducible and eternal core remained a unique vision of God. They also continued to acknowledge the divine source of this vision.[21] Moritz A. Stern, the Göttingen *Dozent*, who contended that the ultimate task of Reform was to destroy the belief in positive revelation, failed to attract any rabbinic support.[22]

Beyond this essential idea, nothing in Judaism was permanent and some, like Sigismund Stern, the noted Jewish educator and one of the founders of the Berlin Reform Association, claimed that even the original Sinaitic revelation was subject to evolution. The implacable law of development governed everything.[23] Accordingly, the national dimension of Judaism was historicized and accounted for in terms of

20. Wolf, *LBIYB*, II (1957), p. 194.
21. Abraham Geiger, *Das Judenthum und seine Geschichte*, 3 vols. (Breslau, 1865–1871), I, pp. 27–36; Samuel Holdheim, *Geschichte der Entstehung und Entwickelung der jüdischen Reformgemeinde in Berlin* (Berlin, 1857), p. 115.
22. Ludwig Geiger, *ZGJD*, II (1888), p. 69.
23. Stern, *INJ*, VIII (1847), p. 378.

function. Many of the early advocates of enlightenment and
reform had received their first taste of secular learning
through the philosophic works of Maimonides. In the third
part of his *Guide for the Perplexed,* Maimonides had
revolutionized the attempt to explain the intention of the
commandments by employing an historical approach for the
first time. The significance of countless biblical institutions
could be ascertained only by a knowledge of contemporary
pagan practice, for their function was strictly prophylactic.[24]
Adopting this line of thought, Reform historians now
contended that the entire Jewish state along with many of its
religious institutions had merely served to shield the fragile
idea of monotheism from the unmitigated depravity of the
pagan environment until it had become sufficiently rooted in
the consciousness of ancient Israel.[25] The destruction of the
First Commonwealth and the Babylonian exile produced a
new exemplar: the Jew who recoiled from the opportunity to
return to his homeland but retained his religious identity.
Wolf considered the rejection of the opportunity afforded by
Cyrus' edict by the majority of Jews

> a remarkable event! Hundreds of thousands remained in the
> dispersion and were not incorporated a second time into the
> Jewish state. But everywhere they preserved the self-same idea
> on which their nationhood depended. They remained adher-
> ents of Judaism and thereby links in a chain.[26]

These expatriated Jews were harbingers of the irreversible

---

24. Amos Funkenstein, "Gesetz und Geschichte: zur historisierenden
    Hermeneutik bei Moses Maimonides und Thomas von Aquin," *Viator,*
    I (1970), pp. 147–178.

25. Sigismund Stern, *Die Aufgabe des Judenthums und der Juden in der
    Gegenwart* (Berlin, 1845), pp. 9–10; Geiger, *Das Judenthum,* I, pp.
    37–39.

26. Wolf, *LBIYB,* II (1957), p. 196. For similar comments, see Jost,
    Geschichte der Israeliten, I, p. xii; Samuel Holdheim, *Ueber die
    Autonomie der Rabbinen und das Princip der jüdischen Ehe,* 2nd ed.
    (Schwerin, 1847), pp. 16–17; Jakob J. Petuchowski, *Prayerbook Reform
    in Europe* (New York, 1968), pp. 53–54 (referring to the Hamburg
    Temple Prayer Book of 1819).

turn which Jewish history would take with the destruction of the Second Temple. The final Reform interpretation of this event was a modified version of a view articulated at the dawn of the emancipation era by Spinoza, whose significance for Jewish history lies in the devastating secular critique of Judaism which he bequeathed to the Enlightenment. On the basis of philosophical argument and scriptural evidence, Spinoza claimed that Judaism should have rightfully perished with the demise of the Jewish state,[27] its illegitimate survival being due solely to gentile hostility.[28] When Mendelssohn took up the argument in *Jerusalem,* he conceded only that the loss of political independence had transformed Judaism into a purely religious system which operated by means of persuasion alone.[29] Moving still closer to Spinoza's original position, Friedländer and later architects of Reform rendered explicit what Mendelssohn had left implicit: the demise of the Jewish state marked the liberation of Judaism from its national origins.[30] More than a century and a half after the *Theologico-Political Treatise,* Holdheim unmistakably echoed Spinoza when he declared that "everything connected with a state qua state must cease once this national entity is dissolved."[31]

In the nineteenth century this reinterpretation was coupled with the idea of mission, an idea still lacking in Jost's *Geschichte der Israeliten.*[32] What former generations had mourned as a national calamity was now celebrated as a providential summons to enter the world to espouse the true conception of God. Exile became the proper locus for Jewish existence. Against the backdrop of a long tradition of

27. *The Chief Works of Benedict de Spinoza,* translated by R.H.M. Elwes, 2 vols. (Dover Publications, New York, 1951), I, pp. 57–68, 72, 245–248.
28. Ibid., pp. 55–56.
29. Moses Mendelssohn, *Jerusalem and other Jewish Writings,* translated by Alfred Jospe (New York, 1969), pp. 99–104.
30. Friedländer, pp. 34–38.
31. Holdheim, *Ueber die Autonomie,* p. 45.
32. It seems to appear first in his subsequent *Allgemeine Geschichte des Israelitischen Volkes,* 2 vols. (Berlin, 1832), I, pp. 8–9.

Enlightenment criticism of Judaism's particularism, the advocates of Reform harped on the universalism of its essence and the nature of its mission. The dissemination of monotheism as Judaism's unique mandate became the major line of defense against collective suicide.[33]

But the destruction of the Temple did not fully release the spirit of Judaism. As in an earlier period, it was again encrusted with separatistic institutions that derived from both internal and external causes. The prolonged disintegration of the state created a vacuum filled by the proliferating regulations of a clerical elite. Holdheim accused the rabbis of having failed to grasp the verdict of history by desperately clinging to the political fragments of a vanished state.[34] With far greater scholarship, the young Geiger tried to show how the rabbis forged new bonds of unity by freely applying an irrational exegetical method which repeatedly violated the simple sense of the biblical text. The result was a vast and stultifying legal system which, despite intensive rabbinic effort, enjoyed no objective biblical mandate.[35]

To handle the extended and diversified medieval experience of the Jews, Reform ideologues appropriated for their

33. Stern, *Die Aufgabe des Judenthums*, p. 17; *PAZR*, p. 74; Geiger, *Das Judenthum*, I, pp. 149–162. The origins and elaboration of the radically new mission theory of the nineteenth century, by which the significance of *Galut* was effectively transvalued, have yet to be traced. The essay by Max Wiener, "The Conception of Mission in Traditional and Modern Judaism," *Yivo Annual of Jewish Social Science*, II-III (1947–1948), pp. 9–24 represents no more than an unfinished start. Years before, Max Nordau, who frequently gave eloquent expression to the Zionist critique of emancipation, had contended that Reform ideologists worked out their theory under the influence of Christian theology which itself had long maintained that Jewish dispersion and survival were intended to provide a witness for the truth of Scripture. There may be more to this intuitive insight than mere polemics. (Max Nordau, *Das Judenthum im 19. und 20. Jahrhundert*, 2nd ed. [Cologne, 1911], pp. 17–19. On the Augustinian origin of this Christian argument, see Bernhard Blumenkranz, *Die Judenpredigt Augustins* [Basel, 1946], pp. 175–181.)
34. Holdheim, *Ueber die Autonomie*, pp. 38–49.
35. Geiger, *WZJT*, V (1844), pp. 58–81, 234–259.

own use the long regnant view of the exile as an era of unrelieved persecution. Whereas ancient and medieval Jewish literature had always perceived the state of *Galut* as fraught with danger, Sephardic historians of the sixteenth century, traumatized by the calamitous end to Jewish life in Spain and Portugal, were the first to construct chronological histories of Jewish persecutions through the ages.[36] In the seventeenth and eighteenth centuries this perception of the past was utilized by the early advocates of emancipation to clear the Jews of responsibility for the reprehensible quality of their social condition.[37] In the biting words of Mendelssohn: "They tie our hands and then reproach us for not using them."[38] In the nineteenth century the Reform theory of Jewish history transferred this same deeply ingrained view of the past to account for the ailing condition of Judaism. Major facets of medieval Judaism were now rendered unessential, for they were no more than a natural reaction to intolerable pressure. The medieval Jew could survive only by living either in the past, in the future, or in a world of fantasy.

In this manner the spokesmen for reform evaluated the institutions of talmudic Judaism and the ideologies of messianic and mystical movements. In an era of relentless persecution, the need for consolation had replaced the free

---

36. Samuel Usque, *Consolation for the Tribulations of Israel*, translated by Martin A. Cohen (Philadelphia, 1964); Solomon ibn Verga, *Sefer Shebet Yehudah*, edited by Azriel Shohet (Jerusalem, 1947); Joseph ha-Kohen, *Emeq ha-Bakha*, edited by Meir Letteris (Cracow, 1895). On the precursors and sources of these sixteenth-century historians of persecution, see the conflicting views of Graetz, *Geschichte*, VIII, 4th ed., pp. 393–399; Isidore Loeb, *Joseph Haccohen et les chroniquers juifs* (Paris, 1888); Fritz Baer, *Untersuchungen über Quellen und Komposition des Schebet Jehuda* (Berlin, 1923); Martin Cohen, pp. 277–287.

37. Jacob Meijer, "Hugo Grotius' Remonstrantie," *JSS*, XVII (1955), pp. 95–96; John Toland, *Reasons for Naturalizing the Jews in Great Britain and Ireland* (London, 1714), pp. 14–16; Christian Wilhelm Dohm, *Ueber die bürgerliche Verbesserung der Juden* (Berlin & Stettin, 1781), pp. 31–35, 107–109; Henri Grégoire, *Essai sur la régéneration physique, morale et politique des Juifs* (Metz, 1789), pp. 1–13, 32–44.

38. Mendelssohn, p. 146.

development of the spirit. The codification of the Mishnah was a typical though early expression of the medieval attachment to the past. Much of the material which it preserved was no longer applicable even at the time of codification.[39] Surrounded by a hostile society, medieval Jews increasingly withdrew behind the protective institutions of the Talmud, a kind of surrogate homeland and the functional equivalent of the Jewish state in pagan antiquity.[40] Holdheim contended that communal autonomy was an anachronism imposed on the Jews by governments which refused to incorporate them into the fabric of society.[41]

Messiansim and mysticism fared little better. Here, too, history transvalued what former generations had cherished. Neither the longing for political redemption nor the pursuit of the mystical experience were regarded as authentic expressions of Judaism, for both could easily be explained as the obvious and unhealthy consequence of physical persecution and cultural isolation.[42]

In sum, the Reform theory of Jewish history offers ample evidence of the extensive interplay between the needs of the present and the perception of the past. It simply bristled with relevance. By historicizing whatever appeared to be a liability, it legitimized the religious accommodation often crudely dictated by German emancipation; its thrust accorded with the perceived mandate of the age. With the end of fanaticism and persecution, the idea of Judaism could be stripped of its institutional armor and delivered to a receptive world. The vision of Sigismund Stern inspired the hearts of many.

. . . and when once the pagan world will be destroyed, not

---

39. Geiger, *Das Judenthum*, II, p. 31.
40. Stern, *Die Aufgabe des Judenthums*, p. 25.
41. Holdheim, *Ueber die Autonomie*, pp. 17–18.
42. Friedländer, p. 38; Wolf, *LBIYB*, II (1957), pp. 197–198; *PAZR*, pp. 74–75, 76, 94, 100; Geiger, *Das Judenthum*, II, pp. 14–15. This alleged connection between oppression and messianism had already been suggested by Grégoire, p. 32.

only by Christianity, but within it as well, then the separation of both religions will cease, and I can't decide which name the religion of mankind will bear.[43]

IV

The decade of the 1840s marked a turning-point in the political fortunes of German Jewry and consequently also in the direction of *jüdische Wissenschaft*. Not only had emancipation failed to bring the millenium, in the 1840s emancipation itself came under severe attack. The political crisis produced five years of enormous ferment which served to clarify opposing religious positions as well as to underscore the continued struggle between rabbis and laymen over the religious leadership of the Jewish community.

In 1843 a population of 206,050 Jews made Prussian Jewry the third largest Jewish community in Europe.[44] But unlike its much larger counterparts in Russia and Austria, large sectors of Prussian Jewry had enjoyed nearly full emancipation since 1812, although as late as 1846, 36.7 percent of the Jews in Prussia, mainly in the border province of Posen, had still failed to attain citizenship.[45] At the end of 1841 the new king, Frederick William IV, who detested the Enlightenment and yearned to reestablish the divine order of the Holy Roman Empire, issued a cabinet order which sent shock waves through Prussian Jewry. Reasserting the long denied identity of Judaism with the Jewish nation, Frederick William IV contended that only legislation which posited this unity and its attendant Jewish separateness could be effective.

The efforts of those who seek an improvement in the social situation of the Jews through their individual assimilation into

43. Stern, *Die Aufgabe des Judenthums,* p. 78.
44. *Vollständige Verhandlungen des ersten vereinigten preussischen Land- tages über die Emancipationsfrage der Juden* (Berlin, 1847), p. xvi. Among the German states, Bavaria with 62,830 Jews had the second largest Jewish population.
45. Heinrich Silbergleit, *Die Bevölkerungs- und Berufsverhältnisse der Juden im deutschen Reich* (Berlin, 1930), p. 9.

the civil life of the Christian population of the land can never
be fruitful and salutary for the mutual relationship between
Christians and Jews, since they stand in contradiction to that
national type.

Accordingly, the king proposed to treat the Jews as a
national minority by organizing them everywhere into
separate corporations, whose corporate interests on the
municipal level would be represented by Jewish deputies
alone. Jews would no longer be allowed to represent a
Christian constituency. In line with their loss of individual
citizenship, the king also advocated releasing the Jews from
the universal obligation of military service.[46]

Prussian Jewry translated its dismay at the pending
renunciation of emancipation into vociferous protest, with the
result that Frederick William shelved his original proposal.
For the next five years the Prussian government deliberated
on the draft of a new Jewish law. In 1845 it invited Moritz
Veit, the president of the Berlin Jewish community, Julius
Rubo, its syndic, Leopold Zunz, the director of its teachers'
seminary, and Joseph Muhr, a banker, to offer their
suggestions in person. Notables and rabbis from across the
land also dispatched memoranda to the government. Finally,
in 1847, the representatives of the provincial estates sitting in
a United Diet ratified a modified version of the government's
proposal.[47]

The agonizing wait kept Prussian Jewry in a state of
unrelieved suspension. In 1843 Holdheim reported:

> The very much feared law of incorporation which still
> threatens the civil and social life of Prussian Jews, or Jewish
> Prussians, has raised the nationality question of the Jews in
> general in many circles. In the past year it variously occupied
> the minds of many.

---

46. *Der Orient*, 1842, p. 187.

47. Horst Fischer, *Judentum, Staat und Heer in Preussen im frühen 19.
Jahrhundert* (Tübingen, 1968), pp. 158–190. See also the highly
interesting memorandum submitted by Michael Sachs and published
by Ismar Freund in the *Festschrift zu Simon Dubnows siebzigsten
Geburtstag* (Berlin, 1930), pp. 251–258.

The views of the king were well known. In 1846, Veit, the learned publisher who served as president of the Berlin community from 1839 to 1848 and who lobbied successfully for the support of the city and provincial governments on behalf of the Jews, still felt that a law reflecting the king's sentiments was a real possibility. His consolation was that the setback would be temporary: laws were no longer legislated for eternity.[48]

An attack from an unexpected corner intensified Jewish anxiety still further. In 1843 Bruno Bauer, the "Robespierre of theology" who had just lost his job at the University of Bonn for trying to undercut the historicity of the Gospels, published an essay in which he declared the adherents of Judaism unfit for emancipation. A left-wing Hegelian, who despised Frederick William's retrogressive ideology of the Christian state no less than did the Jews, Bauer lampooned Judaism as a fossil reflecting the lowest stage in the history of religion. It survived only by fleeing the mainstream of history and immuring itself within its talmudic fortress. But the price was high. The Jew became incapable of any further development. The efforts at reform since the Parisian Sanhedrin in the name of Judaism were fraudulent, for they signified a break and not a return. In the quest for emancipation, the Jews sought only an extension of privilege to cultivate their tribal exclusiveness. Bauer summoned them instead to abandon their parochial concerns and to join in the struggle for universal freedom, a goal that entailed the emancipation of society from religion.[49]

This renewed antagonism toward Jewish political aspirations from both the right and the left unleashed a burst of activity within the Jewish community for religious reform.

---

48. Holdheim, *Ueber die Autonomie,* Vorwort to 1st ed., p. iii; Ludwig Geiger, "Moritz Veit als Kämpfer für die Emanzipation der Juden," *JJGL,* XIII (1910), pp. 140–141.
49. Bruno Bauer, *Die Judenfrage* (Braunschweig, 1843). See also Nathan Rotenstreich, "For and Against Emancipation," *LBIYB,* IV (1959), pp. 3–11. On Bauer's work in general see the fresh reexamination by Lothar Koch, *Humanistischer Atheismus und gesellschaftliches Engagement* (Stuttgart, 1971).

The response was only to be expected, for since the very outset of the emancipation struggle in Germany the underlying issue had always been the nature of Judaism and the fitness of its adherents for admission into the modern state. The initiative to speak on behalf of Judaism was seized by university-educated laymen in Frankfurt, Breslau, and Berlin who organized to issue declarations defining their conceptions of Judaism. Generally, they stressed what they had discarded: the authority of the Talmud, the dietary laws, the medieval hope for national redemption, and a day of rest different from that of the society in which they lived. In a more positive vein, they asserted the eternal truth of Judaism's concept of God as well as its capacity for limitless development. These declarations were intended to persuade the German public and its officials of the existence of a non-Orthodox Judaism, that was entirely commensurate with the duties of citizenship. Its adherents had offered public testimony that they had cleansed their religion of all national vestiges.[50]

But were they, in fact, qualified to testify on the nature of Judaism? Had they not preempted a strictly rabbinic prerogative? Seen in this light, the well-known rabbinic conferences of the mid-1840s constituted an organized effort to regain the leadership of the Jewish community. Since the onset of the emancipation struggle in Germany when Mendelssohn appealed to the rabbis to relinquish their power of excommunication, enlightened lay leaders and traditional rabbis had battled for control over the religious affairs of the community. Now a new generation of secularly educated, liberal rabbis rose to claim their right as the legitimate

---

50. *INJ*, 1845, pp. 131–132; Ludwig Geiger, *ZGJD*, II (1888), pp. 49–62; Holdheim, *Geschichte der Reformgemeinde*, pp. 59–63; David Philipson, *The Reform Movement in Judaism*, 2nd ed. (New York, 1931), pp. 231–234. On the social composition of these Reform groups, a subject as yet almost entirely ignored, see the hints in Holdheim, *Geschichte der Reformgemeinde*, pp. 26, 40, 50, 52; also the significant evidence uncovered by Jacob Katz, *Jews and Freemasons in Europe* (Cambridge, 1970), pp. 91–95.

spokesmen for Judaism. Even Samuel Holdheim, the most radical among them, sharply criticized the Frankfurt declaration issued by a circle of assimilated and anti-rabbinic intellectuals in 1843 as being so negative in character that it could never help generate a religious revival.[51] While laymen clamored for a synod in which both parties would deliberate in full equality, the Frankfurt rabbinical conference of 1845 refused to endorse the Berlin Reform Association, the major proponent of the synod idea, without a promise to abide by the principles set forth by the conference.[52] Although the same political issues that prompted the lay declarations also fed many of the debates at the rabbinical conferences, the rabbis generally accorded more weight to the legacy of the past.

The rash of lay and rabbinic pronouncements on radical reform soon elicited a counter-response. For the first time a handful of men, trained in universities and committed to the practice of *Wissenschaft,* began to challenge the excessive concern with the dictates of the time. In the mid-1840s Zacharias Frankel took the lead. He had served as rabbi in Dresden since 1836, was already hard at work on a lifetime study of the origins and development of Jewish law, and had dramatically walked out of the Frankfurt rabbinical conference in 1845 over the issue of Hebrew in the services. In 1844 he founded what proved to be a short-lived journal openly hostile to Reform in which he formulated a critique of the Reform program based on several grounds.

Politically, he accused the Reform leadership of bartering Judaism for emancipation. Basing his case on a theory of natural law that post-Napoleonic Prussia rejected as a French import, Frankel claimed that equality was a right and not a privilege. Like the tortured victim of the Inquisition who

---

51. Holdheim, *Geschichte der Reformgemeinde,* pp. 63–66.
52. Philipson, pp. 241–244; *Der Orient,* 1845, p. 142. Even Holdheim, the later rabbi of the Berlin Reform Association, opposed the synod idea. The two groups simply did not share the same commitment to the past. (Holdheim, *Geschichte der Reformgemeinde,* p. 122.)

finally came to believe himself guilty of the crime of which he
was accused, many weak-kneed German Jews had come to
accept the oft-repeated argument that the teachings and
practices of Judaism were the real reason for the continued
denial of emancipation. But such demands by the state
violated the principle of freedom of conscience. True
emancipation entailed a triumph of justice and humanity.[53]

To this political argument Frankel added a deeply felt
historical consideration. The willingness to purchase emancipation displayed an appalling callousness toward the countless sacrifices of earlier generations. How many Jews had
withstood the unrelenting oppression of the Middle Ages!
When forced to choose between the cross and the sword, how
many Jews preferred to lay down their lives! And today this
divine legacy sanctified by blood was sold for material
advantage! Such an exchange undercut the very purpose of
emancipation: to grant Jews the freedom and dignity to
dedicate their spiritual and physical resources to the welfare
of society and the state.[54]

Finally, Frankel attacked the Reform program on religious
grounds. Jewish rituals and ceremonies could not be
discarded high-handedly as mere devices to separate Jews
from a hostile environment because they continued to
articulate the religious sentiment of a living people. The
majority of Jews were still able to satisfy their deepest
religious needs through these ancient forms of expression. In
their extreme rationalism, the leaders of Reform blindly
refused to acknowledge the still high level of religious
observance among the Jewish masses, whose religiosity
delimited those areas of Jewish life which must not be
tampered with.[55] By appealing to current religious practice,
Frankel thus employed the same criterion as the spokesmen

---

53. *ZRIJ*, I (1844), pp. 208, 224–228, 283, 331–332; *PAZR*, pp. 34–35.
54. *ZRIJ*, I (1844), pp. 14, 60–73, 208.
55. Max Wiener, *Jüdische Religion im Zeitalter der Emanzipation* (Berlin,
    1933), pp. 256–257; *ZRIJ*, I (1844), p. 302; II (1845), pp. 15–16, 173,
    180–181; *PAZR*, pp. 19–20.

for reform; they merely differed in their judgment. While the latter tended to reflect the alienation of a rising middle class, Frankel spoke for the piety of the *Landjuden* for whom the process of assimilation had scarcely begun.

The attack against Reform soon engulfed its practice of *Wissenschaft* which, till the 1840s, had been primarily a Reform preserve in Germany. As early as 1840 Michael Sachs, a preacher in Prague and a student of Solomon Yehuda Rapoport, one of the luminaries of the Galician *Haskalah*, voiced his disapproval of the tone and direction of Reform scholarship in a personal letter to his close friend in Berlin, Moritz Veit. Trained as a classical philologian at the University of Berlin, Sachs deplored the rationalistic efforts to reduce Judaism to a mere formula. It must be experienced to be understood. Better to observe the minutiae of the ritual codes than to utter a formula which curdles the blood like a lie the moment it's pronounced! Sachs also condemned the thoroughly negative character of Reform scholarship. Its exhaustive catalogue of the sins of which the ancient rabbis were guilty was enough to kill the patient. Lacking any love for their subject, Reform scholars made no attempt to revive contemporary Jewry through positive history. Sachs envisioned an entirely different kind of enterprise.

> This is what I am looking for: to recognize spirit and life, a higher idealistic aspect everywhere; to state the known; to present Judaism in its power and glory as a guide to this higher view of life; to make us conscious of its institutions as an expression of its ideas, of its history in all of its edifying and uplifting might, of the voices of its men of God in their profoundly creative and deeply stirring power, of its significance for the present and that of the present for us.[56]

In 1845, one year after he came to Berlin to occupy the pulpit of the Jewish community, Sachs published a specimen of what he meant by positive history. *Die religiöse Poesie der*

---

56. Ludwig Geiger, ed., *Michael Sachs und Moritz Veit. Briefwechsel* (Frankfurt a.M., 1897), p. 37.

Juden in Spanien attempted to present in translation the pathos and power of Spanish Hebrew religious poetry and thereby to engender some admiration for the creative talent of medieval Jewry. Sachs added a lengthy historical essay in which he offered an effusive appreciation of his subject. In the opening chapter, without ever referring to the name of his protagonist, he delivered a deep-felt refutation of Geiger's scholarly indictment of rabbinic exegesis as arbitrary, faulty, and tendentious. Sachs contended that *Midrash* was the product of unreflective immediacy. Of course the rabbis realized the plain sense of the biblical text, but culturally isolated and still spared the tyranny of foreign methods and ideas, they continued to inhabit the conceptual and emotional world of the prophets. This creative intimacy survived intact until the invasion of Islamic culture and usually yielded a far profounder understanding of Scripture than that gained by the application of an alien science.[57]

The disagreement between Geiger and Sachs was not merely the consequence of a rationalistic versus a romantic approach to the study of the past, but also derived directly from antagonistic views as to the validity and viability of a legalistic religious system that seemed to obstruct the attainment of full emancipation. History had become the arena for resolving the dilemmas that wracked the present.[58]

The ranks of the emerging conservative bloc were significantly strengthened by the addition of Leopold Zunz, whose career had begun a quarter of a century before in the cause of Reform, and whose pioneering history of the homiletic literature of the Jews, which appeared in 1832 also in the service of Reform, had inspired both Geiger and Holdheim with a vision of the social usefulness of modern scholarship.[59]

---

57. Michael Sachs, *Die religiöse Poesie der Juden in Spanien* (Berlin, 1845), pp. 148–164, 195.
58. In another context, Geiger, in passing, rejected Sach's historical approach as superficial and romantic, as aesthetic rather than scientific. (*Literatur-Blatt zum INJ*, 1846, p. 67.)
59. Ludwig Geiger, ed., *Abraham Geiger: Leben und Lebenswerk* (Berlin, 1910), p. 17; Holdheim, *Geschichte der Reformgemeinde*, p. 11.

But in the 1840s he became disillusioned with the thrust of Reform and the quality of its *Wissenschaft*. His private letters bristled with cryptic, caustic remarks about the leaders and activities of the movement. He considered Geiger to be merely a party man and not a scholar. Holdheim was in a class with some of Judaism's most illustrious enemies like Hegel, Paulus, and Bauer. His anti-Jewish program would destroy Judaism. The Berlin Reformers were led by ignorant and simple men, and they stood ready to offer the dietary laws and the messiah in return for emancipation. The statements issued by rabbinical conferences and Reform associations alike smacked of Christianity.[60]

The urgency of the moment drove Zunz to speak out publicly. The original intention of the Frankfurt Reform Association to include a renunciation of circumcision in its declaration had finally been abandoned under pressure, but the controversy continued to reverberate throughout Germany. In 1843 and 1844 Zunz plunged in with two terse, highly charged affirmations of the religious rites of *tefillin* and circumcision. He accused the spokesmen of Reform of being politically motivated. Not a single divine law must be sacrificed for equality, which was after all not man's highest goal and would be achieved in any event. Zunz bitterly attacked the distinction between the national and religious dimensions of Judaism upon which Holdheim rested his case. The dean of *jüdische Wissenschaft* rebuked Holdheim for his exclusive worship of history! The Reform ideologues had rejected the God of Abraham for the idol of history. Jewish symbols would soon wither under the new regime. But Judaism consisted of more than a few disembodied universalistic ideas. To discard the Talmud and the belief in the messiah was to repudiate the Jewish past and future; to renounce circumcision would destroy the act which unites Jews in the present. The Reform program amounted to suicide.[61]

---

60. Nahum N. Glatzer, ed., *Leopold and Adelheid Zunz: An Account in Letters 1815–1885* (London, 1958), pp. 129, 132, 139, 159–160.
61. Zunz, *Gesammelte Schriften*, II, pp. 196, 199–200, 201, 203.

Geiger challenged Zunz's change of heart in a long private letter in which he candidly stated his preference for the dictates of the present. The controversy centered on what should be the decisive force in shaping contemporary Judaism, the cultural level of the present or the legacy of the past? Geiger mourned the loss of Zunz to those in favor of granting the past a normative role. Zunz responded laconically and with evident reluctance. The norms for religion must be purely religious. We must reform ourselves, not our religion. The hue and cry against the Talmud had always been the tactic of apostates.[62]

In breaking with Reform, Zunz, like Sachs, clearly perceived the validating function played by the study of history. In 1845 he published his second major work, *Zur Geschichte und Literatur,* in which he now rendered explicit a theory of *Wissenschaft* that he had adumbrated in his early essays on rabbinic literature and medieval exegesis, and which clashed sharply with that held by Geiger. The volume consisted of a series of essays that dealt primarily with the legal, liturgical, ethical, and exegetical literature of medieval Ashkenazic Jewry and was intended as a corrective to an unwarranted imbalance in the scope of current *Wissenschaft.* Zunz condemned the work of Reform ideologues as selective and tendentious. Brainwashed by the Enlightenment's debunking of Judaism, they defined Jewish literature as religious in character and concentrated only on periods like the Spanish with which they could readily identify. They shunned the literature of Franco-Germany because it seemed too different, too parochial, and too Jewish. In their abhorrence of contemporary clericalism, which Zunz incidentally shared, and in their eagerness for emancipation they had taken to deprecating their past. But if this be the attitude of Jews, would the judgment of Christian scholars ever be more favorable?[63] For Zunz had long believed that the legal

---

62. Geiger, *Nachgelassene Schriften,* V, pp. 180–185.
63. Leopold Zunz, *Zur Geschichte und Literatur* (Berlin, 1845), pp. 1–4, 17, 158.

emancipation of Jews could never effectively precede the scholarly emancipation of Judaism.[64] The prerequisite for all scholarship was objectivity. Yet so many works of Reform history were undertaken for political gain or to buttress a prior point of view.

> Thus we spend time on subjects which appeal to us because they serve transitory ends, while we avoid periods entirely unresearched. And since we do not study men and their actions as an end in itself, but rather for the sake of our anticipated advantage, we remain sunk, no less than our scornful enemies, in unfair prejudice toward many works of the past.[65]

The heart of Zunz's critique was a different concept of *Wissenschaft*.

> History and justice is not the knowledge of a single epoch, of a single stage, of a single event. It is a comprehensive, integrated, and fair understanding. Many a misunderstood century has provided the basis for contemporary life, but since this life no longer pleases those who have fallen away from Judaism, they disdain the men of that age and scorn their works.[66]

To counter the onesidedness of this perception of the past, Zunz devoted the rest of his life to rehabilitating the vast liturgical literature of medieval Jewry. Defying the prevailing irreligious sentiments of his age, Zunz labored to present the synagogue as a national theater in which a living nation gave ample expression to its religious genius.[67]

It was only to be expected that Zunz's indictment of Reform *Wissenschaft* would draw fire from Abraham Geiger, its leading practitioner. In a typically extensive nineteenth-century review of Zunz's book, Geiger set forth his own position

64. Leopold Zunz, *Die Gottesdienstliche Vorträge der Juden,* 2nd ed. (Frankfurt a.M., 1892), Vorrede.

65. Zunz, *Zur Geschichte,* p. 28.

66. Ibid., p. 28.

67. Wiener, pp. 182–183.

with clarity and vigor. Jewish literature did not merit the designation of national literature, for it had always been, even in the days of political independence, heavily weighted toward the religious. The secular subjects on which the Jews may have written in the Middle Ages, when they no longer ranked as a living people, were but a pale reflection of general culture. The fact that Jews wrote about them in Hebrew merely attested to their cultural isolation, for the simple truth was that as soon as Jews began to assimilate to a superior culture they adopted its language. The survival of Hebrew, therefore, signified a cultural lag and not the existence of any national consciousness. Jewish literature had to be defined by its spirit and not its language.

Geiger also candidly challenged Zunz's plea for comprehensiveness. Not all periods were equally important; only some had truly exerted a lasting influence on the course of history, even if all derived from the Spirit. The historian must have the courage to be selective and judgmental. Distortion was not the result of knowing only part of the story, but of knowing the wrong part. *Wissenschaft* turned to the seminal periods of the past to write the history of the spirit of Judaism and to instruct and rejuvenate the Jews of today, but only after the present state of consciousness, nurtured by emancipation, determined what it considered to be seminal. Unwittingly, Geiger had acknowledged that subjectivity lay at the heart of his enterprise.[68]

It should be abundantly clear by now that the 1840s marked a turning point in the history of German Jewish *Wissenschaft*. Under the impact of an intensified emancipation struggle, Reform had moved rapidly further left, with the inevitable result that a countervailing force began to form. While men like Frankel, Sachs, and Zunz did not work in tandem, they did simultaneously rise to denounce the accommodations preached by Reform. What's more, they began to condemn the manner in which *Wissenschaft* was used in behalf of Reform, not by repudiating the discipline as alien to Judaism, but by

---

68. *Literatur-Blatt zum INJ*, 1846, nos. 1,2,14,15,17,18–19.

insisting that it be practiced differently. The emerging conservative bloc had sensed that *Wissenschaft* was an instrument that could be employed to preserve traditional Judaism as well as to revamp it, to resist the price of emancipation as well as to pay it. The Reform monopoly of *Wissenschaft* had been broken. A handful of historians had begun to formulate an alternative program based on a different reading of Jewish history. In the mid-1840s the young Heinrich Graetz threw in his lot with this conservative bloc in resounding fashion. In the following decades he profoundly deepened its perception of the past.

V

Some men can be understood only by identifying their adversaries. Their views were forged in controversy and therefore can never be fully fathomed in isolation. There is no other way to study the work of Heinrich Graetz. His entire career from his earliest days as a university student in Breslau was marked by an unfailing antipathy toward the Reform movement. The evidence is abundant and best summarized by Graetz himself in a letter to Raphael Kirchheim, a remarkably learned Jewish businessman in Frankfurt with an important personal library, who had drawn close to Geiger in the 1860s while remaining on friendly terms with Graetz. In 1869 Graetz wrote him frankly:

> The great question today is, will Judaism survive or disappear? For I regard it as disappearing if it is christianized, or as Heine says, if it spins its צִיץ from the wool of the Lamb of God. I will fight against the christianization of Judaism, which is entailed in the reform of Judaism, to my last breath and with all the weapons at my command.[69]

The most potent weapon in his arsenal was *Wissenschaft des Judentums.* In contrast to his dogmatic mentor, Samson

---

69. S. Unna, "Briefe von H. Grätz an Raphael Kirchheim," *Jahrbuch der jüdisch-literarischen Gesellschaft*, XII (1918), p. 320.

Raphael Hirsch, Graetz challenged the proponents of Reform with their own weapon. His reading and writing of Jewish history were born of opposition and his scholarship was shaped by the determination to provide an alternative view of Jewish history, which would invalidate the claims of the Reform movement to historical legitimacy. If the leaders of Reform in many ways resembled the *philosophes* of the previous century, it is not forcing the analogy to suggest that Graetz assumed the role of Edmund Burke. Like his conservative English counterpart, he approached the past with reverence and held reason in distrust. Human reason was to be tempered by the wisdom of the ages and change enacted in accord with tradition. Neither man accepted the polemical view of the Middle Ages put forth by his adversaries and a pronounced moral strain pervaded the work of both.[70]

Graetz was born in 1817 in a remote eastern village in the backwater of Prussia, the province of Posen, whose 52,000 Jews were still decades away from emancipation. When he arrived in Breslau some twenty-five years later to matriculate in that city's famous non-denominational university, he had not had the benefit of a single year of formal secular education. In contrast to his solid mastery of Jewish sources, which had been acquired with the benefit of some formal instruction, including three years of tutorial work with Hirsch, his broad secular knowledge and linguistic competence were attained entirely on his own through superhuman effort and un-relieved hardship. The intimate diary which he began to keep in 1833 reveals a highly emotional young man, often overcome by moments of religious fervor and afflicted with recurring sieges of self-doubt and feelings of inferiority, but driven at the same time by a burning desire to achieve recognition.[71]

---

70. Edmund Burke, *Reflections on the Revolution in France* (The Library of Liberal Arts, Indianapolis, 1955), pp. 36, 39–40, 42, 62, 90, 99.

71. To date, important selections from Graetz's diary, which spans the twenty-three years of his life from 1833 to 1856, have been published by Markus Brann, *MGWJ*, LXII (1918), pp. 231–265; LXIII (1919), pp. 34–47, 343–363; Reuven Michael, *Kiryat Sefer*, XXXVII (1961–1962),

The move to Breslau brought Graetz, the aspiring, self-educated country bumpkin, face to face with Abraham Geiger, only seven years his senior but already one of the acknowledged leaders of the expanding Reform movement. The confrontation quickly turned into a permanent feud. The differences went far deeper than religious disagreement. Geiger hailed from Frankfurt, had won his academic spurs at Bonn with a prize essay and his doctorate at Marburg, and possessed a far more even temperament than his lifelong younger adversary. Unlike Graetz, Geiger also enjoyed the hard-to-acquire status of a Prussian citizen, for which he had been compelled to wait idly in Berlin for more than a year before it was finally granted in November 1839.[72]

The differences in development and disposition were already strikingly evident in the contrasting reactions of each man to the publication of Hirsch's apodictic *Nineteen Letters of Ben Uziel* in 1836, an event that projected its twenty-eight-year-old author into the limelight as a significant spokesman for a new, modified Orthodoxy favorable to emancipation. The same book, which rescued Graetz's faith from the near fatal challenge of secularism and inspired him to study personally with Hirsch for three years from 1837 to 1840,[73] provoked Geiger to write a devastating review in which he condemned Hirsch for his total lack of any historical sense and for his utterly arbitrary exegetical method.[74] Although

pp. 523–531; *LBIYB*, XIII (1968), pp. 34–49; Shmuel Ettinger, ed., *Heinrich Graetz: Darkhe ha-Historiah ha-Yehudit* (Jerusalem, 1969), pp. 243–265. A complete edition of the diary plus several hundred of Graetz's letters, many of which have already been published, are now being prepared for publication by Dr. Michael. The two best biographical essays on Graetz are still those of Philip Bloch in Graetz's *History of the Jews*, VI (Philadelphia, 1956), pp. 1–86, and Josef Meisl, *Heinrich Graetz* (Berlin, 1917).

72. The best biography of Geiger is still that written by his son Ludwig Geiger in the collective volume *Abraham Geiger: Leben und Lebenswerk* (Berlin, 1910), pp. 1–231.

73. Brann, *MGWJ*, LXII (1918), p. 258; Bloch, pp. 17–22.

74. See in particular Geiger, *WZJT*, III (1837), pp. 77, 81–82. The first two installments were published the previous year. (Ibid., II [1836], pp.

Graetz eventually also came to regard Hirsch as the antithesis of modern *Wissenschaft,* during his first stay in Breslau he was still very much under his influence and harbored a passionate grudge against Geiger for his hostile review.[75]

In the 1840s Breslau was the third largest Jewish community in Prussia (behind Berlin and Posen) and growing rapidly. With a steady influx of rural Jews from Silesia and Posen, the Jewish population jumped from 5714 in 1840 to 7384 in 1849. It was also wracked by the bitterest and most protracted religious controversy of the decade precipitated by the election of Geiger as the community's second rabbi in 1838.[76] By the time Graetz came on the scene, Geiger's forces had clearly gained the upper hand. In the spring of 1842 the board had suspended its first rabbi Solomon Tiktin, his determined Orthodox opponent, following an unseemly demonstration at a funeral at which Geiger was to officiate.[77]

Nevertheless, Graetz's antipathy for Geiger exceeded his aversion to the unenlightened, casuistic Orthodoxy of the Tiktin camp.[78] As the Breslau correspondent of the *Orient* of Julius Fürst, a *Privatdozent* at the University of Leipzig whom Graetz respected for his determination not to convert to Christianity for the sake of an academic appointment, Graetz quickly received the notoriety he sought as a talented and uncompromising critic of Geiger and his movement. His articles were personal, passionate, and pugnacious.[79] In short, long before Graetz was to make his mark as a scholar he had

---

351–359, 518–548.) *Horeb* fared no better. (See, ibid., IV [1839], pp. 355–381.)

75. Michael, *LBIYB,* XIII (1968), p. 42. The year is 1844, not 1848.

76. Salomon Neumann, *Zur Statistik der Juden in Preussen von 1816 bis 1880* (Berlin, 1884), p. 45. Ludwig Geiger, *Abraham Geiger,* p. 56.

77. Ibid., pp. 78–79.

78. Michael, *Kiryat Sefer,* XXXVII (1961–1962), p. 527; idem, *LBIYB,* XIII (1968), p. 42. Graetz also had grown critical of Hirsch's fanatical religious observance and expressed some strong reservations about the supremacy of the *Shulḥan Arukh.* See Brann, *MGWJ,* XLIII (1919), p. 356 and Michael, *Kiryat Sefer,* p. 525.

79. See, for example, his caustic remarks about Geiger in *Der Orient,* 1844, pp. 355-356; 1845, pp. 292, 321, 394; 1846, pp. 111–112. Also his

developed a profound abhorrence for the Reform movement,
fed by an envious dislike for the man who embodied and led
it. The key to understanding Graetz's philosophy of Jewish
history lies in the nexus between this early anti-Reform bias
and the scholarly positions he subsequently adopted. Ideology governed his reading of Jewish history no less than it
governed Geiger's.

The interaction produced a head-on collision in 1844.
Graetz's first published venture in the field of *Wissenschaft*
was nothing less than a lengthy, vitriolic review of a
pioneering study by Geiger on the development of mishnaic
Hebrew. To be sure, Geiger's work was not strictly
dispassionate either. Since his earlier assault on Hirsch's
exegetical method, he had undertaken a critical study of the
history of rabbinic exegesis, with an eye to undermining the
exegetical basis of a legal system which he regarded as alien to
the essence of Judaism.[80] Yet Graetz tore into the book with
all the venom of a jealous protagonist who disdained the
learning but longed for the fame of his adversary.

Aside from a deluge of criticism on details, Graetz
challenged Geiger on three questions of fundamental import.
First, he contested Geiger's assertion that during the Second
Commonwealth Hebrew ceased to be a living language and
that the Hebrew of the Mishnah constituted the artificial
creation of rabbinic scholastics. Refusing to acknowledge that
the prophets were the last Jews to speak Hebrew, Graetz
valliantly marshalled the meager evidence then available,
including the theory that some of the psalms in the Psalter
dated from the period of the Maccabees, to argue that the
Maccabean revolt produced a Hebraic revival. Along with
Aramaic, Hebrew had again been taken up by the masses as a
language of conversation. Second, Graetz denounced Geiger's
presumption to expound the Mishnah objectively and rejected

---

condemnation of the current rabbinical conferences in *Der Orient*,
1844, pp. 179–181; 1846, pp. 229–230, 238, 294–295.
80. Abraham Geiger, "Das Verhältniss des natürlichen Schriftsinnes zur
thalmudischen Schriftdeutung," *WZJT*, V (1844), pp. 53–81, 234–259.

his contention that at times the Talmud itself failed to interpret the Mishnah properly. Like Sachs, whom he admired and quoted at length, Graetz proposed that for the full understanding of certain intellectual works a critical apparatus was insufficient. What gave the "unscientific" rabbinic expositors of the Mishnah a decided edge, he contended, was the benefit of a living tradition which united them spiritually and substantively with the world of the Mishnah. Finally, Graetz rejected Geiger's critical assessment of the Mishnah's biblical exegesis as an argument patently contrived to advance the anti-halakhic program of the Reform movement.[81]

The review unequivocally identified Graetz with the small group of university trained men who had begun to take up the cudgels of *Wissenschaft* on behalf of traditional Judaism. It also brought him the public recognition for which he longed. He proudly recorded in his diary that he received an invitation from Frankel to write for his journal as well as a highly complimentary letter from Sachs. He dreamed of bringing them together with Hirsch to pool their efforts against the rabbinical conferences and Reform associations. Graetz was now more determined than ever to serve Judaism in its hour of need, to join the fight against "malice and sophistry," and he struggled hard to overcome his fears that the jump from a shy, awkward, and unschooled Yeshiva *bochur* to an eloquent national spokesman might be too great.[82]

In 1845 Graetz earned his Ph.D. from the University of Jena for a dissertation on *Gnosticismus und Judenthum* which was published a year later and dedicated to Hirsch, "the profound fighter for historical Judaism, the unforgettable teacher, the fatherly friend."[83] Notwithstanding Graetz's apologies for the utter irrelevance of the subject to the problems currently

---

81. Abraham Geiger, *Lehr—und Lesebuch zur Sprache der Mischnah*, 2 vols. (Breslau, 1845), I, pp. 1–2; II, pp. viii, 4, 7–11, 14, 15, 21–22; Graetz, *Literaturblatt des Orients*, V, pp. 822–827; VI, pp. 631–635.

82. Michael, *LBIYB*, XIII (1968), pp. 45–49.

83. Hirsch Grätz, *Gnosticismus und Judenthum* (Krotoschin, 1846).

tormenting German Jewry, the book does provide a subtle commentary on the contemporary scene. At face value Graetz's scholarly debut was a highly innovative attempt to explore the impact of Gnosticism on second-century Judaism. The very suggestion of any such interaction served notice of the extent to which Graetz was willing to study the history of the Jews in terms of the general context. By locating the most likely historical context, he dated a number of talmudic passages and identified several enigmatic terms and events as the product of gnostic influence. The method of dating on the basis of ideological similarity and historical reasoning, which Graetz used throughout his life, was not terribly refined. It often was arbitrary and hypothetical, with similarities accepted as influence and speculation replacing facts. But at its best, the method could illuminate an undated text brilliantly.[84]

On a symbolic level Graetz's doctoral dissertation mirrored the dilemma of his age. In the introduction Graetz asserted that just as Judaism in the second century had successfully handled the grave challenge of gnostic dualism, so in the nineteenth century it would also overcome the ominous danger of "modern pantheism." Graetz's penchant for reducing historical trends and intellectual currents to personalities was already well developed. The ideological conflict of the second century was embodied in the contrasting figures of Elisha ben Abuya and Akiba ben Joseph, the products of completely disparate backgrounds. The wealthy, well-educated Elisha proved unable to resist the intellectual appeal of gnostic antinomianism and became the prototype of the medieval renegade; the lowly born, uneducated Akiba dramatically surmounted his origins to provide Judaism with the ideological vitality to turn back the challenge.[85] Graetz's spirited and partisan treatment of these

---

84. Among the most successful instances of Graetz's method are the following: *Geschichte*, III, 2nd ed., pp. 494–502; V, 4th ed., pp. 464–471; VII, 4th ed., pp. 430–448.

85. Graetz, *Gnosticismus*, pp. 62–71, 83–85. In the final chapter, Graetz argued that *Sefer Yeṣirah* was a second-century philosophic work,

ancient protagonists strongly suggests that he may have perceived them in terms of his own bitter relationship with Geiger, whom he labeled in his diary as the "miserable spokesman" of an "empty deism."[86] Graetz identified with Akiba, whose creative response to Gnosticism, he felt, was merely one dimension of a career which securely laid the foundation of rabbinic Judaism.[87] Thus the religious turmoil of the present replayed the script of an earlier struggle, with Graetz defending traditional Judaism with novelty and daring against the Elisha ben Abuya of his day.

The book closed on a Hegelian note which would reappear more prominently in Graetz's next work. The confrontation of Judaism with Gnosticism in Graetz's view had had its positive side. It had compelled Judaism to begin reflecting on itself and thereby elevated it to a higher level of self-consciousness.[88]

VI

Graetz's first formative period in Breslau also provided the setting for his initial attempt at a philosophy of Jewish history. Exactly one year after the completion of his doctoral work, the twenty-nine-year-old Graetz published a wide-ranging and coherent prolegomenon to his later history in Frankel's *Zeitschrift*.[89] Ostensibly "The Structure of Jewish History" was an overview to define the nature of Judaism

---

perhaps from the hands of R. Akiba, designed to refute gnostic ideas. He later dated the book in the Gaonic period on linguistic grounds. (*Geschichte*, V, 4th ed., p. 297n. Cf. Gershom Scholem, *Major Trends in Jewish Mysticism*, 3rd rev. ed. [New York, 1954], pp. 75–78).

86. Michael, *LBIYB*, XIII (1968), p. 42.

87. Graetz, *Geschichte*, IV, 4th ed., pp. 50–56.

88. Graetz, *Gnosticismus*, p. 131.

89. Heinrich Graetz, "Die Construction der jüdischen Geschichte," *ZRIJ*, III (1846), pp. 81–97, 121–132, 361–368, 413–421. It was republished again ninety years later (Ludwig Feuchtwanger, ed., *Die Konstruktion der jüdischen Geschichte* [Berlin, 1936]). It was also recently translated into Hebrew in Ettinger, ed., *Darkhe ha-Historiah ha-Yehudit* and now rendered into English.

historically. Actually the essay offered a new theory of Jewish
history carefully designed to refute that constructed by the
advocates of Reform during the previous quarter century. In
nearly every significant aspect, Graetz's theory ran counter to
that propounded by his adversaries, and the cumulative
evidence indicates that Graetz alone among the members of
the emerging conservative camp was the first to realize fully
the nature and function of the Reform theory of Jewish
history.

To be sure, Graetz used the same ideological equipment
employed by his opponents; he remained securely grounded
in the world of German idealism. Ideas were the true
substance and motive power of history, although visible to the
historian only in their actualized form. Thus the idea of
Judaism could be discovered only in the history of Judaism.
What Graetz condemned in earlier efforts was the tendentious
selectivity, the refusal to take into account the entire spectrum
of Jewish history. Whole periods had been treated as
historical mishaps unrelated to the essence of Judaism. Yet if
an idea had forged its way into reality and stamped its imprint
upon an age, then it must represent a genuine dimension of
Judaism's essence. In light of the totality of Jewish history
and in contrast to Reform ideologues, Graetz proposed a
multifaceted essence of Judaism whose different dimensions
shaped different periods of Jewish history.[90]

At the very time when Reform spokesmen were apprehen-
sively protesting the purely confessional character of Judaism, Graetz dared to come out publicly with the declaration
that the essence of Judaism comprised both a religious and a
political factor, a concept of God as well as a theory of the
state. Neither alone could ever exhaust the nature of Judaism.
With respect to its God concept, Graetz adopted a line of
reasoning first developed by Solomon Steinheim, the only
contemporary German Jewish thinker aside from his former
mentor whom he regarded highly. In 1835 Steinheim had
written a fervent but lucid attack against the prevailing

90. See infra, pp. 63–66.

rationalist tendency of the age to reduce religion to the truths of philosophy. The second half of his book juxtaposed what Steinheim felt to be the conflicting views of paganism (i.e., natural religion) and Judaism (i.e., revealed religion) on God, creation, and freedom. Similarly, Graetz posited a fundamental antithesis, arguing specifically that Judaism's perception of God as absolutely transcendent repudiated paganism's theology of immanence.[91] But in contrast to Steinheim and the common Reform view, Graetz insisted:

> that the monotheistic idea is not even the primary principle of Judaism, as it has been widely believed by many up till now, but only the secondary consequence resulting from the extra-mundane concept of God, just as polytheism and idolatry are not the foundation of paganism. Therefore, the idea of monotheism in no way exhausts the entire content of Judaism; the latter is infinitely richer, infinitely deeper.[92]

Part of this wealth was produced by the unique manner in

---

91. S. L. Steinheim, *Die Offenbarung nach dem Lehrbegriffe der Synagoge,* I (Frankfurt a.M., 1835), zweite Abteilung. On Graetz's admiration for Steinheim, see infra, pp. 67, 123. In his *Geschichte,* XI, 2nd ed., Graetz allotted Steinheim more space than any of his contemporaries (pp. 431–437). On Steinheim's work, see Joshua O. Haberman, "Salomon Ludwig Steinheim's Doctrine of Revelation," *Judaism,* XVII (1968), pp. 22–41; Nathan Rotenstreich, *Jewish Philosophy in Modern Times* (New York, 1968), pp. 149–174.

    I am somewhat dubious about Prof. Rotenstreich's contention that Graetz was also influenced by Solomon Formstecher, in light of the latter's well-known Reform leanings. Furthermore, Graetz utterly ignored the man and his work in the volume of the *Geschichte* devoted to his own century. Finally, Graetz's body of ideas, if not their terminology, can readily be derived from Steinheim alone. (See Rotenstreich, *ha-Maḥshabah ha-Yehudit ba-'Eit ha-Hadashah,* 2 vols. [Tel Aviv, 1966], I, p. 77; idem, *Tradition and Reality* [New York, 1972], pp. 54–55.)

92. Infra, p. 69. In contrast, Steinheim had asserted that the unity of God was and is the fundamental proposition of Judaism. (Steinheim, p. 306.) Even Frankel was disturbed by the radicalism of Graetz's position. Witness his long critical note attached to Graetz's essay (infra, pp. 304–305). Despite Frankel's claim that Graetz had changed his view by the time he finished the last installment of his essay, Graetz always remained reluctant to reduce the core of Judaism to the idea of monotheism (infra, p. 309).

which Judaism strove to overcome the dualism inherent in a theology of transcendence and to bridge the chasm between man and God. Against Hegel's critique of Judaism as a "religion of transcendence," Graetz claimed that Judaism was not even a religion, if by that term one understands a relationship to God that will insure personal salvation. It was of the very essence of Judaism to focus on the group and not the individual by translating theology into social practice. The transcendence of God was overcome, Graetz implied, by rendering the idea of God into a suitable social structure. The goal of building a religiously imbued body politic was the way Judaism reunited the spirit with nature. Thus the idea of Judaism comprised a religious and a political dimension, which together constituted the twin axes around which all of Jewish history revolved. The Torah was the soul and the land of Israel the body of a unique political organism. In defending Judaism against the charge that it was guilty of an irremediable dualism between man and God, Graetz arrived at a national definition of Judaism which directly challenged the claims of the Reform movement.[93]

Jewish history, which reflects the idea of Judaism and tests its viability, was divided by Graetz into three distinct periods. Each period realized one aspect of its multifaceted essence. The first period ended with the destruction of Jerusalem and the Temple in 586 and was predominantly of a political character. The second period spanned the Second Commonwealth, and terminated with the destruction of the Second Temple in 70, manifesting a distinctly religious character. The long medieval period of dispersion, which covered some seventeen centuries down to the end of the eighteenth century, revealed still a third dimension of the idea of Judaism.

At first glance, Graetz's periodization did not appear to break new ground, either in the demarking or the characterization of the periods. In both respects it bore considerable resemblance to the scheme outlined just three years earlier by

---

93. See infra, pp. 70–71. On Hegel's view of Judaism, see Nathan Rotenstreich, "Hegel's Image of Judaism," *JSS*, XV (1953), pp. 33–52.

Holdheim who likewise had depicted the first period as
mainly political and the second as religious. Graetz also
resembled his Reform opponents in the common failure to
depart from the regnant Christian periodization of Jewish
history which posited the year 70 as a fateful turning point in
Jewish history. Since the third century the Church had
defended tenaciously the argument that the destruction of
Jerusalem and the dispersion of the Jews which allegedly
accompanied it were the swift divine punishment for the
crime of deicide. In the nineteenth century, few Jewish
historians challenged the historical validity of this weighty
theological legacy; they merely reinterpreted the significance
of this watershed in Jewish history.[94]

The novelty of Graetz's scheme lay precisely in his radical
departure from the significance conventionally attributed by
the Reform theory of Jewish history to the third period. The
destruction of the Second Temple did not climax the demise
of Jewish nationhood nor inaugurate Judaism's mission to the
world. In an omission pregnant with meaning, Graetz
completely ignored the mission concept so central to Reform
thinking. Instead, appropriating a Hegelian category, he
argued that the period of dispersion was marked by a distinct
speculative dimension unknown in the earlier periods.

---

94. Holdheim, *Ueber die Autonomie,* pp. 38–49. On the history of the
Church's interpretation, see Jules Isaac, *The Teaching of Contempt*
(New York, 1964), pp. 39–73. This interpretation was fully retained by
Jacques Basnages, the early eighteenth-century Huguenot historian of
the Jews, in his epoch-making *History of the Jews from Jesus Christ to
the Present Time,* translated by T. Taylor (London, 1708), pp. 2, 53, 61,
145. In the nineteenth century, Reform historians continued to regard
the year 70 as the start of a new era. (Aside from Holdheim, see also
Julius Heinrich Dessauer, *Geschichte der Israeliten* [Erlangen, 1846],
p. 165; and Abraham Geiger, *Das Judenthum,* I, pp. 150–162.) Jost,
however, with his emphasis on the pre-70 emergence of rabbinism,
deserves to be credited with freeing himself at least partially from the
prevailing Christian view. (See his *Geschichte der Israeliten,* III, pp.
180–185.) A less theologically oriented and more historically determined periodization had to await the nationalist historiography of our
own century. (See Gedalyah Alon, *Toldot ha-Yehudim be-Eretz Yisrael
bi-Tqufat ha-Mishnah ve-ha-Talmud,* I [Israel, 1958], pp. 1–11.)

Exposure to conflicting life-styles and ideologies compelled Judaism to reflect upon itself. Although the immediacy of the original religious experience was shattered, exile served to elevate Judaism to a higher level of consciousness. Ultimately the Jews would return to their homeland to translate their profounder understanding of Judaism into a new social reality.[95]

This interpretation of the period of dispersion made it quite evident that there was nothing accidental about Jewish messianism. It was not the natural consequence of persecution but rather, reflected the basic drive of Judaism to translate theory into practice. In a telling metaphor Graetz compared God's exile of the Jews to a father's education of his son.

> Once a son has been educated and matured by his father's guidance and teaching, the father himself sends the boy away from the hearth and ships him out into the world to gather experience and to test his paternal teaching in the thousand conflicts of life. But the father has no intention of letting his beloved boy perish in a distant land. With the strength and independence that comes through bitter experience, the son will return to his house to inherit his father's estate.[96]

Thus Graetz refused unequivocally to historicize the messianic hope, for to abandon the belief in national redemption was to render the exile meaningless.

This Hegelian function of exile as the path to greater self-consciousness also enabled Graetz to challenge the treatment accorded talmudic Judaism by Reform historians.

> There is nothing more absurd and unhistorical than to assert that a force which penetrated as deeply as did the talmudic system is the product of an error, of twisted exegesis, of hierarchical ambition, in short, of an historical accident.[97]

---

95. Infra, pp. 94–96, 124.
96. Infra, p. 98.
97. Infra, p. 100.

If the origins of Judaism lay in protest and true enlightenment came only by plunging into the world, then a certain amount of self-imposed distance and isolation were indispensable for sheer survival. Separation was not imposed by the hostility of an alien environment but counterbalanced the necessity to examine opposing principles at close range.

By implication, Graetz's vision of Jewish history also broke with the basic conceptual assumption of development upon which the Reform theory relied. There is no true notion whatever of development in Graetz. The argument for a multifaceted essence of Judaism amounts to a theory of immanence in which the major changes of later .eras are reduced to the logical unfolding of the original idea. The radical import of Graetz's position is that, unlike the Reform theory, earlier phases of Jewish history are never transcended. The national dimension of the first period or the talmudic system of the third are not abandoned in the wake of subsequent eras. Although every period is shaped by a different dimension of Judaism, and thereby illuminates a part of the whole, none of these dimensions is historicized. All facets continue to remain operative and valid. Even the self-consciousness acquired in exile, which seems to suggest a theory of progress, does not serve to diminish the validity of earlier realizations of the idea of Judaism. Graetz simply refused to accord a higher status to later periods. Thus the proto-Zionist note on which he closed his essay aptly summed up his non-developmental theory.

> And since these three dimensions have assumed historical form, they must have lain in the original idea of Judaism, as the tree in the seed, and according to this view of history, it seems that the task of Judaism's God-idea is to found a religious state which is conscious of its activity, purpose, and connection with the world.[98]

What Graetz did propose was much more akin to a cyclical

---

98. Infra, p. 124.

theory of history. His overview of Jewish history emphasized the formal similarities between periods no less than the substantive differences. The periods of the first two Commonwealths, for example, abounded in parallels. Both periods began with terms of exile, to be followed by a return to Palestine under the inspired leadership of the Judges and the men of the Great Assembly respectively. In each case, Jewish life came to be gravely threatened by the challenge of a foreign ideology, monarchy and Hellenism, while the heroic responses culminating in the reigns of David and John Hyrcanus were cut short by deep internal divisions, in the first era between the kingdoms of Judah and Israel, in the second between the Pharisees and Sadducees.[99]

In the final analysis, what distinguished Graetz's theory of Jewish history from that of his Reform adversaries is what separated Humboldt from Hegel or the historian from the philosopher. In his adamant refusal to impose a rigid developmental scheme on the totality of Jewish history, Graetz heeded Humboldt's astute caveat against a teleological approach to the study of history. In 1821, one year before Hegel began lecturing on his philosophy of history, Wilhelm von Humboldt, the paragon of German humanism, had delivered a brilliant statement on the task of the historian in which he asserted:

> Historical truth is, generally speaking, much more threatened by philosophical than by artistic handling, since the latter is at least accustomed to granting freedom to its subject matter. Philosophy dictates a goal to events. This search for final causes, even though it may be deduced from the essence of man and nature itself, distorts and falsifies every independent judgment of the characteristic working of forces.[100]

Although Humboldt certainly believed in the causal role of ideas and acknowledged the existence of an unknowable

---

99. Infra, pp. 84–92.
100. Wilhelm von Humboldt, "On the Historian's Task," translated in *History and Theory*, VI (1967), p. 64.

cosmic plan, he resisted the philosophic appeal of doing violence to the flux and variety of history. The distinct essence which inhered in every individuality did reveal an aspect of infinity and represented the final goal of all historical reasearch, but the sum total of essences could never be forced into the straitjacket of a progressive model.[101] Humboldt's position, with its respect for the diversity of history, provided Graetz with a theory perfectly suited to take on the spokesmen of Reform who had used the teleology, if not the dialectics, of Hegel to free themselves from the legacy of earlier and lower stages of development.

VII

In 1853 Graetz offered the reading public volume four as the first installment of what was billed as a multivolume *History of the Jews from the Earliest Times to the Present.* In so doing, he defied the scholarly judgment of his day, for Zunz and others had long felt that any further attempt at a comprehensive history of the Jews was premature. The quarter century which had passed since the appearance of Jost's ninth volume in 1828 had certainly witnessed a proliferation of monographs on talmudic and medieval history, but the results merely provided some idea of the vast stretches of the Jewish past still to be explored. Too many documents and manuscripts still lay buried in archives and private libraries, unstudied and unpublished. Graetz himself was clearly aware, as he admitted to his intimate friend Moses Hess in a letter in 1864, of the inevitable shortcomings of his work.

> I am not so modest as not to realize that my history is much better than Jost's which is really none at all. But I know best of all what deficiencies in material, treatment, organization, style

---

101. Ibid., pp. 57–71. See also Georg G. Iggers, *The German Conception of History* (Middletown, Conn., 1968), pp. 56–62.

attend my work. However, I can't help it. I am paving the way for a better work.[102]

Graetz defied the judgment of his peers because an effective refutation of the Reform theory of Jewish history required a shift away from speculative history. Heinrich Heine had once quipped against Hegel that "Life is neither a goal nor a means, life is a right."[103] The most formidable challenge to Hegel's reading of history came from the scientific history of Ranke, who spent a lifetime carrying out Humboldt's conception of a historian. Deeply sensitive to the infinite variety of history, he refused to subsume the wealth of data under a teleological superstructure. "Every epoch is equally close to God."[104] Similarly, Graetz turned to scientific history to undermine the teleology of Hegel's Jewish disciples. Geiger recognized the gulf that separated the two men. In reviewing Graetz's fourth volume in 1866, on the occasion of a second edition, he zeroed in on the fundamental difference:

> The book contains stories [*Geschichten*] which are loosely strung together, but no history [*Geschichte*]. We gain no sense of development, of an inner driving power. I'm not asking for contrived pragmatic history, but just as little do I want a force devoid of ideas. Movements must arise from the depth of a totality rooted in distinct spiritual tendencies. The phenomena must come forth according to an inner law and work their way toward a goal.[105]

That Graetz began with volume four, which covered the turbulent but seminal period from 70 to 500 C.E., was not only a proof of the extent to which he had already worked out his

102. Edmund Silberner, "Heinrich Graetz' Briefe an Moses Hess 1861–1872," Instituto Giangiacomo Feltrinelli, *Annali*, 1961, p. 355.
103. Franz Schnabel, *Deutsche Geschichte im neunzehnten Jahrhundert*, 4 vols. (Freiburg im Breisgau, 1933–1937), III, p. 85.
104. Schnabel, p. 87. See also Iggers, pp. 76–80.
105. Geiger, JZWL, IV (1866), p. 146.

overall conception, but was also evidence of the highly controversial nature of the period itself. The emancipation struggle had seriously threatened the viability of the entire rabbinic system. Reform historians like Jost, Holdheim, Geiger, and the Galician *maskil* Joshua Heschel Schorr had long sought to undermine the divine mandate of rabbinic Judaism by exposing its historical origins.[106] In the 1850s, with the publication of four major works on this crucial period, the level of debate reached a new high. The decade had opened with the posthumous publication of Krochmal's long-awaited *Moreh Nebukhe ha-Zeman* by Zunz in 1851. In 1853 Graetz added his contribution, which was followed in 1857 by Geiger's *Urschrift und Uebersetzungen der Bibel,* and two years after that by Frankel's *Darkhe ha-Mishnah.*

Despite the audacity and ingenuity of Geiger's radical study of rabbinic exegesis, by the end of the decade the conservative scholarship of Krochmal, Graetz, and Frankel had succeeded in presenting a more sympathetic and favorable assessment of rabbinic Judaism. Graetz tried valiantly to portray the disembodied rabbis of the Mishnah and Talmud as vibrant men, each with his own style and philosophy and personal frailties, who collectively resisted the disintegrating forces of their age.[107] In contrast to Jost, who harped on the rise and triumph of clericalism, Graetz invoked the categories of recovery, regeneration, and consolidation. In the wake of national disaster, creative leadership forged new religious institutions to preserve and invigorate the bonds of unity. Graetz berated Schorr and his circle for depicting the founders of rabbinic Judaism like contemporary Polish rabbis.[108] He defended talmudic literature as a great national achievement of untold importance to the subsequent survival of the Jews.[109]

---

106. Wiener, pp. 229–231.
107. Jost had contended that he was unable to detect any coherent intellectual system among individual rabbis. (See Jost, *Geschichte der Israeliten,* IV, pp. 30–45, Anhang, p. 224.)
108. Graetz, *Geschichte,* IV, 2nd ed., p. 480.
109. Graetz, *Geschichte,* IV, 2nd ed., p. 412. See the favorable review in *Der*

The proud and exuberant tone of Graetz's work was as new as the interpretations being expounded, and it reflected the second major reason behind his decision to undertake a comprehensive history. A year before the first volume appeared Graetz had come to Berlin, and in the winter of 1852–1853 he taught a course in Jewish history to aspiring students of Jewish theology who also studied the Bible with Sachs and rabbinic literature with Zunz.[110] When Sachs introduced Graetz to Zunz one evening in his home, he mentioned that his guest intended to publish a history of the Jews. "Another history of the Jews!" sighed Zunz. "Yes," retorted Graetz unperturbed. "But this time a Jewish history!"[111] The significance of this well-known anecdote is not only that it underscores the determination to write a national history, but even more, it suggests one of the sources of Graetz's inspiration.

From the fragmentary evidence which remains it would appear that Sachs exerted a formative influence on his younger colleague. Equally endowed with strong feelings, both men shared an instinctive aversion toward Reform. Graetz had quoted Sachs at length in his review of Geiger's *Lehr- und Lesebuch zur Sprache der Mischnah,* and when Sachs wrote him a highly complimentary letter, Graetz referred to him in his diary as "the hero of the day, who belongs to those people who make a symbolic impression."[112] In the final volume of his history, which covered the events of his own day with a jaundiced eye, Graetz allotted the extraordinary amount of six pages for a glowing encomium on Sachs.[113] Graetz first met Sachs in 1846 and then again in

israelitische Volkslehrer, V (1855), pp. 35–39. Hirsch, on the other hand, bitterly contested the *halakhic* development depicted by his former student. He completely rejected the portraits of R. Yohanan b. Zakkai and R. Akiba as reformers and innovators who rescued Judaism. (*Jeschurun,* II [1855–1856], p. 64: III [1856–1857], p. 403.)

110. Graetz apparently took the occasion to attack Jost's work publicly. (See Glatzer, pp. 253–254.)

111. Bloch, pp. 45, 60.

112. See supra, p. 36, as well as Michael, *LBIYB,* XIII (1968), p. 45.

113. Graetz, *Geschichte,* XI, 2nd ed., pp. 522–527. Salomon Steinheim was

1852 when Sachs introduced him to his learned and close friend Moritz Veit, who agreed to publish the first volume of Graetz's forthcoming history.[114] Above all, Graetz wrote the kind of history for which Sachs had been pleading. In the hands of both men *Wissenschaft* became a vehicle for the recovery of self-respect and a force for the preservation of the Jewish people. Both repudiated an approach to Jewish history that studied the past mainly to escape from its tutelage. The historian had the sacred task to fire his people with a love for the drama and glory of its past in order to strengthen its sense of unity and its resolve to survive.

In their vision of *Wissenschaft* Sachs and Graetz mirrored the prevailing nationalist spirit of contemporary German historiography. Since the frustration of German unity at the Congress of Vienna, German intellectuals led by the retired statesman Baron vom Stein, had begun to unfurl the glories of German history to create a ground-swell for unification. It was hoped that the rediscovery of a common national history would engender a sense of national consciousness. The mood in which two generations of nationalist historians from Georg Pertz to Heinrich Treitschke labored was foreshadowed in the motto which Stein chose for the *Monumenta Germaniae historica,* that vast collection of Latin sources on medieval German history conceived by Stein and carried out by Pertz and then Georg Waitz: *Sanctus amor patriae dat animum* (The sacred love of the fatherland gives courage). To generate that love among the masses became the responsibility of the historian.[115]

The nationalist quality of Graetz's history expressed itself in a variety of ways, quite apart from the open acknowledgment he made at the end of his preface to volume one (which

---

the only other contemporary who received the same enthusiastic treatment (pp. 431–437).

114. I am indebted to Dr. Reuven Michael for the information on 1846. See also *INJ,* 1846, p. 334 and Bloch, p. 45.

115. G. P. Gooch, *History and Historians in the Nineteenth Century* (Boston, Beacon Press, 1959), pp. 60–71, 122–146; Schnabel, pp. 101–105.

appeared in 1874), that the love for the people to which he belonged by birth and convinction sustained him in the execution of his work.[116] To begin with, an unshakable belief in the continuity of Jewish history infused his entire enterprise. Graetz lashed out against Christian theologians and historians for depriving the Jews of any legitimate history beyond the destruction of the Second Temple.[117] He also rebuked Jost for denying any continuity between the prophets and the rabbis.[118] In contrast, Graetz emphasized the legal character of the Bible and claimed, without effectively proving his case, that medieval Jewish history continued to show a national dimension.[119] In brief, the substance of Graetz's work was the story of a single people, still very much alive, whose unique historical experience spanned some three millennia.

Second, Graetz fully identified with his subject. When the Jews endured defeat and persecution, he shared the agony of their fate. On occasion, his quill faltered in recounting the brutality of their hardships.[120] Not surprisingly, Graetz also

---

116. Graetz, *Geschichte*, I, 2nd ed., p. xiii.
117. Infra, pp. 93–94. *Geschichte*, XI, 1st ed., p. 581.
118. Ibid., p. 456.
119. Graetz, *Geschichte*, II, 1st ed., Part One, pp. 192–200, 300, 303. Also infra, pp. 133–139.
120. Graetz, *Geschichte*, III, 2nd ed., pp. 405–406; VIII, 4th ed., pp. 355–392. A notable exception to this identification is to be found in Graetz's handling of the Chmelniccki persecution of 1648. In fact his pronounced aversion toward Polish Jewish culture and society induced Graetz to suggest that the disaster was not entirely undeserved. Greed had blinded the Jews to the precariousness of their position in the Ukraine and the dangers inherent in abusing the Cossacks. The consequences of the ensuing pogrom transcended the immediate loss of life. The refugees from Poland, with their medieval ways, now swarmed westward at the very moment that the nations of the West were entering the age of Enlightenment. The Polandization of western Jewry retarded its entry into the modern world for more than a century. (*Geschichte*, X, 3rd ed., pp. 49–76.) It is instructive to compare this treatment with Graetz's attempt to absolve German Jewry of the eleventh century of any responsibility in setting off the persecutions which attended the First Crusade. (*Geschichte*, VI, 4th ed., pp. 82–83.)

harbored an ill-concealed hatred for the enemies of his people. His history is replete with outbursts and expletives against Roman, Christian, and German oppressors.[121] He measured the character of renowned non-Jews like Luther, Voltaire, and Fichte in terms of their attitudes toward Jews and Judaism.[122] Similarly, Graetz did not hesitate to pour his wrath on Jews whom he regarded as having betrayed the cause of Jewish survival. He railed against Hellenized Jews, Herod, Josephus, apostates, Friedländer, and Holdheim among others.[123] As was frequently the case in nineteenth-century national histories, empathy ended in partisanship.

Coupled with such self-righteous indignation 'at national degradation and treason was an eloquent effort to accentuate the ideal of national recovery. The Maccabees had effected a national revival which made Hebrew again a living language.[124] Rejecting the invidious portrait of the Zealots by Josephus, Graetz depicted them as noble, brave, and idealistic men inspired by faith to regain national independence.[125] The

---

121. Graetz, *Geschichte*, III, 2nd ed., pp. 50–51, 136; XI, 1st ed., pp. 377, 514, 520, 537. M. Brann cleaned up this final volume somewhat for the second edition in 1900. (See ibid., pp. vii–viii.) The intimate correspondence with Hess provides ample evidence of Graetz's unmitigated hatred for the Catholic Church and the Germans. (See Silberner, pp. 349, 353, 369, 377, 384, 387–388, 395, 396.) Understandably, Graetz laid the blame for many of the misfortunes of medieval Jewry on the steps of the Church. (*Geschichte*, VII, 4th ed., pp. 176–182, note 11; VIII, 4th ed., pp. 105–106, 283–284, 343–344.)

122. Graetz, *Geschichte*, IX, 4th ed., pp. 297–302; XI, 1st ed., pp. 53–54, 246–248. At the end of his essay on Voltaire, Graetz reiterated his conviction that "one can test quite accurately the integrity of the apostles of freedom and of the philosophers by their relationship to the Jews." (*MGWJ*, XVII [1868], p. 223.)

123. Graetz, *Geschichte*, III, 2nd ed., pp. 49, 151, 376; XI, 1st ed., pp. 170–175, 377–378, 561–566.

124. Graetz, *Geschichte*, III, 2nd ed., p. 70.

125. Ibid., pp. 339–340. See also his ingenious reconstruction of the evidence for an alliance between the Zealots and the Shammaites in 66 C.E. (Ibid., pp. 494–502.) For recent confirmation of Graetz's theory, see Saul Lieberman, *Greek in Jewish Palestine* (New York, 1942), pp. 179–184, and Gedalyah Alon, *Meḥqarim be-Toldot Yisrael*, I (Israel, 1957), pp. 44–45, 266 n.63.

subsequent revolts against Rome in the second and fourth decades of the next century were cast in terms that echoed the contemporary European scene. The Jews loathed subjugation. Filled with an indomitable spirit of freedom and memories of independence, they rose in an epic struggle against the Roman colossus. "The beginning resembled every national uprising."[126] Graetz believed that in his own day one could detect the first sign of yet another national revival in the universal Jewish outrage and action in the face of the Damascus blood libel of 1840 and that this turning point in modern Jewish history should have been commemorated annually in the synagogue.[127] As modern Greek and Italian nationalists were reviving the glories of Pericles and Scipio, Jews must rediscover the heroic moments of their own history. The road to the future led through the past.[128]

Finally, Graetz as a national historian mounted a subtle argument for the importance of Jewish history for the understanding of general history. This rather bold proposition was the reverse of the more widely acknowledged realization that a proper understanding of the Jewish history of any given period required careful attention to the larger canvas of general history. And Graetz from the very beginning of his scholarly career repeatedly tried, sometimes with striking success, to account for particular Jewish develop-

---

126. Graetz, *Geschichte*, IV, 2nd ed., pp. 125–126, 149–151, 161. Quotation p. 126.

127. Graetz, *Geschichte*, XI, 1st ed., pp. 509–510, 553–554. In 1840, a depressed and inferiority-ridden Graetz had collected six thaler from the indifferent Jews of Ostrowo, where he was serving as a house tutor, for Moses Montefiore's efforts on behalf of Damascan Jewry. (Michael, *Kiryat Sefer*, XXXVII [1961–1962], p. 525.) Geiger, on the other hand, refused to consider the plight of Damascan Jewry as more than an isolated humanitarian problem. The plight of Judaism disturbed him far more, and he believed it could be relieved only through the intellectual and religious revitalization of German Jewry. (Max Wiener, *Abraham Geiger and Liberal Judaism* [Philadelphia, 1962], pp. 87–88.)

128. Graetz, *Geschichte*, XI, 1st ed., p. 581. This passage was omitted from the second edition. (Cf. ibid., XI, 2nd ed., pp. 530–531.)

ments in terms of the non-Jewish world.[129] But as a proud, assertive Jew, Graetz also was eager to show the Jewish impact on general history. All too frequently, this meant a forced and unhistorical comparison between Jews and Christians or Moslems to the decided advantage of the Jews, as if for the moment Jews remained the sole carriers of civilization.[130] But on other occasions, his claims were more substantive. Rabbinic sources, for example, were indispensable for illuminating the origins and early history of Christianity.[131] The Jewish revolts in the Diaspora and Palestine during Trajan's Parthian campaign might seriously have threatened the survival of the Empire, if they had only been coordinated.[132] The Jewish tribes of the Arabian peninsula helped shape the character of Islam.[133] The expulsion of 1492 deprived Spain of its middle class and thus insured its imminent decline.[134] And the prolonged Pfefferkorn-Reuchlin battle over the nature of talmudic literature, which engulfed the Holy Roman Empire and the Church, paved the way for the Reformation by creating a state of mind in Germany that was receptive to Luther's revolt against Rome.[135] These attempts to explain significant aspects of

---

129. Besides the aforementioned study of Jewish gnostics, see also, for example, his essay "Die mystische Literatur in der gaonäischen Epoche," *MGWJ*, VIII (1859), pp. 113–118, 140–144; *Geschichte*, V, 4th ed., pp. 464–471; VII, 4th ed., pp. 35–36.

130. Graetz, *Geschichte*, V, 2nd ed., pp. 268, 317; VI, 4th ed., pp. 2, 66, 67.

131. Graetz, *Geschichte*, IV, 2nd ed., pp. viii, 77–116, 455–458.

132. Ibid., p. 128.

133. Graetz, *Geschichte*, V, 4th ed., pp. 100–119. Geiger had been the first scholar to put this proposition on a sound historical footing in 1833 in his brilliant prize-winning book *Was hat Mohammed aus dem Judenthume aufgenommen*, 2nd rev. ed. (Leipzig, 1902). (See the prolegomenon by Moshe Pearlman to the English edition of Abraham Geiger, *Judaism and Islam* [New York, 1970].)

134. Graetz, *Geschichte*, VIII, 4th ed., p. 351.

135. Graetz, *Geschichte*, IX, 4th ed., pp. 64, 171, 174, 179, 477. A somewhat similar argument had been put forth by Samuel Usque in the sixteenth century to the effect that the Lutherans stemmed from Jews who had been forced to convert to Christianity (Usque, p. 193).

general history in terms of Jewish history implied a confidence in the continued centrality and uniqueness of the Jews. Graetz had recast the religious concept of chosenness in secular terms.

Yet during the very decades when Graetz poured his energies into the production of a patriotic narrative history of the Jews to counterbalance the kind of history being written by Reform ideologists, his own theory paradoxically began to approximate that of his adversaries. To be sure, the emotional antagonism toward Reform remained as intense as ever; witness the overtly polemical treatment accorded the precursors and founders of the movement in the final volume of his history.[136] But ideologically Graetz moved somewhat closer to Reform's conceptualization of the past. Not all of Graetz's later views were articulated or adumbrated in his schematic essay of 1846. The occasional essays in which he subsequently speculated on the nature of Jewish history along with certain tendencies of his comprehensive work reflect several significant departures from his initial effort at conceptualization.

In 1846 Graetz had maintained a pregnant silence on the central issue of a universal Jewish mission, which dovetailed perfectly with the essay's particularistic tone. That silence was abandoned in 1853 in the Introduction to his first

---

136. In 1869 when Graetz became the editor of the highly respected *MGWJ*, its pages suddenly began to reverberate with anti-Reform polemics. In the light of this unexpected change in editorial policy, the Institut zur Förderung israelitischer Literatur, which had assumed publication of Graetz's history with volume three, refused to commit itself to publishing the forthcoming eleventh volume, which was to deal with the emancipation era. The board of the Institute, headed by Adolf Jellinek and Ludwig Philippson, feared that Graetz's treatment of the Reform movement might fall far short of the dispassionate research required of a scholarly study. To reassure itself, the board requested Graetz to submit his manuscript in advance for examination. When Graetz ignored the request, the Institute withdrew its support. (On Graetz's editorial policy, see Silberner, pp. 391, 393; on the controversy itself, see Philippson's version in the *AZJ*, 1869, pp. 387–389 as well as Graetz's inadequate rejoinder in the *MGWJ*, XVIII [1869], pp. 284–286.)

published volume. Graetz now also invoked the standard Reform argument: the redemption of mankind hinged upon the dissemination by the Jews of their unique theological and ethical systems. The traumatic events in the closing years of the Second Commonwealth were now interpreted by Graetz in terms of an apostolic role which necessitated dispersion. A consciousness of their mission and a confidence in their ultimate success served to sustain the Jews through centuries of frustration.[137] This line of reasoning became steadily more prominent in Graetz's later essays, simply because within the hostile context of German society Jewish existence was not a self-evident right but a privilege to be justified. Ludwig Philippson, the pro-Reform editor of Germany's leading Jewish weekly, summed up the Jewish dilemma in 1847:

> That which desires to exist will be asked about the causes and content of as well as the justification for its existence. And only in so far as it can legitimately establish its rights, is it acceptable. . . . Judaism exists; it desires to and will survive. Thus it must make clear to both its adherents and others why it exists and for what reason it hopes to survive.[138]

The tragedy of the Jewish predicament was that to make a case for continued group survival inevitably entailed denigrating the faith of the very society into which Jews sought to integrate. Judaism's right to survive could only be established at the expense of Christianity. In formulating his case Graetz was merely not as politic and tactful as the leaders of Reform.[139]

A second feature of the Reform theory which Graetz quickly came to adopt was the undue emphasis on persecutions.[140] Ironically this version of the medieval Jewish experience is most often identified with Graetz. And yet his

---

137. See infra, pp. 125-132. *Geschichte*, III, 2nd ed., pp. 131, 216, 281-282.
138. *AZJ*, 1847, p. 2.
139. See, for example, "The Significance of Judaism for the Present and the Future," infra, pp. 275-302.
140. See the introductions to volumes IV, V, and VII of his *Geschichte*.

undeniable preoccupation with Jewish suffering led to a radically different conclusion. While articulating the same position, men can sometimes intend wholly different meanings. Unlike Reform historians, Graetz's perception of exilic history in terms of humiliation, oppression, and violence did not stem from a desire to exonerate his contemporaries from any alleged character defects or to provide a rationale for discarding aspects of Judaism which now seemed to be a liability. In the case of Graetz, the vivid and charged narration of Jewish suffering was intended to intensify the attachment to Judaism, whose institutions and beliefs had been sanctified by the blood of countless martyrs.[141] Graetz believed that persecution strengthened the bonds of faith. Catholics were always more devout in countries swept by the Reformation.[142] By extension, Graetz hoped that the vicarious experience of degradation and martyrdom which he sweated to convey to his readers would fortify their commitment to Jewish survival.

It is altogether likely that Graetz's excessive attention to the precariousness of Jewish existence in the past was also intended to question the exuberant and facile faith of his fellow Jews in the promise of the present.[143] Graetz never lost the awareness of being in exile. His skeptical view of human nature denied him the comfort of the prevailing faith in progress and the perfectibility of man. In the opening chapters of Genesis he saw the inevitable fate that awaits men who confidently conduct their lives solely by the canons of reason, arrogantly rejecting divine counsel.[144] Reason alone would never overcome the passions—it certainly was not on the verge of success in the nineteenth century. Graetz decried the immorality and materialism of western civilization and denounced the illiberalism and anti-Semitism of German

---

141. This had been the view of Frankel. See supra, p. 24.
142. Graetz, *Geschichte*, III, 2nd ed., p. 458. See also pp. 49, 79.
143. *Verhandlungen der zweiten israelitischen Synode zu Augsburg* (Berlin, 1873), p. 253. Also Schorsch, pp. 69, 232.
144. Graetz, *Geschichte*, II, 1st ed., part one, pp. 166–174.

society.[145] In 1866 he confided to Hess his desire to settle in Paris and to teach at the École Rabbinique de France.[146] Long before most of his optimistic coreligionists, he sensed the gravity of the anti-Semitic backlash which engulfed the newly founded Empire.[147] In sum, Graetz simply did not share the state of mind which gave rise to the Reform theory of Jewish history. His conception of man led to a modified cyclical theory of Jewish history based on the sober realization that the darkness of a former age could descend again.[148]

That realization turned into personal reality for Graetz in 1879 when he became the object of a public attack by Heinrich Treitschke, the *"praeceptor Germaniae."*[149] In truth, such a collision was inevitable, for sooner or later Graetz's one-sided history was bound to offend the sensibilities of German nationalists. Treitschke and Graetz were cut from the same cloth and used history for the same ends. Extremely apprehensive about the fragile sense of unity and inchoate sense of national purpose from which the Reich still suffered, Treitschke condemned the divisive prominence of Jews in German society. Their presumption and insensitivity were typified by Graetz's *History of the Jews,* a work that insulted the religion and the cultural giants of the German nation. The import of Treitschke's remarks, which not only tried to vindicate the current anti-Semitic resurgence but effectively intensified it, was clear: the time had come for German Jewry to keep its side of the emancipation agreement. Assimilation meant dissolution.[150]

---

145. See infra, "The Correspondence"; Silberner, pp. 375, 384, 387–388.

146. Ibid., p. 369.

147. Schorsch, p. 71.

148. Graetz, "Die Schicksale des Talmud im Verlaufe der Geschichte," *MGWJ,* XXXIV (1885), pp. 529–541. See especially p. 540.

149. The sobriquet is applied by Andreas Dorpalen, *Heinrich von Treitschke* (New Haven, 1957), chapter 9. A convenient selection of essays from this far-flung literary debate is to be found in Walter Boehlich, ed., *Der Berliner Antisemitismusstreit* (Frankfurt a.M., 1965).

150. Boehlich, pp. 7–14, 33–47.

The spate of Jewish responses to the portentous intervention by Treitschke served only to underscore Graetz's isolation. No one dared to defend his work openly. In his own two immediate replies Graetz ignored the larger issues and chose to defend himself against Treitschke's specific charges.[151] Not until 1883, and then only anonymously, did he deliver an impassioned argument on behalf of Jewish survival. *The Correspondence of an English Lady on Judaism and Semitism* was Graetz's final reply to Treitschke. Against the background of a devastating indictment of the moral degeneracy of the nineteenth century, Graetz asserted that the unfinished mission of Judaism was to convince mankind to accept the rigorous ethical system that was the key to Judaism's survival. Furthermore, the maintenance of talmudic Judaism with its pronounced legal and ritual character was still essential. While conceding that ritual would no longer be of value in the days of the Messiah, Graetz insisted that there was nothing messianic about his own day. Talmudic institutions still protected Jews from the virulent hostility of the outside world. A certain amount of ritual was being sloughed off by life itself. But to interfere with this natural process would only shatter Jewish unity so vital in the face of a hostile society. On the positive side, Jewish ritual helped to preserve a sense of unity. Borrowing a page from Mendelssohn, Graetz added that it also functioned as a vast pedagogic system ever reminding Jews of the ethical core of their religion. Before Jews could carry their message to the world, they had to actualize it among themselves. Graetz appealed directly to the sense of responsibility of Jewish intellectuals, who felt that they had already internalized Judaism's ethical teachings. They must continue to subject themselves to the dictates of the ritual system for the sake of the masses for whom it remained indispensable.[152]

---

151. Schorsch, pp. 11, 45–46, 62, 70; Boehlich, pp. 27–33, 47–54.
152. [Heinrich Graetz,] *Briefwechsel einer englischen Dame über Judenthum und Semitismus* (Stuttgart, 1883). Mendelssohn, pp. 73–94. The structure of the book, as the title implies, is an exchange of letters

Graetz ended this deeply felt declaration on Jewish survival with a veiled allusion to the future possibility of a renaissance of Jewish life in Palestine. It was a typically defiant finale, for Treitschke had explicitly warned that Germany could not tolerate dual loyalty.[153] But Graetz was steeped in Jewish national sentiment. Despite his embrace of the mission theory, he never ceased to regard Judaism as anything but a national religion. He spoke for the ancient and traditional twofold character of Judaism with its capstone of national messianism. When Hess wrote in *Rome and Jerusalem* that "the pious Jew is above all a Jewish patriot," he pinpointed the source of Graetz's nationalism.[154] Graetz had first

---

between an inquiring English Jewess and her male friend, a knowledgeable and committed Jew. Graetz may have been prompted to choose this English setting by George Eliot's ideological novel *Daniel Deronda* which had appeared in 1876. Eliot had startled the literary world with an unexpectedly moving portrayal of Jewish character and destiny, in the course of which she not only insisted on the right of Jews to retain their identity but boldly averred the inseparableness of Judaism's spiritual and national strands. Against the backdrop of European nationalism, she envisioned the creation of "an organic center" in Palestine which would revitalize the Jews and benefit mankind [George Eliot, *Daniel Deronda* (Penguin Books, 1967), pp. 575–599]. Graetz's enthusiasm for the book is well attested: as editor of the respected *Monatsschrift*, he published David Kaufmann's exuberant review [*MGWJ*, XXVI (1877), pp. 172ff., 214ff., 255ff.] and in the *Briefwechsel* itself, he referred to it warmly [infra, pp. 205, 213, 255, 258.]

153. Boehlich, p. 46.

154. Moses Hess, *Rome and Jerusalem*, translated by Meyer Waxman (New York, 1945), p. 55. Hess's return to Judaism inaugurated an extraordinary friendship with Graetz, who had read the manuscript of *Rome and Jerusalem* with great excitement and without whose help it would probably have remained unpublished. Graetz's letters to Hess over the next eleven years reveal an affectionate, frank, and meaningful relationship. Both men shared a deep antipathy toward the Germans and the Catholic Church, conceived of Judaism in a similar manner, and longed for national regeneration. They also readily came to each other's assistance. Hess provided Graetz with a number of relevant passages from rare nineteenth-century French pamphlets for volume eleven of the *Geschichte*, which he selected and copied personally, since to have the pamphlets copied by someone else in their entirety was too expensive. Graetz repeatedly invited Hess to join

articulated his national conception of Judaism in 1846, and his final reply to Treitschke, in 1883, confirms that he could not be intimidated to relinquish it. German pressure could only force him to mute and disguise it.[155]

Above all, Graetz remained committed to the rejuvenation of his people. His faith in God's guiding presence throughout Jewish history, as witnessed by two earlier instances of national recovery, assured him of the future.[156] His own work, he hoped, would contribute to the revival of Jewish consciousness. He succeeded beyond measure. As a young man Graetz had once failed to acquire a rabbinic pulpit because he was unable to complete the delivery of his sermon.[157] There is more than a touch of irony in the

---

him on his projected trip to Palestine, on one occasion expressing the hope that he would soon be able to offer his friend an advance to help defray the expenses. In sum, the rich correspondence bespeaks a lasting friendship which was securely based on a common world view. (See Silberner, pp. 326–400.)

155. The extent to which the German scene compelled Graetz to write in allusions, projecting his true sentiments on to the past, is strikingly evident in his two popular essays on Jewish messianism. At the very same time that Graetz was concealing his beliefs behind a guise of historical learning and religious rhetoric, Hess, living in Paris, was able to expound his national conception of Judaism without inhibition in one of the leading French Jewish periodicals. (Cf. Hess, "Lettres sur la mission d'Israël," *Archives Israélites*, XXV [1864].)

Graetz's resignation in 1885 from the governing committee of the recently formed international organization of Hibbat Zion must also be understood in the context of the German setting. In his letter to Leon Pinsker, which he threatened to make public if his name were not removed immediately from the membership of the committee, Graetz articulated his opposition to the increasingly nationalistic tone of the program to settle Russian Jews in Palestine. German anti-Semitism did not permit Graetz the freedom to determine his public posture solely according to his personal convictions. (See A. Druyanov, *Ketavim le-Toldot Hibbat Zion ve-Yishuv Eretz Yisrael*, I [Odessa, 1919], cols. 405–406; Moses Lilienblum, *Ketavim Autobiographim*, III [Jerusalem, 1970], pp. 33–34.)

156. See Graetz's revealing letter to his Hebrew translator, S.P. Rabinowitz, published by Meisl, p. 179 as well as infra, p. 263.

157. Bloch, p. 32. On Graetz's fear of the rabbinate, see Ettinger, ed., *Darkhe ha-Historiah ha-Yehudit*, p. 255.

remarkable fact that the reception accorded to Graetz's history by Jews around the world made him the greatest Jewish preacher of the nineteenth century.[158]

---

158. Besides the bibliography of Graetz's work prepared by M. Brann, ed., *Heinrich Graetz: Abhandlungen zu seinem 100. Geburtstage* (Vienna & Berlin, 1917), pp. 124–171, which lists the countless translations of his history, see also Hess, *Rome and Jerusalem*, pp. 37, 73–74; B. Rippner, *Zum siebzigsten Geburtstage des Prof. Dr. Heinrich Graetz* (Magdeburg, 1887), pp. 4, 26, 27; Meisl, p. 69; Richard Lichtheim, *Toldot ha-Zionut be-Germania* (Jerusalem, 1951), p. 72; Solomon Grayzel, "Graetz's *History* in America," in Guido Kisch, ed., *Das Breslauer Seminar* (Tübingen, 1963), pp. 223–237.

1

The Structure of
Jewish History[1]

An Overview

What is Judaism? This apparently naive question may
puzzle many of those who, standing in the midst of Judaism,
believe they know its contents exhaustively, no less than the
question "What is truth?" has always embarrassed many who
were positive that they had swallowed truth by the spoonful.
What has not yet been proposed as Judaism since it became
the object of systematic thought! How many fundamental
interpretations of Judaism have recently seen the light of day,
claiming exclusive meaning and venturing to order religious
life! One moment, Judaism is the complete embodiment of
speculative theology, a kind of incipient Hegelianism
traversing every dialectic stage (Hirsch).[2] Then, again, it is
exactly the opposite of a priori thought, namely an a posteriori
revelation of peculiar, seemingly anti-rational dogmas which
by virtue of their clarity compel the recognition of speculative
reason (Steinheim).[3] Then, too, Judaism is a thoroughly
systematic program for cultivating an obedient disposition, a
submissive subordination to the absolute will of God, its
ultimate good being the inculcation of religious feeling (Ben
Uziel).[4] Then, again, the precise opposite of religion: a kind
of cold shower for the innate religious fanaticism of the
human soul, a program directed more to practice, a secure
"balancing-rod" against the pernicious onesidedness of
conflicting inclinations (Mises).[5] Some contend that Judaism
is an ethically oriented religion of pure reason; others argue

63

that Judaism is a mystagogic guide to a contemplative life, a religion of immortality which prepares one for the life to come.

All these different, often conflicting, conceptions of Judaism do not fail to base themselves on adequate proofs drawn from the richly stratified content of Judaism. Indeed, all contain some kind of truth which lends them an appearance of validity. However, these divergent interpretations of Judaism simply prove its rich intellectual content. They are true when they are conceived as individual aspects of the fundamental principle of Judaism. But each is rendered false the moment it attempts to pose exclusively as the fundamental idea of Judaism, for such an effort always omits a larger or smaller part of the totality of Jewish institutions which is not covered by this common denominator and which can find its sufficient explanation on the basis of this fundamental idea only by force or not at all.

Till now, the deeper study of Judaism's fundamental character has been pursued in several ways. Either one stresses its dogmatic, metaphysical character, its abstract side and makes this principle supreme—considering the other part as a nonessential form into which the idea was poured to make it accessible and familiar to the popular mind and every fluctuation of which consequently alters the idea somewhat. Or one emphasizes its concrete character, its legislative nature, in which case Judaism is broadly conceived as an ethical system. To prove its philosophic character, some limit the evidence to the concepts of the Bible, or they invoke, for this purpose, the entire rich field of Jewish literature, including the Midrash and philosophical exegesis, without ever considering that these sectors bear the traces of foreign influence and therefore are of little use in determining purely Jewish concepts. To substantiate the practical character of Judaism, others return to the written word, thus ignoring all subsequent tradition, or they take their position in the present form of Judaism and view it as the natural outgrowth of the immanent principles of Judaism.

Even from this inadequate analysis, it is quite apparent that the basic views about the idea of Judaism must necessarily differ according to different points of view. It is another question whether these differences in interpretation reside in the object itself, whose multifaceted essence defies logical synthesis. In that case we would have to despair of ever discovering the soul which animates and guides the organism of Judaism. However, before our judgment submits to this despair, we must still test several other methods of analysis which might help us to penetrate the sealed depths of the root idea of Judaism.

It is clear as day that all the attempts to determine the ideological basis of Judaism, which we have just briefly analyzed, share a single defect. None have submitted the totality of Judaism to examination. On the contrary, all of them have insisted on concentrating on a single section, thereby often misunderstanding the factors involved and not infrequently confusing cause and effect. But the totality of Judaism is discernible only in its history. Its complete nature, the sum of its powers, becomes clear only in the light of history. Every vital idea must create for itself a solid existence. It must work itself out of the monotonous, dormant state of the ideal into the changing, turbulent world of reality. Thus, history is not only the reflection of the idea, but also the test of its power. For even the idea, in the best sense of the term, must possess enough flexibility and inner indestructibleness, not only to endure life, with its alternating ebb and flow, but also to master it and imprint its stamp upon it. If an idea has fought its way through into reality, if it has moved through the manifold configurations of history, then we may assume that all the actual forms brought forth were originally immanent. For history merely ripens the seeds of an idea, and the variety of forms which history yields are only concrete manifestations of the idea.

It is not our intention here to discuss at length these facts of the still young discipline of the philosophy of history. But these facts can be used to show that Jewish history in all its phases, even in the apparent aberrations of the moment, exhibits a single idea, that in fact, it constitutes a concrete explication of a fundamental concept. If one surveys Jewish history, both its active and passive ideas, using rather broad categories, if one grasps the natural nodal points which punctuate its path while also, in some way, extrapolating from the facts their driving ideas, then one comes across the primary causes which produced them and the seeds which the idea of Judaism actually bore since its beginning. We would like to try this method and thereby to attempt a conceptual construction of Jewish history.

At the moment of its entrance into history, Judaism appears as a negative force. It negates paganism. It rises in protest. Maimonides had already perceived this truth, though he remained at the surface. His conception of paganism was limited entirely to externals, to the concrete manifestation of its essence, and his interpretation of Judaism as opposition thereto, especially to the immoral cult of paganism, was likewise limited to externals. Maimonides' highly superficial conception of Judaism's sacrificial system is well-known. However, even the excesses of pagnaism, its crude, often ethically offensive practices rest on an idea. All manifestations of pagan life must be reducible to one fundamental idea and Judaism is called upon to negate this idea. It should nullify the utter insignificance of paganism as far as truth is concerned as well as its damaging effect on society, at least within its own small group, and then not in the speculative style of the classroom but in the concrete and clear manner of life. Thus the fundamental idea of Judaism could be discovered at the very outset, if we could determine indisputably the essential difference between Judaism and paganism. In fact, nothing is easier than showing the dividing line which separates these two forms of religion. For this purpose it is not necessary to undertake an extensive comparative study of their dogmas, as for example juxtaposing the Jewish concept of יש מאין with the pagan metaphysical principle of *ex nihilo nihil,* or comparing the other dogmatic differences as Steinheim did so penetratingly in his impressive book, *Die Offenbarung,* which is a lovely contribution to the philosophic comprehension of Judaism. A single glance already reveals the enormous contrast: paganism and Judaism constitute the same opposites as nature and spirit.

Paganism rests on the prior assumption and condition that nature in its broadest sense, operates on an immanent force. The pagan notion of God is identical with nature. The pagan god remains forever idealized nature, even in its highest stage of development where it is stripped of every animal and plant form and becomes humanized, even in the world of the Greeks where art supported religion and idealized the Olympian inhabitants. Pagan immortals are subject to necessity no whit less than mortals. The omnipotent law of nature is an irresistible power also for the gods, and Tyche—the blind, ruling goddess—governs both gods and men.

I do not wish to belabor the point here that the necessary consequence of this pagan concept of God was the absence of moral freedom. Human action, good or bad, constructive or destructive, was viewed as a necessity like the law of nature, unalterably predestined by fate. Rather, let us immediately examine the opposite of paganism, Judaism. Here God is the only authority, the only determiner, the essence of self-determination. The natural and the divine are separated. Compared to God, nature is nothing. Only by decision of the divine will, by the free act of creativity was it brought into existence, though its life and duration remain dependent forever on the breath of God and could again be reduced by Him to nothing. The idea of God constitutes, therefore, the pinnacle of Jewish life. All activity, all interests must first be incorporated into the framework of the divine in order to be considered of value.

The totality of Jewish life is enveloped by the glory of God. It receives its grace only after the spirit of God has suffused it. Moral freedom, complete self-determination, therefore, is the first consequence of the Jewish principle. Nothing is a greater abomination in Judaism than paying the manifestations of nature the respect due God. In fact, it is precisely when nature momentarily appears as an active force that it must be repudiated as unworthy, unholy, and insignificant. A considerable number of the commandments of Judaism bear this negative character and emphasize the subordination of nature. Products of nature, particularly those drawn into the circle of human life, to be taken and used by the human organism, must first be subjected to a process of sanctification.

This fundamental difference in the conception of the divine can be developed still further. To the pagan, the divine appears within nature as something observable to the eye. He becomes conscious of it as something seen. In contrast, to the Jew who knows that the divine exists beyond, outside of, and prior to nature, God reveals Himself through a demonstration of His will, through the medium of the ear. The human subject becomes conscious of the divine through hearing and obeying. Paganism sees its god, Judaism hears Him; that is, it hears the commandments of His will. It is only one step from the perception of a god to the representation of its likeness. Just as the pagan cult of idols is an entirely natural consequence of the pagan God-concept, so is it alien to Judaism to represent visually the divine "which has no form."

Furthermore, artistic expression also develops differently according to the different concepts of God. The artistic act created in Greek paganism, in accord with its sensuous God-concept, the art of sculpture, that lovely fragrant blossom of the pagan form of perception. In Judaism, on the other hand, which perceives its God in the alternatingly loud and soft sounds of the movement of the waves, in the rhythm of word sounds, the artistic drive, in harmony with this particular view of God, gave birth to music combined with religious poetry. But even in the peculiar development of poetic forms, the deep difference between the pagan and Jewish spirit manifests itself, though we can only develop this point later.

It is unnecessary to dwell on this viewpoint any longer, for the entire structure of Judaism attests it. The sharp opposition of Judaism to a paganism sunk in idolatry and immorality, traits which are conspicuously evident at a single glance, is nothing but the broad antithesis between the religion of the spirit and the religion of nature, divine transcendence and immanence.

On the basis of these introductory observations, it is already apparent that the monotheistic idea is not even the primary principle of Judaism, as has been widely believed by many until now, but it is the secondary consequence resulting from the extramundane concept of God, just as polytheism and idolatry are not the foundation of paganism. Therefore, the idea of monotheism in no way exhausts the entire content of Judaism; it is infinitely richer, infinitely deeper. Not even the repudiation of the deification of nature exhausts Judaism; it marks only the beginning of its career, a fact that becomes fully clear in the course of its long history.

Thus Judaism in no way remains fixed in this negative capacity, in its oppositional character. Its essential mission is to prove positively its special God-concept. This stamp is imprinted on all the commandments of Judaism, so that they may always remind us of this duality, sometimes in a negative and at others in a positive form. Another peculiarity of Judaism is also exhibited clearly enough by them, namely that the abstract, ideal teachings are immediately put into practice. Thus the concept of an extramundane God does not hover in the ethereal region of thought, but creates for itself a living people: an adequate political constitution must serve as the living carrier of this idea, which must ultimately become the moral code for society and the way of thinking for the individual. The revealed idea of God exists not for itself, in order to be known merely in a theoretical fashion, but seeks, at the same time, to be a holy institution which furthers earthly happiness. The concept of God must immediately become a concept of the state.

The political constitution of the Jewish state is usually characterized as theocratic, in the unfavorable sense of the word, but on this point as well as on many others, Judaism is misunderstood. Indeed, the divine stands at the head of the Jewish political system. All actions of state life begin from Him and eventually return circuitously to their point of departure. However, although God is the beginning and the end of this *Civitas Dei,* He is not its purpose. The purpose is rather eudaemonistic, as Mises somewhat crassly though correctly described it in his original pamphlet, *Ein Beitrag zu den gegenwärtigen Wirren im Judentum.* " . . . that you may fare well in the land which the Lord your God is giving you," [Deuteronomy 5:16] this is the constant refrain in the most dissimilar commandments. It concludes the ceremonial law of sparing the mother bird [Deuteronomy 22:6–7] as well as the moral injunction of loving one's parents [Deuteronomy 5:16]. It makes little difference whether Aher expects the promised happiness immediately for the individual who fulfills the commandment or whether R. Jacob, his grandson, postpones the reward till the world to come; both views clearly rest on faulty exegesis. For Judaism is not a religion for the individual, but for the community, and the promises and rewards attached to the fulfillment of commandments do not refer to the individual—for then the broken promises would serve to contradict Judaism at any given moment—but rather are apparently intended for the entire people. The unity and welfare of the Jewish state is dependent on the extent to which the commandments are observed. Likewise Judaism does not promise any other-worldly happiness for faithfulness. Immortality is not its concern; the survival of the soul has as little place in Judaism as the dogma of transubstantiation, and who knows whether this deficiency is not precisely its strength. We repeat: Judaism is not a religion of the individual but of the community. That actually means that Judaism, in the strict sense of the word, is not even a religion—if one understands thereby the relationship of man to his creator and his hopes for his earthly existence—but rather a constitution for a body politic.

On the other hand, these material and social purposes are

permeated by metaphysical ideas, formed by and interwoven
with religious dogmas. Judaism definitely does not lack
dogmas, although they do not manifest the usual bony rigidity
and furious religious obstinacy. From this point of view, we
are driven to conclude that Judaism has a religious character.
Precisely this twofoldness characterizes the nature of Judaism. Knowledge of God and social welfare, religious truth
and political theory form the two components of Judaism
which are destined to flow through history thoroughly mixed.
The dogmatic and the social or, to put it another way, the
religious and the political, constitute the twin axes around
which Jewish life revolves.

The concrete expression for these abstractions is the
revealed Law—the Torah—and the Holy Land. The attention
of the people is directed to these two possessions. The Law is
the soul, the Holy Land the body of this unique political
organism. The precisely defined territory provides the wide
space for the limitless unfolding of the Law, which is
stamped with the idea of God in all its fullness, and the Law
in turn serves to advance the social welfare of Israel. The
Torah, the nation of Israel and the Holy Land stand, one
might say, in a mystical relationship to each other; they are
inseparably united by an invisible bond. Judaism without the
firm soil of national life resembles an inwardly hollowed-out
and half-uprooted tree, which still produces foliage at the top
but is no longer capable of sprouting twigs and branches.

You may subject Judaism to a process of refinement, extract
modern thoughts from the fullness of its contents and trumpet
forth this essence as the heart of Judaism with stupefying,
resonant phrases and brilliant clichés; you may build a
church and accept a creed for this refined and idealized
Judaism "in a nutshell"; nevertheless, you still will have
embraced only a shadow and taken the dry shell for the
succulent fruit. You possess neither the Judaism taught by the
Bible in unambiguous terms, nor the Judaism molded by
three thousand years of history, nor, finally, Judaism as it still
lives in the consciousness of the majority of its adherents.[6]

Judaism is not a religion of the present but of the future. As its patriatchs once lived in a world of promises and viewed their contemporary circumstances merely as a preparation for the future of their progeny, so Judaism struggles toward a present which it currently lacks. Aware of this imperfectness and the corresponding ineffectiveness, Judaism looks back to the burning bush of Sinai and forward to the time envisioned by the prophets, when the knowledge of God, justice, and happiness will unite all men in brotherhood. Remembrance and hope form the pillars of cloud and fire which lead Israel toward the future. In the hope of acquiring the promised land as a showplace for the gradual growth of the knowledge of God, the patriarchs on their towering camels wandered about this strange, often hostile land. In this hope their descendants, the enslaved tribes in the Egyptian school of suffering, comforted themselves, and in this hope the young nation matured, without home, without fame, in the nomadic tent life of the Arabian desert, defying the experience of every national body politic. The Bedouin life of the tribes in the wilderness actually represents the embryonic stage of the future nation. The history of the Jewish nation begins only at the last station of the wilderness; the Jordan represents the transition from tribal to national organization.[7] A logical thread goes through the history of this nation, and if one surveys it in sufficiently large divisions, this history will render visible the changing activity of the two factors which constitute Judaism.

As long as the playing field of the totality of Jewish history is the national homeland, it can conveniently be divided into two large parts which, upon comparison, resemble each other only slightly. The first half, the pre-exilic period, has a predominantly political character; the religious dimension is only minimally present at the beginning. The second half, the course of history following the exile, is characterized by an overriding religious stamp, while the political-social tendency, which is only barely still visible, disappears entirely at the end of this period. The bearers of the first historical era are political citizens, war heroes, and kings with only a touch of religious sentiment; those of the second era are pious men, sages, teachers, students, and sectarians who manifest only a passing social interest. A single glance can reveal this fundamental difference. You are convinced that in the post-exilic period you are dealing with an entirely different nation with entirely different institutions, and this fundamental difference has misled even a Jewish historian into splitting Jewish history into a history of the Israelites and a history of the Jews.[8] However, is there no connecting link between these two divisions? Does not the influence of the pre-exilic period extend into that following the exile? Did not the prophets lay the groundwork for the piety of the second period? Judaism knows itself to be one and the same in both eras; it bears within it the self-consciousness that, despite all the differences resulting from external experiences and internal metamorphoses, it represents for itself an indivisible unity.

Thus these two components, the religious and the social, must inhere in the nature of Judaism, in its original idea, for them to emerge in the course of its history at first separately and onesidedly and subsequently together and integrated. The fusion of the religious and the political, the union of a transcendent God-idea with a political life must become in Judaism, a reality, even though both these forces in another sphere might give rise to constant friction and struggle or even appear to be irreconcilable. The naturalness of social life with its higher and lower aspects should be borne and illuminated by the idea of God. The vision of a political life conducted within the framework of Jewish institutions remains the distant ideal of Judaism; the Messiah as envisioned by the prophets, transmitted by the tradition, and embraced by the consciousness of the Jewish people is the capstone of Judaism.

Our task in this survey is to measure the sequence of Jewish history, its peaks and nadirs, by this criterion, and to order it

according to the fundamental idea of Judaism, according to
the indisputable principle that history is the reflection of an
idea.

Just as surely as Judaism postulates the fusion of the
religious and the social, it is also obvious that both these
factors stand far apart at the beginning of its history, much
like theory and practice or story and deed. The Torah was
handed over to the tribes in the wilderness; perhaps, in a
theoretical vein, they had already assimilated some of it. But
they could not yet attain the level of practice, of actual
realization. The first page of Jewish history begins with the
Book of Joshua, with the crossing of the Jordan, with the
encampment at Gilgal. The Pentateuch, the slavery in Egypt,
and the miraculous survival in the wilderness up to the death
of the man of God with the radiant face constitute the
interesting introduction and preparation thereto. This pre-history constitutes, so to speak, Judaism's years of service as an
apprentice and journeyman.

In the first period, which ends with the Babylonian exile,
we see a double struggle to reach a twofold objective. The
loose tribal confederation, which still has no popular center
toward which the particular tribal interests might gravitate,
must raise itself to the level of a common national life, to a
rounded-off and well-organized state. But it must also elevate
the natural life of the people, which is still marked by a
primitive, physical sensuality, to the soaring heights of a
spiritual life and it must place the cult of the transcendent,
nature-ruling, holy God at the center of the state. But the
coarse naturalness of the people obstructs the attainment of
this goal, and this first period of Jewish history records the
fluctuating interaction between the naturalness of the masses
and the God-idea struggling to be realized.

The First Phase. In the forefront of this period stands the
political-social factor, while the religious dimension is
shoved entirely into the background.

The tribes among whom Joshua divided the land and who

allowed foreign elements to remain in closest proximity to them, participate vigorously and exclusively in the natural aspects of life and even marry with the Canaanites, who were spared though mired in immorality and crude nature worship, thereby losing the core of their existence. They desert their own idea and as a result of this desertion, weaknesses begin to appear in the still not very firm national edifice. The individual members fly apart like atoms; the bond which should unite the tribes begins to loosen and it becomes a simple matter for their neighbors to defeat the fragmented tribes one by one. But when the disgrace and oppression have reached their peak, when they have surpassed the limits of endurance, a reaction sets in, inspired by a heroic individual in whom the original God-consciousness is not entirely extinguished. This hero repulses the danger for the moment and points out the actual causes of the decline. The people return to their God and the hero withdraws again into the background without a trace. This is the leadership type of the period of the Judges which fully accords with this heroic age in the governmental history of the people.

The religious life in this age of the Judges does not move in a straight line but jumps from point to point. Despite the apparent paltriness of religious life in this stage which is not yet separated from tabernacles and sacrificing priests, and despite the fact that the people could easily jump back and forth from the lewd Baal and Astarte cult to their own cult without changing their life-style in the slightest, the religious dimension was still not entirely lacking. Also, in this period, the difference between paganism and Judaism, between the cult of nature and the religion of the spirit was evident. The heroes of other nations, whom the Judges so closely resembled, still differed from them in an essential point. The hero of the emerging pagan nation knows the deed to be his own, he can boast about it; and, also, his people acknowledge the act of heroism, express their amazement, sing praises and enjoy hearing its praises sung. The Jewish Judge, in contrast, steps back from his own act; he is entirely aware that the rescue of his people did not spring forth from his own power but was brought about by God's all-powerful arm. The poetess Deborah does not sing of Barak's acts of heroism but of God's wonderful help. The Greek Hercules is a demigod who performs his heroic acts by virtue of his inherent divinity; Samson, the Jewish Hercules, is only able to carry out his heroic deeds by virtue of the spirit of God resting upon him, which externally is connected to his Nazarite head of hair; and, for his final heroic act in which he finds his death, he must implore God for strength. Thus the full historical life of heroism does not emerge from the spontaneity of the hero but derives from God. This awareness lives in the people, and this dimension is the thin thread of the religious factor which goes through the entire historical phase.

The Second Phase. The political side still dominates the historical expanse, but the religious side is already breaking through. It begins with the last Judge, the levitical prophet Samuel.

The people, robbed of all independence by tribal rivalries and internal divisions, perceives the lack of unity in its political life and attempts to achieve this unity through the institution of kingship. It has already looked around in foreign circles and found all nations to have an earthly rather than a heavenly king. It demands from Samuel a king who would lead it on the model of all other nations. In this demand is revealed the deep gulf between the reality of this people and its ideal destiny. Instead of the God-idea and its consequences forming the basis of political life and fusing the political unity with the divine, this people showed itself to be so little affected by the idea that it wished to introduce an omnipotent earthly power between itself and its God.

The frequently misunderstood Samuel, in whose actions a keen-scented rationalism has sensed hierarchical pride and priestly arrogance, profoundly realized the gaping hole which the introduction of an alien, disruptive element threatened to open in the finely woven fabric of Judaism. The prophet from Ramah, who fought for the religious unity of his people till old age, depicted for it this deviation from the eternal idea with clear, sharp words. In vain! A king was chosen by lot. In vain were also the efforts of this prophet, who stands on the same level with Moses, to subject the absolute will of the king, the royal power to the decisions of God's will and thereby to neutralize this potentially disruptive influence. Saul's petty jealousy toward the promising, handsome shepherd-boy David, his melancholy-rooted fits of insanity frustrated all hopes; bloody crimes against the priests who represented the religious idea were the end result of the monarchically organized state.

The religious aspect at this stage is also entirely external and while it becomes more extensive it certainly does not become more intensive. The sacrificial cult is continued at Shiloh and the actions of the priests, who serve also in a judicial capacity, give rise to numerous complaints. The Ark of the Covenant is not regarded as a shrine for divine instruction but rather revered like Palladium in an almost idolatrous fashion. The seer is questioned like an oracle regarding insignificant domestic matters and is expected to provide information about missing donkeys. Only the tribe of Levi, which from the beginning had received the task to disseminate God's teaching among the people and to serve as a unifying bond between priesthood and people, seems to have vividly preserved the idea of God in its consciousness.

Samuel and his school of prophets at least manifest a high degree of Jewish conviction. From this school emerged the singer of psalms, Assaf, who may well have created this poetic genre and served as the model for the royal singer. Assaf is older than David and his psalms deal with historical subjects that are pre-Davidic. This school also seems to have developed and perfected a simple, graceful prose; and from this time dates the first work in the long series of historical narratives in that exceptionally balanced and delicate style which bequeathed to the Hebrew language as much fervor as flexibility.

It appears at first glance as if under David's rule the

religious dimension would become more important and that with the consolidation and securing of national life, with the imposing position which the state, by virtue of its monarchical structure, had likewise achieved in the realm of foreign affairs, religious life might also rise to a higher level and attain more effective influence on the hearts of the masses. And, in fact, David's predominantly religious character, his particularly gentle disposition, his sensitive poetic soul might well have been suited to reflect in his own life the unity of the social and religious dimensions in their interaction. He subdued with the sword Israel's dangerous neighbors and sang the most uplifting hymns on the harp and lyre. He provided for the physical welfare of his people, for a prospering situation and, at the same time, laid the foundation for a central building for religious life. Thus the Davidic period, in which the twofold character of Judaism appears in at least one individual, becomes the high point of history, the ideal for all subsequent generations, the beloved memory which evoked in poets and prophets alike the most tender chords.

The days of David constitute the classical period for the religious and poetic figures of subsequent generations, a spring blossom which sprouted from the soil of a genuine Jewish spirit only to break and wither quickly through the adversity of a rugged environment. How limited this influence was on national life and how little the people were capable of appreciating this fresh spirit is most clearly evident in the troubled relations in the poet-king's own household. Immorality, fratricide, plots against father and king make up the tragic thread that ran through David's life, threatening even his old age, and the people willingly lent a hand. Yet the political maturity of the people continued to develop; the process of building a united national life out of the fragmented tribal state was completed in David's time, and this pervasive consciousness of national unity expresses itself in Joab's heroic words: "Let us be brave for our people and for the cities of our God" (II Samuel 10:12).

The level of political consciousness continued to rise still higher in the glorious reign of his son, the philosopher-king. But the growing power and international respect opened a channel for foreign influences and pulled Judaism out of its isolation, which is so salutary for the development and preservation of its inner spirit. Prosperity leads to sumptuous living and produces immorality; observing the life-style of other nations awakens reflection at the expense of religious fervor.

To be sure, the religious dimension gains immeasurably through the centralization of the cult. The fragmentation of religious life through different cultic centers now comes to an end. The king dedicates the Temple and in his dedicatory address he gives expression to certain cosmopolitan ideas. Religious poetry, as crystalized in the two poetic forms of the psalm and the proverb, celebrates its springtime. But nowhere in the Solomonic period do traces of religious thought appear in the life of the people; the glory radiating forth from the Temple captivated and blinded the people more than it enlightened and warmed them. Only the band of Levites worked itself ever more deeply into the Jewish idea and it, in turn, awakened their artistic nature to the lyrical outpouring of the Psalms. The Temple hymns and the flowering of the proverb came in this historical phase, the one form cultivated by the sons of Korah and the other by the king himself. Also in the actual form of Jewish poetry, which has its analogue in pagan Greece, the fundamental difference between the Jewish and pagan forms of perception is evident. The artistic sense of the Greeks, who regard their history as their own spontaneous act, transforms historical deeds poetically into epic and drama. In contrast, in Judaism, where the experiences of history are attributed to God and where the saving God and not the hero or the deed forms the object of exaltation, the product of the poetic drive is precisely the lyrical effusion, the psalm of praise. The philosophical spirit also created a poetic form in Judaism, the reflections of the proverb, which is similar to the first attempts of Greek philosophy, which, as is well known, likewise expressed itself in poetic form. But Greek philosophy in its early stages focuses on the relationship between the natural world and its ultimate cause, while the proverb focuses on the relationship of the ethical world to the divine will.

However, despite the richness and sincerity of the poetic creativity which the awareness of God inspired, too much was still missing to allow the life of the people during the Solomonic period to become intensively religious. It was in fact in many ways dissipated by the penetration of foreign customs and the resulting love for luxury.

The Third Phase. The religious dimension is elevated precisely by a factor that causes a decline in political life, namely the division of the Jewish kingdom. How little allegiance the people had for its religious institutions is shown by the ease with which the ten tribes broke off from the sacred House of David, the Jerusalemite Temple, and by the bold act of Jeroboam in erecting an almost pagan sanctuary against the one in Jerusalem. But the division of the kingdom, while weakening its political power and sowing the seeds for the eventual demise of the state, did cause the religious factor to penetrate life more deeply. For Judaism was thereby thrown into internal conflict, in consequence of which the inimical elements which thus far had operated side by side undifferentiatedly could now be separated and purified.

If up to this point the monotheistic institutions had stood in close contact with the pagan way of life, now, as a result of the division, these elements came to a decisive separation: the Jewish element focused on the Temple in Jerusalem; the pagan element centered around the animal cult at Bet-El and Dan. While Jeroboam, scornful of history, sanctioned a pagan cult on Jewish soil and raised it to national significance by associating it with the Golden Calf of the wilderness, the Jewish king Abijah could declare to him and his followers: "You have driven out the priests of the Lord, the descendants of Aaron and the Levites; you have chosen for yourselves priests in the manner of the pagans; the first good man

becomes your priest. We, however, remain faithful to the
eternal, our God; we have not forsaken Him" [II Chronicles
13:9–10]. As a result of the friction between the kingdoms of
Judah and Israel, the former identified more and more with
the divine law upon which its cult rested and its interest
therein grew steadily. And even though the Judean kingdom,
infected by the coalition and the marital alliance with a
thoroughly paganized house of Ahab soon produced a series
of kings who really yielded little to the kings of Israel, there
still arose within the people a nucleus, aroused precisely
because of the spreading disregard of God, an elite band
whose lives reflected Judaism and to which they lent the
magic power of the word.

Prophecy in general and the last stage in particular, namely
that which unquestionably emerged in the wake of national
division, constitutes the glory of the Jewish spirit. The last
prohpets were, henceforth, the bearers of the religious aspect
in Judaism; in them the revealed idea of God found its
interpreters, its defenders, its panegyrists and its most worthy
representatives. The long line of pre-exilic prophets starting
with the school of Isaiah and closing with that of Jeremiah,
who did not emerge only from priestly circles but also directly
from the midst of the people, left behind a powerful and
inspiring spirit in their immortal works, in which richness of
thought and perfection of form are thoroughly interwoven.
Prophecy became an educational force for posterity. In the
prophetic discourses, truth and poetry, simplicity and
loftiness alternate; on one occasion they aroused the dulled
senses of the people with thunderbolts, on another they
soothed their agitation with heart-warming words which
salved the wounded hearts like the balm of Gilead. They
painted the picture of a future in which the Davidic period of
peace and intelligence would be universalized. They foretold
of the loss of political independence, although with the
consolation that when the present nation would go down, the
idea of God would not be dragged down with it but rather
would educate a more amenable and mature generation. They

foretold further that the Jewish concept of God, the sacred heritage of Judaism, would not remain restricted to Israel alone but would spread throughout mankind. From all over the nations of the world would pilgrimage to Mount Zion; discord among men would disappear and nature itself would be sanctified, coming to reflect the image of God.

We can assert that with the decline of the political factor the religious dimension did take an upswing and, precisely during the exile of the ten tribes and the demise of the Kingdom of Israel, the religious side manifested its power in the prophetic quartet of Isaiah, Hosea, Micah, and Amos. But the prophets did not restrict their interests in any way exclusively to religion; they turned their attention to the social and political arena with the same fervor. They often raised their voices for or against an alliance with a powerful conqueror. Isaiah warned against submission to Assyria; Jeremiah pressed for yielding to Chaldean power, but both zealously fought against a coalition with the decaying state of the Pharaohs. Thus Judaism created for itself in the prophets a powerful, pulsating heart, and this heart lacked only a national body whose higher and lower functions would be governed by it.

In the form of prophecy, the ideal of Judaism had fully articulated and explained itself, and its task was now to transform the ideal into reality. But the people, the masses of that time were, according to the repeated complaints of the prophets, unfit for a lofty mission. They thus envisioned in the future an ideal Israel which would be permeated by the spirit of the revealed Law, which would be ready to endure martyrdom for the sake of truth. "This Israel is My servant, on whom I can rely, the chosen one who gives me pleasure; I have bestowed My spirit upon him and he shall bring justice to the nations. He shall not cry nor lift himself up, he shall not let his voice be heard upon the street; a battered reed he shall not break, a barely burning wick he will not extinguish but only justice shall he bring to truth. He will not dally nor rush until he shall have established justice on earth and the inhabitants of distant islands will await his teaching" [Isaiah 42:1–4].

The people of that era, who had directed the entire energy of their national resources toward the natural, had to be reeducated, their political existence had to be smashed, and they had to be prepared to accept the religious side of their faith. A long time before, the early prophets had already threatened exile from the homeland and uprooting from the political base as the only way to ready the people for its spiritual mission. Now the fulfillment came. The Holy Land spewed forth its children and, with the murder of Gedaliah and the departure for Egypt of the last remnants of the lowest class under Jeremiah, the last trace of Jewish political life was obliterated.

The Babylonian exile, the analogue of Egyptian slavery, was a second period of preparation for the unfolding of an aspect of Judaism. Which side it was is immediately apparent. We really lack the historical data through which we might uncover the causes behind the surprising revolution in national consciousness. We know only the unexpected result of the transformed mentality of the people to the extent that we do not even recognize this people as being the same who dared to tell the prophet: "We wish to offer incense to the queen of heaven, for since we have stopped we have fallen badly" [Jeremiah 44:17–18]. In the wake of the exile, the pagan deification of nature from which the masses had been unable to break away, was swept aside.

To what influence may we ascribe this total disappearance of polytheism from the midst of the people? The Sabian dualism, which assumed a cosmic world view and was not entirely free of idolatry, could hardly have effected this result or advanced the monotheistic consciousness. Much more natural is the assumption that the echo of the prophetic words, the fulfillment of the exile threatened by the prophets only now made a deep impact, powerfully gripping the mood of the people.[9] Admittedly, the people in the exile did pick up Persian elements, such as the belief in angels—an accommo-

dation of the Persian *Amshaspand* and *Ized* to the highly
amorphous Biblical concept of מלאך —and, for example, the
belief in evil spirits שדים —corresponding to the *Div* of
Zoroastrianism—and, finally, the idea of Satan, borrowed
from Ahriman which only in the post-exilic writings plays a
personal role. However, it is just impossible that the fire religion of the Magis with its division of divine power and its
views of life could ever have impressed the genuine Jewish
notion of God on the people! In fact, precisely in the second
section of Isaiah, the dualistic God-concept is attacked and
the Jewish idea of God is bluntly contrasted with this view.
"I, the Creator of light and the Begetter of darkness, I, the
Creator of good and the Begetter of evil, I, the Eternal, make all
these." [Isaiah 45:6–7].

In any case, let us stick to the undeniable fact that in the
wake of the Babylonian exile the entire mass of the the people
was permeated by the pure God-idea of Judaism, by the
recognition that His being transcends the world of nature.
And herewith begins the second period of Jewish history,
whose hallmark is that the religious factor now achieves
predominance and the social and political concerns assume a
subordinate role. If in the first period matters of state fully
dominated, in the second period religious interests gained
exclusive control, to the point of negating all political
independence: Judaism ceased to be the constitution for a
state and became a religion in the usual sense of the word.
However, wheareas in the first period the exclusive political
interest, dependent on natural necessity, begins at its high
point and follows a declining course, in the second period, the
religious exclusiveness, like a phenomenon totally divorced
from nature, reaches its peak only at the end and follows an
ascending course. Incidentally, I wish merely to mention here
that both these manifestations of onesidedness and extremism
can never fully present the nature of Judaism, and, in much
the same way as the purely political acts can hardly exhaust
the content of Judaism, similarly the purely religious side
does not correspond to the whole idea.

Inevitably, the religious period of Jewish history has analogies to the political era in that both stages of development reveal the same characteristics. Let us accompany the small band of returning exiles, scarcely 100,000 in number, whom Cyrus permitted to return to the homeland in a manner as benevolent as it was incomprehensible, and let us see which interests move them on their native soil. The historical actions are of an entirely religious character. The first task of the returnees is to erect provisionally an altar at the spot where the Temple had been reduced to ashes and to restore the sacrificial cult as commanded. The festival of Sukkot is celebrated, the choirs of Levites are organized, the foundation stone of the Temple is laid, and all hopes are directed toward its completion. The three last post-exilic prophets no longer raise their voices for political purposes, but rather now impress upon the people religious values. Haggai condemns the sluggishness with which the Temple is built; Zechariah addresses himself to the problem of fasting and foretells that one day all nations will participate in the festival of Sukkot; Malachi brings the phenomenon of prophecy to a close with the words: "Remember the teaching of My servant Moses, which I gave him at Horeb for all Israel" [Malachi 3:22]. Eighteen years after the return, the Temple is completed and dedicated with a religious celebration. Consider the situation: both the highest and final act of public religious life in the first period was the building of the Solomonic Temple, in which a love of splendor was as evident as religious interest, whereas in the second period this was the first action taken, accomplished only in the face of danger and by great sacrifice. All this characterizes the dominant religious spirit of the second period.

The First Phase. The religious component, which stands in the foreground of the history, strives toward consolidation. With deep historical insight, the Talmud assigns the role of Moses to the indefatigable Ezra in the following words: "Ezra really deserved to receive the revealed Law, had not Moses preceded him" (TB Sanhedrin 21b). Furthermore, Moses gave the Law to only a single group, the Levites, while Ezra made it the common property of the entire nation, "an eternal possession," as a guideline for both its public and private life. Moses totally isolated the people from the surrounding paganism, and the Canaanites had to be sacrificed to this system of isolation; Ezra, however, removed the paganism with which the people had entered into a close relationship and tore away the pagan wives from the hearts of their Jewish husbands. But then Moses had to work with an uncivilized mass, with bands of slaves who constantly yearned to return to the fleshpots of Egypt, while Ezra could rely on the Lawbook revered by the people and thus make greater demands on them.

Like Joshua, Nehemiah had to achieve security for the people against their neighbors: Previously the indigenous Canaanites were political enemies, now the half-Jewish race of Samaritans loomed as religious adversaries, who under the leadership of the cunning Sanballat intrigued to thwart the fortification of Jerusalem whose inhabitants had excluded them from any religious fellowship. Despite the preponderance of the religious factor, in the days of Nehemiah the religious situation was still fluid, murky, and uncertain. Nehemiah was still compelled to resort to forceful measures to maintain the Sabbath and to dissolve the mixed marriages, and such measures for preventing religious transgressions or inculcating religious practices, once sanctioned and accepted, henceforth acquired the value and force of new commandments next to the divine prescriptions.

At this juncture, then, the function and significance of the Men of the Great Assembly in Jewish history become apparent. Some have, in fact, contested or at least doubted the existence of the *ecclesia magna,* but without justification. Its activity, which may well have extended beyond Simon the Righteous, is actually proven in the protective measures and enactments which we already meet with in the period of the Maccabees and which, therefore, could have derived only from this assembly. We must, however, be careful not to imagine this *ecclesia* to be a closed body with a defined

function and purpose, something akin to a consistory. Its
significance is crystallized in a single sentence ascribed to it
in the *Ethics of the Fathers,* an admonition to posterity:
"Train many students for the Law and build fences around
the Teaching" [1:1]. In this sentence, which represents the
beginnings of the later development of the two sides of
Judaism—transmission and protection, הלכה למשה מסיני and
סייגים —the historical significance of the כנסת הגדולה is
articulated. Our history shows here a gap of one hundred
years, from Nehemiah to Simon the Righteous, which we
usually fill in with the *ecclesia magna,* a period which even
Josephus and the Talmud telescoped and erased. But perhaps
this period simply did not bring to fruition much that was
worth handing down; for the audible fact will always create
for itself an organ which will transmit it to posterity, an
Achilles will always find his Homer.

In fact, the historical activity of this period was actually
internal, silent and, I might even say, inexpressible. To have
religion take root among the masses through enactments and
measures, to attend to immediate needs, to protect religious
Judaism against transgressions, to uphold the integrity of the
Law—toward these ends the Great Assembly seemed to direct
its efforts. From this viewpoint, the Men of the Great
Assembly formed the counterpart and analogue of the Judges.
Their common character is temporary relief. The Judges
preserved political independence in the face of severe danger,
rescuing it for the moment; the Men of the Great Assembly
secured the continuation of the religious commandments in
the face of severe violations, guarding them for the moment
with protective measures. We could readily designate both
periods as anarchical, the former political and the latter
religious in character, which are momentarily and improvisa-
tionally alleviated by a few unofficial personalities.

The Second Phase. The religious dimension creates for
itself a center and a following.

Thus far in the course of events, the religious life lacked
enthusiasm, a sacrificing ardor; the almost artificial means of

hedging were only briefly effective. As in the first period, when political Judaism achieved unity and centralization by means of a monarchical system that was alien even inimical to Judaism, so now, again, enthusiasm was kindled and spiritual unity attained as a result of the penetration of an alien, even inimical element into the heart of Judaism. This alien element, which evoked a deep movement and continuous vacillation in Judaism, was Hellenism. Both monarchy and Hellenism were reluctantly adopted by Judaism, both threatened to destroy its character, but both were eventually assimilated and incorporated, once their damaging influence had been overcome.

The triumphal march of the Macedonian conqueror, the bright student of Aristotle, who, like a "winged leopard"[10] tore through and subdued the lands from the Hellespont to the Ganges and from the Oxus to the sources of the Nile, implanted in all these lands the seed of Greek education and civilization. Hellenism with all its alluring forms flourished along the banks of the Euphrates and Orontes and along the shores of the land of the mummies. An elongated Palestine lay wedged in between the courts of Antioch and Alexandria, which were quite equally matched in sumptuousness and perfidy. As a result of the touchiness and imperial ambitions of these courts, a politically neutral Judea was inevitably dragged into all the entanglements and scrapes. At the court in Alexandria, where the Jews fared well as long as they paid their annual tribute, they became familiar with a more attractive side of Greek culture. Soon they had not only mastered the Greek language into whose forms they poured a much distorted and impoverished spirit of Judaism and in which they produced the bastard literature of the Apocrypha, but had also appropriated the easy and pleasurable life-style; the sons of Tobias, related to the family of the High Priest, were Jewish only by descent.

Hellenism, which the pensive poet of the divan strikingly characterized as bearing only blossoms but no fruits,[11] steadily attracted ever more admirers from among the Temple officials. Refined paganism was no longer abhorrent in the eyes of many and they gladly welcomed it. Antiochus Epiphanes's violent attempt to impose paganism found a ready counterpart among numerous representatives of Judaism, for otherwise his crazy schemes would have been useless from the very outset. But precisely as a result of this friendly reception of paganism did the people fathom the extraordinary danger which threatened their spiritual treasure and for the first time they died as martyrs for their religion. There followed the first violent confrontation of these two religious world views in their historical embodiments. Paganism had on its side an imposing material power, seductive charm, and the entire naturalness of man. Judaism, on the other hand, relied solely on the power of the idea and it transformed victims who feared the use of weapons into military heroes, it aroused a family of heroes and kindled enthusiasm in the hearts of the people. Judaism came to recognize its own nature through the opposition of paganism. It committed its blood and might to the fight for self-preservation and in the wake of this life-and-death struggle with paganism, it acquired that dedication which has operated so beneficially and effectively ever since.

The Maccabean period paralleled the glorious era of David except for its prevailing religious hue. John Hyrcanus is the David of the second period, though he is not king but High Priest, and his wars have a religious rather than a political intent. The religious tensions at this time intensified to the point of intolerance. The destruction of the Samaritan temple on Mount Gerizim, the imposing of circumcision on the defeated Edomites were consequences of what might be termed national religiosity. Yet with all the greatness of independence which Judaism achieved under the successors of the Maccabees, it still did not arrive at a noteworthy political life. First the religious side had to penetrate the historical process to its fullest extent. Political interests were pursued only secondarily, so that even the rulers themselves easily let the scepter be pulled out of their hands.

The Third Phase. The foreign element, which had penetrated to the very core of Judaism, separated, manifesting itself outwardly in the form of religious divisions.

Greek civilization, that foreign challenge which forcibly tried to eradicate everything Jewish, was fortunately overcome. But it continued to survive in the hearts of many and produced ferment within Judaism itself. Refined pagan views, mediated through Greek civilization, were accepted as criteria by which to judge Judaism. In short, the conflict between Sadducees and Pharisees erupted, a historical phenomenon that has the same background as the division of the kingdom into Israel and Judah, whose analogue it is, except that in the latter case the political dimension predominated, while in the former the religious prevailed. Both dimensions of Judaism lay at the basis of this division. Both aspects, which Judaism strives to bring together and integrate, namely religious truth and social welfare, the fear of God and the enjoyment of life, were torn asunder by these parties.

But before I come to speak of Pharisaism, I must first counter an unfortunate secondary meaning which later generations unjustly attached to this term. Hypocrisy and sanctimoniousness are as far removed from the principle of Pharisaism as is the commercial spirit from Judaism, and the occasional instances of degeneration in this sect are more penetratingly denounced and scourged by the Talmud, which is itself decried as Pharisaic, than by the religious founder from Nazareth. Pharisaism, to return to the point, aligned itself more with the religious side of Judaism, whereas Sadduceeism identified with the political and social side. According to the Pharisees, or *Perushim,* who were rooted in a Judaism rescued from Syrian tyranny by the Maccabean wars, life existed for the sake of religion and ought in all its dimensions to be thoroughly permeated by religion. Wherever life appears devoid of the idea of God—that is of the Law—it is unholy and impure and can only be hallowed through intense religious practice. Regarding the present, the Law with all of its emanations, protective measures, and even self-imposed hardships should encompass the breadth of life. Every step must be religious in character or it is unholy. As far as the future, the Pharisee, building on prophetic promises, awaits the universal spread of the knowledge of God; a life shaped according to the Law and ritual purity, which at the moment is observed by only a segment of the people, the חברים , will be adopted by ever larger circles and the Messiah will come to fulfill a religious mission. The rewards promised in Scripture do not entail a state of social happiness in this world but rather a state of supernatural blessedness in the world-to-come. The characteristic traits of Pharisaism are a careful observance of the Law, an exaggerated concern with ritual purity, tradition, separation from the coarse, lower elements of the people, and finally the dogma of a future life and resurrection.

The Sadducees, nourished by Greek elements and subscribing to the enjoyment of life, regarded religion only as a means toward an end, which is life itself. Religion should advance and justify happiness.[12] The laws set down in Scripture are entirely adequate for this purpose. Every addition, whether introduced as a tradition or a protective measure, circumscribes the freedom of life and obstructs the happiness toward which Judaism strives. In the contemporary scene, Sadduceeism made itself felt by opposing the totality of oral tradition and especially the laws of purity and the separatistic system of the Pharisees. As for the future, it awaited a rebirth of social harmony, a Davidic kingdom of peace, as the prophets had foretold, but entirely in accord with the laws of nature in this world. Because of its minority status, the characteristic traits of Sadduceeism are likewise negative and oppositional, namely a negation of tradition and of the doctrine of rewards in a future life.

It is impossible within the framework of a mere survey to explore more fully the differences between the Pharisees and Sadducees, but it is entirely apparent that the fundamental difference came out of Judaism itself, that it rests on the onesidedness of each of the factors operating within Judaism,

and that it was finally brought to the surface in a historical
form through the conflict with Greek civilization. This
difference was at first confined only to the schools; however, it
certainly did penetrate public life as a result of the
intervention of the ruling High Priests of the Maccabean
House, initially with the Sadducees on top. Simon ben Shetah
paved the way for the triumph of the principles of the
Pharisees and founded a center for religious concerns in the
Sanhedrin.

What the prophetic schools were in the first period, namely
the focus of the religious interest of the nation, the
Hillelite-enlarged Sanhedrin in the Hall of Hewn Stone in the
Temple became in the second. Every public religious act
required in advance its authorization and approval. The
Jewish diaspora under Roman and Parthian rule spontaneous-
ly recognized the religious decisions of this highest religious
tribunal as inviolable. In this way, the religious dimension
acquired in the Patriarchate a completion, compactness, and
concentration which could protect Judaism against the
consequences of growing dispersion and denationalization.
For political life declined steadily since Rome had arrogated
to itself direct rule over Judea when the half-pagan,
anti-nationalist Herodian dynasty had played into its hand.
And with political dissolution around the corner, powerful
messianic sentiments arose in the hearts of the people, which,
like the prophets before the demise of the first state, provided
the exiles in their wanderings with the consolation and hope
of a political-religious rebirth. Jesus of Nazareth was not the
only one who had striven to make the messianic ideal a
reality. Messianic expectations were rife as the state disinte-
grated, and, as Jesus addressed the people about the kingdom
of heaven, they asked him if he was the son of David. But the
people entirely failed to understand his proclamation that his
kingdom was not of this world; they lacked all the necessary
presuppositions. The people were expecting a Messiah who
would carry them further into Judaism rather than out of it
and who, at the same time, would rejuvenate and strengthen
the decaying state.

It is noteworthy that the fall of the state, the burning of the Temple, did not make the same dreadful impression on contemporaries as did the demise of the first state. No Jeremiah poured out his profound elegiac *kinot* over the ruins of the Second Temple. The zealous self-sacrifice of the patriots did not even find a historian who would transmit their acts of heroism without distortion to posterity. Instead they fell into the hands of the treacherous Josephus Flavius, who, fawning before his imperial patron, transformed the heart-rending convulsions of true patriotism into criminal acts. In truth, the leaders of Judaism had come to view political survival with considerable indifference. R. Yoḥanan ben Zakkai was satisfied with the permission received from Titus to continue the Sanhedrin and Patriarchate in Yavneh. Judaism fled to the academies; therein it concentrated all its strength, and religious life was thenceforth conducted according to the results of the insulated controversies of the schools.

With these events, with the normalizing of the religious factor according to the theoretical discussions in the academies, Judaism enters upon a new course. A new dimension appears which will complete the earlier results of history—the intellectual now becomes the predominant force in the historical formation of Judaism. This third period, which Jewish history undergoes on foreign soil, also has nodal points and phases analogous to those in the earlier periods, which, if the present survey should be favorably received, will be more fully developed.

The Christian conception of history, as is well-known, fully denies to Judaism any history, in the higher sense of the word, since the loss of its national independence, an event which coincided with another of great importance to the Christian world. It scarcely grants Judaism a few lines and believes to have discharged its obligations as soon as it refers, in a meager footnote, to a few disparate facts of Jewish history in the margin of the annals of world history. The stylus of the world historian races cursorily over the martyrdom of Jewish history, as if he feared to arouse through these bloody recollections the conscience lulled to sleep by sophistry, as if he feared to conjure the spirits of vengeance through a loud word. And, indeed, the brisk activity of Jewish history, the immortal creations which Judaism brought to life behind the sealed gates of the ghetto, within the gloomy seclusion of its academy, how can these possibly find recognition and appreciation? Furthermore, this habit of lowering Judaism into the grave, of issuing Jewish history a death certificate is also quite convenient; one thereby avoids the difficulty which would loom before any strictly Christian construction of world history. Thus, all the more urgent is the demand on us to vindicate the right of Jewish history, to present its tenacious and indestructible character, to prove that Jewish history reveals no Middle Ages in the pejorative sense of the word, that, in fact, the apparent state of death of Jewish history in the darkest days of the Middle Ages was merely an assumed disguise to escape from bloodthirsty brutality, or even a healthy, invigorating winter sleep, which fitted Judaism to enter into a daring, universal race against a more fortunate, younger opponent.

It is not even difficult to show that Judaism, during its period of dispersion which has still not ended, has produced, in addition to a passive history of severe trial and martyrdom also an active history which gives the most striking evidence of infinite vitality and flexible energy. In the same way that the first two periods of Jewish history, the pre- and post-exilic, revealed to us, on the one hand, a uniform character, while on the other, despite all unity, a characteristic singularity, so too does the third period which we shall call that of the Diaspora because it did not take place in the homeland, manifest, despite its apparent disunion and fragmentedness, an organic unity as well as a fundamental difference from the post-exilic period, which it does resemble and which we regarded as essentially religious in character.

If we should briefly delineate the content, the basic difference and, in general, the character of the period of the

Diaspora, it would consist of the following aspects: the historical activity of Judaism in the seventeen hundred years of its dispersion was theoretical, directed to the intellectual formulation of its teachings and contents, an activity which would not let itself be disturbed and overpowered by the tragic blows of history.

And in this regard, it was essentially different from the second religious period. In the former period religion was cultivated in reflectionless immediacy; it followed an entirely external, naive course. In contrast, in the later period religion immersed itself in the inwardness of reflection; it pursued the study of its own being and significance. The idea of Judaism, which till then had striven toward embodiment and consolidation and therefore had completed its work outside, in the marketplace of world history, involved and interested in all the conflicts of the world scene, now withdraws into itself. It seeks to grasp itself consciously, it seeks to ascertain its contents, it seeks to explain itself in a mediated and theoretical manner.

If in the second period pious men, sages, and sectarians appear before us as the bearers of history, they are also not missing in the third period of the Diaspora. But they are more than that now, they are scholars, thinkers, religious philosophers, systematizers, even skeptics and apostates—for skepticism is a necessary component in the purifying process of the understanding. The course of history in this period is distinguished by the organization of schools and systems: Judaism becomes scientific scholarship. All the data of its historical experience till then, the laws of the Pentateuch, the teachings of the prophets, the tradition of the scribes are now seized and reworked by the intellect. Religious practice, the symbol, no longer remains ensconced in a state of latency but is freed as truth and idea by thought and understanding.

It is obvious that the main direction of Jewish history in this period, which still continues into the present, attempts to transform the facts of Judaism into rational truths, of course not to rest satisfied with this abstraction or that theory and thereby to become a metaphysical theorem, but rather out of a state of self-consciousness to produce a system of practice rooted in theory, in short, a religious-social reality.

If this postulate be granted: that just as Judaism possesses a social and religious tendency which it manifests in history it also has a theoretical-speculative dimension to which it likewise strives to give historical form, then the necessary existence of two phenomena of Jewish history suddenly becomes clear. For by nature antagonistic, they have, since the beginning, produced an atmosphere of tension and uneasiness in the synagogue, and the efforts to mediate and reconcile them still occasion in our own day passionate outbursts and party struggles. These two phenomena, which I regard as the consequences of the tendency to fathom Judaism theoretically, are: the thorough dispersion of the Jewish people, with its attendant cosmopolitan existence for Judaism, and the talmudic system whose purpose is to isolate Judaism. The necessity of both consequences can be accounted for by the following line of thought.

Should Judaism ever bring itself to the level of consciousness and clarity, should it ever emerge from the restricted state of immediacy and be exposed to the mediation of thought and scientific scholarship, then it must temporarily be torn out of the quiet center of its life, out of the narrow limits of its birthplace; it must be brought closer to the field where the various national spirits do battle. The civilized world in all its manifoldness must be unlocked for Judaism so that it might come to understand itself by seeing and experiencing the opposite. From its central position on the world stage, it should observe the countless figures of world history pass by; it should garner experience from the rise and fall of nations and tendencies and derive therefrom encouragement or admonishment. From this high vantage point of quiet contemplation, as if placed on the Archimedean point outside the earth, Judaism could discover through comparison and contrast the full depths of its content and the loftiness of its own tendency. Wherever the course of world history

went, wherever a seed of universal significance was sown,
there Judaism was also to be found. Along with the Romans,
Judaism settled down on the Iberian peninsula, in Gaul, and
along the Rhine and then moved ever deeper into the steadily
expanding borders of the Franco-German kingdom. With the
raging flood of Islamic peoples, Judaism also entered new
lands and situations, and as the tribal waves from Europe and
Asia smashed against each other, Judaism suffered as well as
benefited. With the discovery of the New World, Judaism
again found a home of freedom in the primeval forests of
America. And whenever a new truth surfaced in the particular
character of a national group or even a new form for an old
truth, Judaism could appropriate it in order to test its own
content and accept it with the expectation of either
discovering the same in its own store of truths or perceiving
that its own teachings contained a contrary idea far more
convincing and powerful.

But in this worldwide experience of Judaism and in the
atomistic dispersion of its adherents there loomed the danger
of self-estrangement, disintegration, and dissolution. The
danger threatened that the God-consciousness of Judaism
which had created suitable institutions to render it imperish-
able, when set in an alien environment in the midst of foreign
influences and amid a host of world powers, would be
crushed. Or, what amounts to the same thing, that it would be
exchanged through joining or adjusting to an alien tendency.
This apprehension was justified; it was not the mere product
of excessive anxiety. To be sure, Judaism had survived a
life-and-death struggle with Greek paganism at a time when it
was still firmly rooted in its own soil and supported at least by
a touch of worldly power. And now uprooted and fragmented,
robbed of all power and support and thrown entirely on its
inner, idealistic resources, Judaism should embark on a
similar or rather much more ominous struggle without
preparation or equipment? But no, Judaism was prepared and
equipped to counter the dissolution and estrangement of its
own principle—its weapon was the talmudic system.

Once a son has been educated and matured by his father's guidance and teaching, the father himself sends the boy away from the hearth and ships him out into the world to gather experience and to test his paternal teaching in the thousand conflicts of life. But the father has no intention of letting his beloved boy perish in a distant land. With the strength and independence that comes through bitter experience, the son will return to his house to inherit his father's estate.

With staff in hand, the son takes to the road to cover the earth. He mixes with the sometimes friendly, sometimes hostile world; he takes part sometimes freely, sometimes unwillingly in its concerns and collisions. Accompanied by vivid recollections of his father's house and paternal admonishments, he does not lose himself in these interests at first; his gaze will remain resolutely and longingly directed toward his beloved home. He will pour out his yearning for his homeland in secret outbursts and silent soliloquies, for he is fully conscious of his pilgrimage; he knows that the goal of his own eternal wandering is none other than to return to the arms of his father inwardly purified and enriched, self-aware and mature. But, alas, the son is only flesh and blood. Although the paternal education was intensive and the paternal teachings penetrating and convincing, they did not yet dominate the son's heart to the extent that he would be able to withstand every trial. Was there not a real danger that led astray by the enticements of the world, the sophistry of the passions, and the abstruse reflections of the mind, the son would abandon his course and become unfaithful to his convictions and life style which essentially contradict the way of the world? Was the fear not justified that the vivid memories of the father's house would slowly be diluted and obliterated by the growing physical and temporal distance and that the bond which bound the son to his father's house and its ancient traditions would be loosened? Was there not real danger—and now let's finally drop the metaphor—that God's first-born son, subjected to the influences, pleasures, and concerns of the world, would forget his lofty mission, the purpose of his pilgrimage through the tumult of the world and barter his birthright for a dish of lentils?

A dividing wall had to be built in the midst of this international existence which would keep Judaism from entering into too intimate a union with a world that deified nature. The same function which the natural borders of Palestine—the high Lebanon in the north, the sandy deserts in the east and south, and the partial ocean border of the west—had served, namely, to cut off the Holy Land from too close contact with the polytheistic world, was now served by the protective measures of the Talmud. These talmudic injunctions turn every Jewish house, anywhere in the world, into a precisely defined Palestine; they isolate Judaism even in the most lively centers of the world and draw immovable boundaries between the life style of Judaism and contrary world views. When the borders of Palestine were first breached and Judea stood open to the incursion of Greek elements from the north and south, from Syria and Egypt, the Men of the' Great Assembly enunciated the principle "Surround the Law with fences." This warning was increasingly taken to heart the more the borders of Palestine were transgressed and the natural barriers fell. The Talmud replaced artificially the inoperative system of natural isolation, and whatever criticisms one may have against it, Judaism owes its survival solely to the Talmud. We could apply to this situation the traditional adage "The sage is preferable to the prophet" (חכם עדיף מנביא). What prophecy only partially succeeded in doing, to distance the Jewish people from the nature religion of paganism and to douse it with the sap of Judaism, the talmudic sages accomplished with their protective system.

The talmudic restrictions and, in fact, the entire talmudic system—for even the later expansions and stringencies of the law were added in the spirit if not according to the letter of the Talmud—are not to be seen as something foreign forced upon Judaism, as an outgrowth of Jewish history and a beclouding of the Jewish spirit, but rather they are to be seen as a logical consequence deriving from the premise of Judaism's basic idea. If Judaism is a protest against the nature consciousness rooted in polytheism or paganism, if it constitutes the counterforce of the free ethical spirit to the immoral bondage of nature, then it must also in its external historical appearance be separated from its opposite, all the more so when the proximity increases and the number of points of contact between them multiplies. There is nothing more absurd and unhistorical than to assert that a force which penetrated as deeply as did the talmudic system is the product of an error, of twisted exegesis, of hierarchical ambition, in short, of a historical accident! As the dogmatic controversies of Christianity derive naturally from its basic structure, so too is the talmudic system an authentic child of Judaism; it could secure its survival only in the presuppositions of Judaism.

The talmudic system, therefore, constitutes the most effective counterbalance to the necessary international existence of Judaism. The one is the creative, the other the preserving principle; the one serves an assimilating, the other a separating function. When new elements and ingredients coming from the nations and the world are brought to Judaism to be incorporated, then the talmudic system rejects those parts damaging to Judaism and excises the disintegrating elements with an instinctive sense of revulsion. Endowed with sensitive antennae, the sages of the Talmud quickly detected an un-Jewish practice or an un-Jewish viewpoint and rejected them as "the ways of the Amorites" or as "Gentile laws." But in addition to this negative side, the talmudic system also had a positive one, namely, that it stamped as Jewish many neutral acts and practices because of their affinity to the spirit of Judaism and accepted them as part of Judaism. Thereby Jewish life gained a particular hue and a distinctive style which made it more difficult and dangerous to pass over to any of the more powerful surrounding principles. My intention here was not to offer an *apologia* for the talmudic spirit, but merely to vindicate its historical necessity, a necessity which of course depends on the circumstances.

The more the talmudic system penetrated the life of Judaism, being altered all the time, the more distinctly religious in character did it become. However, that was not the sole task of this period. The very process of determining and deciding the Halakhah, or that which was a genuine need and accorded with the spirit or letter of Judaism, already required some theory, and only the decisions which were accepted in the academies after passionate and thorough discussion were adopted in life. These halakhic academies flourished immediately after the burning of the Temple on the native Palestinian soil of Yavneh under the Patriarchate of the House of Hillel and later in the Galilean north, in Tiberias and Sepphoris, where a complete collection of many halakhot, the Mishnah, arose. From here, that is the academy of R. Judah the Prince, this development moved on to the Babylonian-Parthian empire along the shores of the Euphrates and Tigris. There the famous academies of Nehardea, Pumbedita, and Sura arose and served until the eleventh century as a training ground and model for the European schools in Spain, Italy, and Germany—for Cordova, Otranto, and Mayence. Regarding the activity of these schools, we ought to stress that although religious practice was certainly one motivation behind these studies, it was by no means the only one. Study for its own sake, a knowledge of Jewish Law, the theoretical mastery of Scripture and Tradition were all regarded as equally useful and obligatory, as a way of fulfilling the commandments. The theory of the Law is known under the name Talmud or, with some variation , Midrash. The theoretical aspect was so highly valued vis-à-vis religious practice that the greatest mishnaic authorities could even ponder the question whether the theoretical examination of the Law might not be more important than the performance of the religious act itself: תלמוד גדול או מעשה גדול ? From this stems the remarkable zeal for the study of the Law, תלמוד תורה, which brought troops of students to study with famous scholars, both of whom set aside the joys of family life and all practical life for its sake, a phenomenon still evident in the last century. Most of the martyrs of the Hadrianic period bled solely for this theoretical activity, for the forbidden study of the Law, for the proscribed assemblies of teacher and students, as, for example, the staunch R. Ḥananiah ben Teradion, the glorious R. Akiba, even the so-called ten martyrs, עשרה הרוגי מלכות or the הרוגי לוד with all their students.

These facts must be borne in mind if we wish to determine the center of Judaism's historical activity in this period of the Diaspora. The historical labor of Judaism concentrated on the theoretical explication of Judaism—and therein this period differs decisively from those that preceded.

This speculative aspect of halakhic studies, however, constituted only the beginning; the continuation and expansion is to be found in the Aggada. The Aggada (i.e., the philosophic Aggada) deals like the Halakhah with the given, with the content of Judaism as expressed in Scripture and Tradition. But at the same time it independently transcends this material in order to harmonize it with the categories of understanding. It seeks to illuminate and render comprehensible the dry letters of Scripture or the strange and abstruse character of religious behavior, discovering a deeper meaning in the letters and a higher relationship in religious behavior. If the Targumim (the Aramaic translations of Scripture) alter obvious anthropomorphisms in Scripture by substituting other expressions that will not mislead the reader, this is part of the aggadic enterprise and implies that the interpreters and their age have already become philosophically aware of the purely spiritual nature of God. If already in the Mishnah the distinction is made between purely religious duties (עבירות שבין אדם למקום) and social duties (עבירות שבין אדם לחברו), this again constitutes aggadic thinking. Thus at the beginning of this period, there is discussion regarding the rational and so-called irrational commandments of Judaism, with the latter appearing to the skeptics as perplexing and unessential.[13] Not infrequently, aggadic speculation arrives at the viewpoint that some of the positive prescriptions of Judaism are superfluous and appear to be unconnected with the rest of the commandments.[14]

This inclination to treat speculatively the facts of Judaism, the words of Scripture, and the prescribed religious practices constitutes *the first phase* of the theoretical perception of Judaism.

It cannot be denied that this philosophical Aggada is attributable not only to internal ferment but also to external influence. Greek metaphysics, especially the dominant Platonism of the neighboring Alexandrian school, the polemic against Christianity, the rapidly spreading Gnosticism—all these phenomena together awakened in the synagogue the spirit of contemplation and penetration.

If we can assume the information about the Essenes in Josephus and Philo to be historical—an assumption by no means certain—then they may actually have been the first to attempt to explain the Bible and the commandments philosophically, that is, allegorically, symbolically, and, typically, and to extract from them a higher truth.[15] At any rate, it is certain that already prior to Philo there were Jews who concerned themselves with the aggadic-philosophic exposition of Scripture and the allegoric meaning of the commandments and whose interpretations Philo often quotes in the name of "some" or "pious men." The historian Josephus allegedly wrote such a commentary to the Pentateuch in which the verse in Genesis [1:5] which reads "it was evening, it was morning, *one day*" rather than "the first day" merited his philosophical explanation. But this aggadic-philosophical school reached its high point in Philo, the Jewish Plato, about whose plastic style and poetic-philosophic bent the ancients already said: "Either Philo platonizes or Plato philonizes." Philo fully reveals the aggadic character in his commentary to the Pentateuch (for all his writings must be viewed as such), and only from this point of view can his interpretations be considered if they are to be properly appreciated.[16] At first glance, Philo and the Aggada have in common the exegetical techniques of interpreting every letter in a single word (נוטריקון) and of computing the numerical value of the letters (גמטריא), two fruitful methods of interpretation by which anything can be read into or extracted from the text. Although a large part of the Philonic Aggada is preoccupied with discovering foreign thought patterns in biblical literature, such as the Pythagorean symbolic system of numbers, ratios, and harmony, the Platonic theory of Ideas (the Logos theory), and Platonic ethics and politics with their system of four virtues, he still extracted some genuinely Jewish ideas in opposition to certain pagan views. Philo particularly stresses the unity of God, *creatio ex nihilo,* and the ethical and ennobling character of Jewish law. At the expense of consistency, Philo teaches enthusiastically the unalterableness and eternity of Judaism which he then ·juxtaposes to the changeableness of human institutions. "But the laws of Moses, permanent, secure, inviolable, as if stamped with the seal of nature, have remained fixed since the day they were first recorded till now, and we are confident that they will remain immortal into the most distant future like the sun, the moon, the sky, and the universe. For no matter what good or evil fate the Jewish people has already experienced, it has not altered the slightest commandment, but rather properly revered the laws as holy and divine. Neither hunger nor pestilence, neither war nor a tyrant, neither physical nor spiritual suffering, in fact, no cruel fate ever succeeded in abolishing the Law; how could it not continue to remain holy and desirable above all else?"[17]

Philo already occupies himself with the problem of whether the religious acts of Judaism must still be performed if one has fathomed their inner meaning and ideal significance, and he assumes an affirmative position. "There are some people who, since they believe that the prescribed laws are only symbols for ideas, consider the ideas carefully but thoughtlessly disregard their performance. But I wish to condemn this disregard; for both must be carefully observed, the precise study of the concealed truths as well as their irreproachable, visible containers. These people violate what the people hold dear and search for the naked truth, as if they lived alone in a desert or were bodiless spirits who knew neither city nor house nor in fact human society. This is actually what Scripture teaches: to appropriate an excellent idea but also not to abandon any of the customs. For we are not allowed by virtue of the fact that we understand that the Sabbath (the numerical system of seven) signifies the uncreated, or the Sabbath rest signifies becoming, to set aside the laws of the Sabbath and thus to kindle fire, work the land, carry objects, summon to court, render a decision, collect debts, and perform all the labors of the work-day. On the contrary, we must assume that the practical commandments correspond to the body, the ideas to the soul. And just as we regard the body as the dwelling place of the soul so likewise with the prescribed commandments."[18] This aggadic-philosophic genre is not, however, merely the beginning of a tendency to conceptualize the Jewish idea, but actually represents the starting point of a movement which will become richer and more competent in relation to the times and places it will traverse. It is enough that in this historical expression of Jewish life the urge is already apparent to uncover the inner meaning behind the externals of religious practice.

We should not conclude, however, that this kind of activity was restricted only to the academies and occupied only the circles of the learned. On the contrary, from many sides the aggadic viewpoint with all its lights and shadows impinged on national life. When talent was exhausted, mediocrity and imitation took its place. Aggadic interpretation became fashionable, and a comprehensive midrashic literature arose, which we do not even fully possess. Aggadic creativity continued till the ninth and tenth centuries and this literature was used to instruct and edify the masses, acquiring thereby a popularity which it has not fully lost to this day.

A derivative of this genre is Jewish mysticism with its fundamental text, the Zohar—a creation of gnostic and theosophic views to which a number of still other unknown factors also contributed. In the seventeenth century Jewish mysticism helped spawn the movement of Sabbatai Zevi; it took on new life through Isaac Luria and his disciples and to this day dominates the circles of the Hasidim.

The Aggada entered national life from still a third side. Poetic talent took possession of aggadic material and reworked it into religious hymns and liturgical pieces for the festivals according to the canons of versification. Kalir's original works of art stimulated emulation, the literature of the *piyyut* rapidly grew and disseminated both mature and immature notions of the Aggada in the synagogue. Aggadic thought amply betrayed immature and crude elements even in Philo, its most gifted representative, the most serious being that with this method it is impossible to arrive at a system of Jewish concepts; its very character is epigrammatic and unconnected. Since the Aggada takes as its starting point the very letters of Scripture, striving to expound them and reconcile them with ideas adopted from elsewhere, the result is that it moves only within this sphere; it jumps from verse to verse without regard for continuity or consistency, without the slightest attention to the contradictions into which it must inevitably fall. To the loose threads of the verses seriatim, it attaches its reflections, whatever idea can be connected to the verse at hand, only to drop them immediately in order to seize others which would suit the next verse better. If the sense of the verse defies the imposed interpretation, then it must have recourse to more arbitrary means such as allegory or the manipulation of the numbers and letters which now take the place of logic.[19] As a result, this literary genre acquired an arbitrary, incongruous and childish character, a circumstance which often provokes bitter criticism of the Aggada, Talmud, and Tradition itself, because many thoughtless critics confuse the external form of the Aggada with the entire Talmud and in turn, the Talmud with Tradition. Finally, this genre is also crude because it dragged foreign ideas and assumptions into the interpretations of Scripture without ever realizing what it was doing. As much as it manifested a dimension of reflectiveness, it still was firmly rooted in a state of immediacy and indeterminateness; it still did not know how to separate foreign matter from its own.

The Second Phase. The continuation of this theoretical elaboration of the conceptual content of Judaism took place, first of all, by transforming ecstatic enthusiasm into sober analysis, poetic embellishment into prosaic conceptual clarity, in short, by rendering aggadic commentary into philosophy. If the aforementioned aggadic-philosophic school still fully manifested a poetic nature, if it rested more on intellectual observation than conceptual clarity, if it still betrayed the traces of that free-floating curiosity without any center or objective, then the next genre to appear in Jewish history is characterized by the discarding of this crude and incomplete form. Saadia is indeed the last to write a commentary to the Pentateuch filled with philosophic reflections and, at the same time, the first to round out these philosophic reflections into a system. And thereby a new theory of Judaism rooted itself in Jewish history. Henceforth it would be necessary to discover a principle by which Judaism could establish and justify itself, and to derive from this principle the particulars of Judaism as its consequences and conclusions; henceforth it would be necessary to traverse the expanse of Jewish concepts with a sober mind, with grammar and sound exegesis and with logical acuity.

While in Palestine and the other lands which reflected the same spirit, aggadic creativity still continued to flourish, clinging firmly to the scriptural text and reading into it all the experiences of personal and group life, there now stirred in the lands of the caliphate, the home of the Babylonian Talmud, a new fresh spirit which banished the semi-darkness of the Aggada and its perversions by means of strictly logical concepts. Saadia the Fayumite, whom the proud academy of Sura felt compelled to call from Egypt to become its Gaon, is the first representative of this spirit. The historical circumstances behind this phenomenon are varied: contemporary masoretic and grammatical studies; the predominance of Aristotle in Asia, who through the generous patronage of the Abassid caliphs became the philosophic darling of the Arab-Oriental world; the conflicts with Karaism which made it necessary to pursue the simple meaning of Scripture and thereby to find support for the Tradition which was being sorely challenged; and finally the more sober temperament of Babylonian Jews, who in this regard were quite distinct from the emotional Palestinians.

By the prime of Saadia's life, this purely rational spirit had already reached the level of skepticism, of disbelief in revelation, of unabashed violation of religious commandments.[20] The need was felt not only to view Judaism in the traditional manner as the customs of the fathers and the instructions of the sages, but at the same time to subject it to reflection and conviction. Saadia also made concessions to this demand of the times that Judaism must justify itself rationally; he recognized reason as the highest authority, which in the first instance must decide the proper interpretation of Scripture. Indeed his religious-philosophic system intended to harmonize Judaism with the categories of reason. His book *Emunot ve-Deot, Faith and Reason,* is the first attempt in the Jewish world to reconcile faith and reason or, more correctly, revelation and philosophy. Although it must be reserved for the still unwritten history of Jewish religious systems to describe these systems and, in fact, it would suffice for our task merely to point out that this or that idea has now entered the historical continuum, still it may not be superfluous, as long as that work remains a pious wish, to present the outlines of the major systems which constitute turning points in Jewish intellectual life, because this attempt will reveal most clearly and convincingly the inner connection and interrelationship between these systems. A system of thought, however, never belongs entirely or even partially to its creator; it is rather a product of the time, and the function of the thinker is often only to gather the scattered sparks of an idea into a single focal point. Thus in speaking of Saadia's or Maimonides' system, we are not considering the views of this or that individual but of the spokesman of the time, views which then, in turn, must be seen as the product of countless different factors.

In the midst of the unclear ideas of his contemporaries,

Saadia developed a highly simple system, partially borrowed
from Arab theologians.[21] He takes no step without first
proving it or refuting its opposite; the assortment of his proofs
and counter-arguments he draws from the storehouse of
reason, מן השכל , and from the grammatically purified apparatus of Scripture, מן הכתוב .

The visible world is created: the proofs being its finiteness,
the endless divisibility of its parts, and the instability of its
substance. If the world is created, then it must have a creator
who has produced its existence out of absolutely nothing.
This creative power can only be one. The unity of God
implies omniscience just as His creative activity implies
omnipotence, and these together, spirituality (incorporeality).
The purpose of creation was to make manifest God's
greatness, wisdom, and goodness. In the order of creatures,
man assumes the highest position, even superseding the
angels; for the best and most important is always to be found
in the middle (כל דבר חשוב שמור באמצע); the seed is enclosed
in the middle of the plant, the yolk in the middle of the egg.
Now, the earth occupies the center of the heavenly spheres,
thus its inhabitants represent the highest among created
beings and the actual purpose of creation. But the favored
citizen of the earth is unquestionably man by virtue of his
spirit and gifted nature.

By means of his spirit, however, man recognizes his
dependence on God, a state which derives from his feeling of
gratitude and which immediately imposes upon him certain
duties: to honor and to love God and to recognize the rational
laws of morality. At the same time these duties advance his
temporal and eternal happiness (הצלחה גמורה וטובה שלמה). If
man, however, deduces these duties through reason, what is
the need for revelation? This revelation spares man the
arduous task of coming to recognize the basic rationality of
his nature and to live according to its dictates (וטובתו בדרך
ההיא ועל ידי צווי ואזהרה] יותר טוב להם בעבור מה שנסתלק מעליהם
מעניני הטורח). Those who believe in the unity of God
(קהל מייחדים) are, therefore, compelled to recognize revelation,

partly because of its reasonableness and partly out of thankfulness to God.

Alongside the rational part of revelation(מצוות שכליות)stands, however, also another part composed of nonrational practices which acquire value only through God's commandment (מצוות שמעיות). The obligatory character of this part stems from the conviction that since they come from God, they are intended for the best. And it is even possible that they may contain a rational and partially useful basis (ועם זה אפשר שיהיה להם תועלת חלקית ועלילה מעטה מדרך המושכל). Thus we might be able to imagine plausible reasons for the holy days (festivals), for the holy men (priests), for the proscription of many kinds of animals, for the various forbidden marriages and finally for the numerous regulations for daily consecration—although they would be unconvincing reasons. Divine wisdom may well have incorporated in them entirely different ideas.[22]

However, revelation as a historical fact, if it is to be believed, must be authenticated. Judaism has such documentation in the miracles of Egypt and Mount Sinai. But miracles alone, which have no rational purpose, prove nothing; for just as miracles cannot set aside the laws of morality, they cannot abrogate the laws of thought. The revelation of Judaism, the Torah, is forever indissoluble, a point which Saadia confirms on the basis of internal evidence: the prophets promised the Jews eternal earthly existence (Jeremiah 31), yet a Jewish people without the Torah is sheer nonsense (כי אומתנו אינה אומה כי אם בתורתה). From these principles Saadia derived several additional dogmas which no religion at the time could afford to omit. From the concept of God's mercy and justice, he developed the principle of reward and punishment for virtuous or wicked living, and in turn from this he came to the belief in the immortality of the soul. From the concept of God's omnipotence, whereby the world was created *ex nihilo*, he developed the doctrines of resurrection and messianic redemption.

In this systematic form Judaism comprehended itself as a

unique totality, and no matter how inferior it may be to later systems, it was still of infinite importance. By virtue of the fact that an authority like Saadia, the celebrated Gaon of the academy at Sura, the successful opponent of the Karaites, the prolific writer, translator, and exegete, undertook to comprehend Judaism philosophically, the philosophic examination of Judaism received an indisputable sanction. Henceforth philosophic studies became part of Judaism. Many who followed Saadia took up problems of Jewish philosophy, expounding anthropomorphic and anthropopathic biblical verses and aggadic passages according to metaphysical principles. From the banks of the Euphrates and Tigris both philosophic and talmudic studies made their way to the Iberian peninsula. Kairowan in north Africa, the ancient Cyrene, formed the bridge between Babylonia and Spain. This blessed peninsula, the home of religious fanaticism and the Inquisition, became, under the tolerant scepter of the Moorish caliphs who craved both learning and comfort, the classical land of Jewish studies. It produced a long line of Jewish personalities at home in all fields of human and divine learning: Jewish mathematicians, doctors, statesmen, grammarians, philosophic exegetes, poets, and religious philosophers appeared in great numbers on this stage. Two individuals towered over all the others: Judah ha-Levi and Moses ben Maimon, and both their contemporaries and posterity have paid tributes to their genius.

Saadia's sketchy and incomplete system tended to explicate individual dogmas of Judaism rather than its full nature. Precisely the characteristically Jewish, its unique physiognomy, the large body of "traditional commandments" remained unexplained or were treated only tangentially. This gap left by Saadia was now filled by Judah ha-Levi with a consistency and completeness which again disturbed the balance between revelation and philosophy.

Judah ha-Levi, the prince of poets, the Jewish Plotinus, whose intense longing for the Holy Land, for the cradle of Judaism where inspiration and prophecy were born, caused him to regard his birthplace as a foreign land, began his speculations about Judaism from precisely the opposite principles. In his book, the *Kusari*, modeled after the Platonic dialogue, he put his convictions into the mouth of a Jewish sage (חבר).Reason and the syllogisms of metaphysics are in no way sufficient to construct a positive way of life, because metaphysical truths are subject to constant fluctuation and philosophers themselves cannot agree. Reason plays only a negative corrective role. Thus pure reason rejects from the very outset every religious expression, every emotional relationship of man to God and God to man, which remains nonetheless an urgent human need. There must, therefore, be still another source of knowledge for truth. A far more powerful means of persuasion than that which is available to syllogistic demonstration exists in undeceiving observation, in tested first-hand experience (הראייה אין צריך עמה לא ראיה ולא מופת). Upon such a convincing visual, personal experience rests the revelation of Judaism. The extraordinary events in Egypt, at the Red Sea, at Mount Sinai, and in the forty years of wandering in the wilderness, the endless acts of mercy which God performed for the Jewish people, and, finally, the visible presence of the divine spirit in the prophets—all took place within sight of millions of people, who obviously did not fail to examine whether these amazing occurrences were not simply illusions or tricks. This direct, tested, and undeceiving impression of revelation was transmitted through an authenticated tradition from father to son, and here as well neither deception nor trickery were possible (התברר אצלם המעמד ההוא בראות עיניהם ואחר כך הקבלה הנמשכת שהיא כמראה העין).

In this regard revelation is comparable to newly discovered important phenomena in physics, which reason a priori would never have granted, but once convinced by actual observation it will labor to confirm them rationally.

If revelation and a direct relationship between God and man are secured through personal experience, thereby also providing a criterion to distinguish between a genuine and a false experience of revelation, then it becomes possible on this basis to construct a system of Judaism. Adam, the protoplast, directly created by God with physical and spiritual beauty, undamaged and unaffected by the disruptive experience of birth, was also endowed with a divine nature which manifested itself in the direct comprehension and assessment of present, past, and future situations without the paltry assistance of involved syllogisms. This specifically prophetic nature was transmitted naturally to those of his descendants who by virtue of their physical and psychological make-up were suited for it. In this sense Adam was called God's son and his descendants sons of God (בני אלהים). They constitute the heart and core of mankind (לב האדם וסגולתו). Those not suited, however, bear only a slight resemblance to their original ancestor and have the same relationship to those who are suited as the shell to the core (והשאר כקליפות אינם דומים לאבות). Thus Adam's nature passed down through Seth, Noah, and Eber to Abraham and from him it subsequently concentrated in the Jewish people.

The Hebrews, the descendants of Eber, are not only qualitatively but also genetically different from other nations. Only in their midst were the Prophets possible, in their midst were preserved the traditions about the origin of the world and the pre-history of mankind, and from them did they reach other nations, though distorted, debased, and diluted with myths. As a result of this inherited nature they were qualified and worthy to receive God's word at Sinai for all humanity. The Jewish people is thus the core of mankind (ואנחנו הסגולה מבני אדם) just as the prophets and righteous men are the kernel of the core (הנביאים והחסידים סגולת הסגולה). Therefore, even converts can never come to possess the nature necessary for prophecy, although they do share in the happiness promised the Jewish people. The purpose of the Torah is to preserve and cultivate this nature in Judaism. The Ten Commandments constitute the prototypes and categories for the other commandments.[23]

These divine prescriptions of the Torah must be fulfilled without reflection or arbitrary alteration if they are to achieve their objective, which is none other than to preserve the clarity of the prophetic vision, the direct observation of the divine glory and the continuation of God's merciful rule over Israel. But how this divine nature breaks through in an individual man remains a mystery. For this to happen certain prior conditions must be present. Besides the careful observance of the biblical commandments, they are the sacred soil of Palestine, the heart and core of the earth, and the holy tongue, in which God communicated to man.

The rational laws of Judaism (חוקים שכליים) in no way, therefore, constitute its essence; they are merely external conditions without which the commandments that sanctify and elevate man would remain without influence, for indeed no society, not even a band of thieves, can survive without a definite social ethos. Thus, not the rational commandments are characteristic of Judaism, but precisely those peculiar prescriptions which defy reason (הם התורות אשר התיחדו בהם בני ישראל תוספת על השכליות). Still, in every single commandment of the Torah the wisdom of God is mirrored (תורתכם נכלל בה כל דק ועמוק מהחכמות), and even the sacrificial cult of the Temple rendered certain ideas visible. The Sabbath, for example, testifies to a vital awareness of the creation of the world (ושמירת השבת כאילו היא הוצאה מעשית בחדוש);likewise circumcision is a reminder to control the sex drive (המילה היא אות אלהית . . . באבר התאוה הגוברת לגבור עליה).[24]

According to these principles the entire body of Jewish religious law can be seen as a logical development. The promised Messiah will restore the relationship between the Jewish people and its God which was disrupted by the violation of the Law and the subsequent exile. Living in the Holy Land and guided by laws which sanctify, the people will again become a holy nation in which God's presence will be reflected and prophets inspired.

It is not an accident that this system of Judaism, which throughout does not rest on alien assumptions and which, I might observe, is thoroughly nationalistic in character, succeeded in exercising only a relatively small amount of influence on Jewish posterity, despite the high regard in which this poetic philosopher was constantly held and which is aptly expressed in the biblical allusion "Be sure not to neglect the Levite" [Deuteronomy 12:19], an allusion preserved by tradition to this day. Besides a not very significant influence on the views of Moses ben Nahman (Nahmanides) and a few traces found in the *Zohar,* this system produced no echo, evoked no religious response. In an age when Aristotelian rationalism and pure intellectualism dominated Arabs and Jews alike, this nationalistic, mystical interpretation of Judah ha-Levi could not find the proper soil. First this orientation had to fully expire; history had to show that the facts of Judaism simply did not correspond to the ideas produced by the categories of an imprisoned and finite mind. A beginning was made by Saadia; Maimonides completed and perfected the system.

If Philo was already called by the ancients the Jewish Plato, then Moses ben Maimon certainly deserves to be called the Jewish Aristotle. The entire intellectual output of Maimonides clearly betrays the calm and clarity, the systematic mind and the universality of the Stagarite philosopher. Although Aristotle had disciples among all the nations, in all regions, and among all religious persuasions, none mirrored the Peripatetic School more truly than Maimonides. Even when he appears to wander independently, or deviates entirely from Aristotle's philosophy, or handles material that lies entirely outside Aristotelian philosophy, the Aristotelian thinker is unmistakably present. Maimonides is a systematizer through and through; every block of material which his mind masters is turned by him into an organic unit. We meet the same articulate, clear mind in all the fields in which he works, in the commentaries, the halakhah, and philosophy. In every intellectual subject he extracts the principles, the starting point, which he places at the center and around which the details line up logically. He has, therefore, for every subject which he treats, an illuminating introduction (הקדמה) which gives the reader a personal guide to lead him reliably into the unknown.

True to the Aristotelian principle, indeed even more so than Aristotle himself, Maimonides presents theoretical wisdom, the metaphysical understanding of God, His substance and attributes, a life lived according to reason, in short, theology (in the philosophic sense: חכמה אלהית) as the highest good and the ultimate purpose of all human activity. But since the highest level of knowledge can be reached only through propaedeutic training, that is, through the study of physics (חכמה טבעית), mathematics (חכמה לימודית), and, finally, logic (חכמת היגיון), these sciences also become an objective of human activity, but only insofar as they are a means to the highest science, the First Philosophy. Judaism called the highest science, metaphysical theology מעשה מרכבה (the vision of God's throne-chariot), and designated the subordinate sciences, specifically physics, מעשה בראשית (the account of creation), both of which had to be withheld from the ordinary man and made inaccessible because of their profound and lofty character.[25] Thus the final purpose of divine revelation can only be to make known the highest truths of metaphysics regarding the unity of God, His incorporeality, and similar divine attributes.

Moreover, true to the teleological philosophy of Aristotle, Maimonides sought to show the existence of definite reasons in the Torah as a whole as well as in its details. Just as it is impossible to agree with the Arabic dogmatists (Mutakal-limun— מדברים) who contend that the divine act of creation had no specific purpose, on the contrary, that it was wholly an act of the absolute divine will (אחר הרצון לבד לא לבקשת תכלית כלל),likewise one cannot concede to the timid Jewish thinkers that the Torah has no definite purpose. They fear that to subsume the Torah under rational categories might lead to the conclusion that Judaism is in fact a product of human reason.[26] But precisely because the Torah stems from God is one forced to assume that it pursues generally as well as particularly a rational purpose. The ultimate purpose of

Judaism is none other than the spiritual and material perfection and ennobling of man (תקון הנפש ותקון הגוף). The ennoblement of the spirit is theologically the highest priority, though its realization occurs last; in contrast, physical perfection, which is only a secondary objective, in actuality occurs first.

The highest purpose of Judaism is, therefore, the teaching of the philosophic truths about God, such as the necessity of His existence, His unity, omniscience, and omnipotence, His absolute will, His eternity, and then, the scrupulous discarding of all views about God which are inappropriate to the concept of God (נתינת דעות אמיתיות ולהסיר דעות פחותות). After this main purpose come the political purposes. Man as a social animal (מדיני בטבעו) requires a social setting for his survival, without which he would lack the strength, the means, the desire, and the leisure necessary to strive after life's highest goal. The ethical commandments of Judaism, therefore, have only relative value, for without them as the basis of existence the heights of knowledge could not be scaled.

On the basis of these principles and also the assumption that the historical task of Judaism had been to oppose directly Sabianism (אמונת הצאבה) with its corrupt, highly unethical views and practices, which was already flourishing at the time of Judaism's birth, Maimonides was able to find for most of Judaism's commandments a reasonable and purposeful foundation and to make them available to reason. With systematic clarity, Maimonides succeeded in classifying the entire range of Jewish law into fourteen categories and in providing each category with a plausible explanation. His method of explaining Jewish law (טעמי המצוות), however, lacks a unified character, and it is hard to describe it as anything but thoroughly rationalistic. When an unusual commandment or detail does not readily yield to any of his assumptions, then Maimonides has a handy remedy—its intent was most likely anti-Sabian.[27]

This is not the place to examine the strengths and

weakenesses of the Maimonidean system. Our only purpose is to draw attention to the great influence which it had on Jewish history. As a result of the *Guide* which soon became the basic text of all Jewish thinkers, a deep internal split divided Jewish communities in three parts of the world. Religious intellectuals, who wanted to justify Judaism philosophically, and simple believers, who feared the worst from any philosophic examination of Judaism, began to square off against each other. The controversy was generally ignited by the subordinate position which Maimonides had assigned Judaism vis-à-vis Aristotelian philosophy, but specifically by the doctrine of creation, regarding which Maimonides held no firm position. He did not wish to accept Aristotle's view of the world because it did not seem to him sufficiently demonstrated to assert it against the clear sense of revelation, yet he would not adopt, along with Saadia and other dogmatists, the temporal creation of the world as the basis of his system, because it had still to be proven metaphysically. "If the eternity of the world had been proven by Aristotle, then the apparent contradiction of revelation would not be overriding, for we could interpret the conflicting verses accordingly (היינו יכולים לפרש הפסוקים ההם ולהעמיד קדמות העולם). The gates of exegesis are not closed." This was the conclusion of the Maimonidean system. From France, from Montpellier, the storm against this conclusion quickly spread. The *Guide* was banned despite the highest regard which people generally felt for the enormously talented, nearly ideal figure of Maimonides.

As a result of this controversy over the *Guide* and over the relationship of philosophy to Judaism, in which the giants of an entire century participated, the theoretical elaboration of the idea of Judaism gained at least in breadth if not in depth. What formerly had occupied intellectuals in the quiet isolation of their study, now broke out in the open, stirred the people and became a catalyst of Jewish history. Even misuse and caricature were not missing. The ancient days of Alexandrian Judaism returned; the dry facts of the biblical narrative were again transformed into allegory, this time according to the model of Maimonides; the metaphysical catchwords of "matter, form, active intellect, and passive intellect" (חומר, צורה, שכל הפועל, והנפעל) appeared all over, and exegetes claimed to discover them in every biblical verse and aggadic passage, a travesty which the noble Solomon ibn Adret finally felt compelled to restrict. Skepticism also surfaced in the works of Samuel Zarza and Joseph ibn Caspi, as was only to be expected in the course of such a heated controversy; and had not the fanaticism of the Catholic Ferdinand and the Grand Inquisitor Torquemada halted this development in the middle by means of bloody edicts of expulsion, torture, and the stake, this theoretical clarification of Judaism might well have advanced much further. Along with the Spanish exiles and the persecuted victims of the Inquisition, Maimonidean philosophy found refuge and acceptance in the Turkish Empire, the Italian states, and the Dutch emporium. The vestiges of this dispersed philosophy contributed to the birth of Spinoza's philosophy, just as Philonic-aggadic thought helped create Neoplatonism. The history of philosophy should not treat Judaism so coldly and arrogantly; many of the stones in its various systems were taken from the ruins of Judaism.

Once the supremacy of Aristotelian philosophy was finally broken by English naturalism and by the boost which philosophy got from the Cartesian principle of "I think, therefore I am," Judaism also had to search around for another principle. The Aristotelian-Maimonidean system could no longer satisfy. Admittedly, the need for a philosophic justification of Judaism was little felt during the century from Menassah ben Israel to Mendelssohn. This century had a thoroughly tedious character, whose barrenness may have been caused by the new Lurianic mysticism. But as the need became appreciable and a gifted personality grasped the problem, a new philosophic trend immediately emerged.

The Third Phase begins with Mendelssohn, the manager of a silk business. Jewish thinkers generally held no public office and filled no official position connected with their intellectual work; Philo, Judah ha-Levi, Ibn Ezra, Maimonides, and Naḥmanides were theologians without office, they distributed the fruits of their intellectual efforts without compensation as Moses had done with the Torah received at Mount Sinai. With Leibniz and Wolf, philosophy became firmly established in Germany. Mendelssohn played an important role in freeing philosophy from the rigid and unwieldy formalism in which it had operated till then, rendering it flexible and enjoyable, and in this sense he deservedly bears the name "the Jewish Socrates." As Socrates had brought philosophy down out of the stars into the homes of men, so did Mendelssohn free it from the tedium of its formalism and humanize it. But also in another sense can Mendelssohn be called the Jewish Socrates. Like Socrates, he was through and through a philosopher, every inch a sage, without, however, having a philosophic system; like him, he was stimulating and fructifying, he fulfilled for philosophy the Socratic function of a midwife. How enormously influential his productivity was for the outer and inner history of Judaism is well-known to the present generation. Mendelssohn is regarded as one of the luminaries of Jewish history. He also wrote a great deal for and about Judaism, but his system of Judaism is only sketchily developed, even in his *Jerusalem,* which an external occasion seemingly forced from him. Nevertheless, as sketchy as his system may be, it still reveals a new trend in the understanding of Judaism. This trend no longer appropriates a principle whose justification lies outside Judaism, but rather desires a center of gravity within itself. Although Mendelssohn, like many Jewish thinkers such as Solomon Maimon, for example, was trained in philosophy by Maimonides' *Guide,* his first principle is still a direct contradiction to that of Maimonides.

"Judaism is not a revealed religion, but rather a revealed legislation." That means Judaism does not have the function to teach "eternal truths" but to provide guidelines for behavior: "Act, do not act"—that is the pivotal point of

Judaism. The goal of this revealed legislation is to advance the national welfare of the entire Jewish people as well as the individual well-being of its adherents. This particular legislation, however, is rooted in several metaphysical assumptions and historical facts which ought not to be forgotten; on the contrary, the faithful must be ever aware of them if they are to exercise the desired influence on the people. To insure the uninterrupted remembering of the eternal truths and historical events, Judaism has a proper and useful means: the ceremonial law which consists of behavioral prescriptions. By means of a mnemotechnic system of acts, the written prescription and visual presentation of these truths and facts, which sooner or later would lead to the idolatrous worship of texts and pictures are, on the one hand, circumvented, while on the other, the system does encourage reflection and study because the objectively meaningless nature of these acts necessarily points to something higher.

In Judaism, state and religion are rooted in the same soil, or more correctly, they are one. God, the Creator of the world, is likewise the Lawgiver and King of the nation: the civil component is at the same time religious and holy, while the religious is also a civil obligation. Serving the state is serving God. A religious transgression is not punished by religion, which as a matter of conscience possesses no coercive power, but by the state. With the loss of its political character, Judaism lost also its civil powers to impose discipline and to excommunicate. But the religious side will preserve its unalterable value until the same Divine Being who originally commanded the laws publicly will choose to revoke them publicly.

This is roughly the outline of Mendelssohn's view of Judaism, which in regard to its limited scope, to be sure, is comparable to the system of Saadia which similarly sets up only general categories; but it is far superior to Saadia's by virtue of its historical, national point of departure. However, this trend of thought could not immediately be developed further. Judaism had first to recover from the state of exhaustion produced by the chase to which it had been subjected for seventeen hundred years. During this period it became estranged from itself; the hard blows of fate partially brutalized it. Its body became dehydrated and needed first to be revived by the humor of education. It lacked a language, the vital carrier of ideas, and had first to learn one. It lacked any understanding for the written records of its experience and had to be retaught the Bible; it had lost all trace of self-esteem and this too had to be relearned. Thus, a certain period of time was required for Judaism to orient itself in the world, until it could find itself once again.

In the meantime, the circle of "eternal truths" was enlarged and enriched through the advances of the critical-speculative schools. Men now discover eternal truths not only in the ideas of the spirit but also in the far higher realm of the actions of the spirit, not only in the formalism of logic, in the abstractions of metaphysics and the externalism of nature, but especially in the concrete forms of art, science, religion, in the composite of all these factors, in the formation of the state, and particularly in the developments of history. Thus Judaism must merely appropriate this point of view, and its philosophical justification will be a simple matter. From this viewpoint of an objective and unbiased historical examination, the outcome is assured.

To be sure, Hegel still treated Judaism with crude prejudice. In his philosophy of religion he dismissed it as "the religion of transcendence," a subordinate manifestation; in his philosophy of history he tossed it into the *olla podrida* of "the Persian views of religion," where he also places the totally contradictory views of the Egyptians.[28] But Judaism is definitely not a product of the Orient; on the contrary, it constitutes a blunt contradiction to it. Judaism has already been able to extract a fairer treatment from Braniss, at least the Judaism "before the birth of Christ." He regarded it as a generically different historical phenomenon from paganism which had completed its course in five stages of national development, the Chinese, Indian, Egyptian, Sabian-Persian, and the Greek: freedom of the spirit versus subjugation by nature. But both Judaism and paganism traversed parallel stages of development until they began to draw closer together and were eventually mediated and reconciled by Christianity, that is, absorbed and dissolved.[29]

But it is just as unlikely that Judaism will be expunged from the book of the living by such a view of history as by the most recent trends in the midst of the synagogue to consider it a slightly embarrassing abstraction or to shift it from the power of the deed to the vagueness of religious feeling. However, recently, a good beginning has been made on the Jewish side to raise to the level of consciousness the different sides of Judaism in all their abundance and fullness. This impetus came independently from three talented men. Steinheim stressed the metaphysical side, Hirsch (ben Uziel) the religious, and Salvador[30] the social-legislative side. The only thing still missing is a comprehensive principle of Judaism, which would encompass and unite all these sides, a principle which would be mirrored in all the appearances of Jewish life, the dogmatic, religious, political, and historical down to the lowliest form. But this consideration does not belong to the structure of history, since it anticipates the future.

My task was only to show that the last period of Jewish history, which I have called that of the Diaspora, had a distinctive, specific style different from earlier ones, and this style has proven to be speculative. From the imperceptible start of halakhic discussions through three other phases—the aggadic-philosophical, the rational and the speculative schools—we have followed the course of this style down to the present. This theoretical dimension could develop fully only in the international arena, in exile, although it still needed a counterbalance in the talmudic system against too rapid a development. Exacting religious observance always toned down and rendered harmless the dangerous conclusions of the theory. Thus, the course of Jewish history has produced three dimensions:

1. The political-social in the first pre-exilic period;
2. The religious in the post-exilic period and;

3. The theoretical-philosophic in the last period of the Diaspora.

And since these three dimensions have assumed historical form, they must have lain in the original idea of Judaism, as the tree in the seed, and according to this view of history it seems that the task of Judaism's God-idea is to found a religious state which is conscious of its activity, purpose, and connection with the world.[31]

2

Introduction to Volume Four of the *History of the Jews*[1]

The long era of the dispersion, lasting nearly seventeen centuries, is characterized by unprecedented sufferings, an uninterrupted martyrdom, and a constantly aggravated degradation and humiliation unparalleled in history—but also by mental activity, unremitting intellectual efforts, and indefatigable research. A graphic, adequate image of this era could only be portrayed by representing it in two pictures: the one represents subjugated Judah with the pilgrim staff in hand, the pilgrim pack upon the back, with a mournful eye addressed toward heaven, surrounded by prison walls, implements of torture and red-hot branding irons; the other exhibits the same figure with the earnestness of the thinker upon his placid brow, with the air of the scholar in his bright features, seated in a hall of learning, which is filled with a colossal library in all the languages spoken by man and on all the branches of divine and human lore—the figure of a servant with the proud independence of the thinker. The one represents the external history of this era, a history of suffering, the like of which no other people has endured in such an aggravated degree and to such an immense extent; the other exhibits the inward history, a comprehensive history of the mind, which, like an immense river, springing from the knowledge of God as its fountainhead, receives, appropriates, and blends all the tributary sciences—again a history peculiar to this people alone. Studying and wandering thinking and

125

enduring, learning and suffering, fill the long space of this era.

Within this space of time universal history has thrice changed its costume. The senile Roman Empire languished and sank into the tomb; in its mouldering body the chrysalis of European and Asiatic nations was developed; they attained the brilliant butterfly-form of Christian and Moslem chivalry; and from the ashes of its castles the phoenix of civilization soared triumphantly aloft. Universal history thus underwent a triple transformation—but the Jews remained the same; they changed at most their outward form. But universal history also thrice changed its spiritual standard. From the refined, but hollow culture, mankind degenerated into barbarism and dark ignorance; from ignorance it again arose to the luminous sphere of a higher civilization: but the spiritual standard of Judaism remained the same and was only enriched by new subjects of thought and ideal forms. If the Judaism of this era presents the most glorious martyrs, compared to whom the persecuted sufferers of other nations and creeds may almost be pronounced happy, it has also produced eminent thinkers, who have not remained an exclusive ornament of Judaism. There is scarcely a science, an art, an intellectual province in which Jews have not taken a part, for which Jews have not manifested an equal aptitude. To think was as much a characteristic feature of the Jews as to suffer.

In consequence of the chiefly compulsory, seldom voluntary, migrations of the Jews, the Jewish history of this era comprises the entire habitable globe, extending to the snowy region of the north, the tropical heat of the south, crossing every ocean, and settling in the remotest corners of the earth. As soon as a new part of the earth is occupied by a new people, the dispersed of this race forthwith make their appearance, defying, in their adaptability, every adversity. If a new continent is discovered, Jewish congregations here and there constitute themselves and coalesce by a spontaneous process of crystalization, without foreign aid, without external force. Around the temple, sacred even in its ashes, the dispersed into all parts of the earth form a vast circle, whose circumference is identical with the ends of the habitable globe. Through these migrations the Jewish people gathered new experiences and the eye of the homeless became practiced and keen; thus, even the accumulated sufferings were instrumental in extending the horizon of Jewish thinkers. Jewish history of this era has passed, passively and sometimes actively, through all the momentous events and occurrences of universal history from the time that all the terrors of barbarism were discharged at the overrefined Roman Empire, to the point when the spark of civilization was again struck from the flint of barbarism. Every storm in the historical atmosphere has also deeply affected Judaism, without shaking its foundation. Jewish history of these seventeen centuries represents universal history in miniature, and the Jewish people became a cosmopolitan people, which, because nowhere, was, on that very account, at home everywhere.

What has prevented this constantly migrating people, this veritable Wandering Jew, from degenerating into brutalized vagabonds, into a vagrant horde of gypsies? The answer is at hand. In its journey through the desert of life for eighteen centuries, the Jewish people carried along the ark of the covenant that breathed into its heart ideal aspirations, and even illuminated the badge of disgrace affixed to its garment with an apostolic glory. The proscribed, outlawed, universally persecuted Jew felt a sublime, noble pride in being singled out to perpetuate and to suffer for a religion that reflects eternity, by which the nations of the earth were gradually educated to a knowledge of God and morality, and from which is to spring the salvation and redemption of the world. The consciousness of his glorious apostolic office sustained the sufferer and even stamped the sufferings as a portion of his sublime mission. Such a people, which disdains its present but has an eye steadily fixed on its future, which lives, as it were, on hope, is on that very account eternal like hope. The Law and the hope of a messiah were two angels of protection and comfort, upholding the humbled and guarding them from despair, degeneracy, and national suicide. The Law for the present, the messiah-hope for the future—sustained by study and the exuberant effusions of poetry—instilled balm into the lacerated hearts of this most unfortunate people. While the wide world shrank for the enslaved people into a dark filthy dungeon in which its energies were shackled, the more gifted of this people withdrew into the inward world of thought which expanded in inverse proportion as the boundaries of the outward world were narrowed and drawn around their lacerated body. And thus arose the certainly rare phenomenon that the persecuted became superior to his persecutor, the tortured almost pitied his torturer, the prisoner felt freer than his jailer.

This most profound meditative life is reflected in Jewish literature, which grew more copious as it satisfied the needs of the more gifted, while also serving the entire Jewish people; as the latter settled over the whole habitable earth, Jewish literature grew into a veritable cosmopolitan literature. It constitutes the kernel of Jewish history, which their sufferings have wrapped in a bitter shell. In this gigantic literature, the whole people has deposited its intellectual treasures and its emotional life. The doctrines of Judaism are exhibited there, ennobled, pellucid, visible to the weakest eye, and only appearing trivial to him who is accustomed to drag a sublime, stupendous, patent miracle into the sphere of common, everyday phenomena. On the thread of this literature, the successive facts and events must be strung; it indicates the pragmatic connection and must, therefore, not be treated as a secondary branch, as an appendix to the principal history. The appearance of a new, important literary production was not regarded as an interesting isolated phenomenon, but became, in this circle, a deed, followed by fruitful results. Jewish literature, born with pain and in the throes of death, became diversified like the homes of its origin, varying like the costumes of the nations in whose midst it grew, rich and multiform like the recollection of a thousand years' experiences. It bears the unmistakable marks of a single progenitor of Judaism; a homogeneous characteristic feature is imprinted upon all its forms which reflect in their every surface and sides the ideal whose rays they have absorbed. Jewish literature is thus the inalienable property of this era, which in its essential aims, in its characteristic peculiarity, may therefore be called the theoretical-religious era in contradistinction to the second post-exilic one, which was rather of a political-religious nature, and to the first pre-exilic era, which bore an emphatically political character.

However diversified and extensive this literature may be, it can be classified under three principal headings, three distinct currents, which, though fed by tributaries from other regions, have but imperceptibly deviated from their course. Each of these principal directions may be regarded as a principal science to which the others stand in the relation of auxiliary branches. The predominant aims of this long era were first, the gradual accretion of the Talmud; secondly, philosophical interpretation of Scripture and independent philosophy; and lastly, the rabbinical activity per se, completely ignoring biblical research and independent inquiry. The era is therefore divided into three extended periods: the purely talmudic, the scientific rabbinical, and the rabbinical per se. It is obvious that these three principal directions were not suddenly initiated, but were prepared by gradual transitions. The development of the purely talmudic direction, which reaches into the epoch of the Geonim, suffers a slight deflection by the opposition of Karaism, which denied the authority of the Talmud, and again by the polemical attacks of rabbinical thinkers. Thus, the interest for biblical exegesis and philosophy was awakened, but only reached its full sway with the extinction of the Geonim. Upon the meridian of Judaism purified by philosophy, the dark clouds of a current inimical to knowledge are already gathering which descend in a thick vapor of rabbinism, inaccessible to light, and a confused, mysticism.

I. The talmudic period extends from the founding of the

Sanhedrin and the academy in Yavneh to the extinction of the Gaonate and the Babylonian talmudic academies (70–1040).

II. The rabbinical-philosophical period reaches from the establishment of rabbinical and scientific schools in Spain to the dissensions between intelligent faith and blind orthodoxy (1040–1430).

III. The rabbinical period per se is developed in the struggle against free inquiry, and ends with the dawn of the new era under Mendelssohn (1230–1780).

THE TALMUDIC PERIOD

In this period of nearly one thousand years, Jewish mental activity is principally, and almost exclusively, occupied with the theoretical construction of the religious life, the fixing of the dogma received by tradition in all its ramifications and applications. In the beginning of this period, it is true, there is an evident desire to risk another attempt to regain the lost political life. This desire produces collisions, insurrections, wars, and defeats. But this political movement is soon abandoned, giving full scope to purely intellectual efforts. Then begins the bee-like industry, to collect, sift, expound, and apply the Tradition; to arrange and form into a whole the comments and applications newly added; and, lastly, to extract from this enormous amount of accumulated material rules for practical life. This gigantic talmudic fabric, in the construction of which more than twenty generations of teachers and pupils, officers and artisans, Palestinian and dispersed Jews, employed all their mental faculties, sacrificing the joys of life, must not be regarded as the mental sport of idle scholars or as a forging of chains by ambitious priests, but as a genuine national work of intellectual aspiration, in which, as in the structure of a national language, not this and that individual, but the whole nation had a share. This view is corroborated by the changed direction in the course of development in Jewish history, that is to say, by the conspicuous display of intellectual activity and the descent into the shaft of inquiry, transmitting, expounding, comparing and discriminating, altogether theoretical occupations, that, from this time forward for a thousand years, constitute the principal aim which nothing could disturb or divert from the course once taken. Repressed for a moment, the impulse burst forth in direct proportion to the pressure which was brought to bear upon it. But this talmudic activity was, at its inception, so predominant, and exclusive, that no other branch of knowledge, not even such a one as might have served for its support, could find room at its side. Even exegesis, the correct understanding of the sacred text by a thorough knowledge of grammar, was but superficially glanced at. A Jewish philosophy, a free inquiry into the cardinal doctrines of Judaism, the eternally true and eternally valid in the Law, could not make headway at a time which aimed at recovering from the wreck and guarding against new storms, notwithstanding that the Alexandrians, with Philo at the head, had already begun the foundations for a philosophical structure. In order to draw exegesis joined with Hebrew grammar and philosophy into the sphere of study, it required the impulse of a new element which was hostile to the talmudic system. Karaism was this new, fermenting element which produced new forms and situations. The first period of this era may, therefore, properly be called the talmudic, because the principal aim of history was directed at the construction of the talmudic system and at the Talmud as the textbook. It was only at the end of this period, stimulated and promoted by the karaitic schism, that the taste for auxiliary sciences, for exegesis, grammar, and even for the construction of a Jewish philosophy awoke, without, however, ripening into maturity. Outward and inward disturbances meanwhile supervened, which guided the stream of Jewish history into another channel; after that time, it changed its form both outwardly and inwardly. Judea and Babylonia and the cities on the Jordan and Euphrates, until then the only theatre of history, lose their importance. Jewish intellectual activity migrates from the extreme East to the extreme West, from Babylonia to Spain, and there unfolds new blossoms and ripens new fruits. The first period of the era of the dispersion (diaspora) is talmudic in its spirit, and Judean-Babylonian in its geographical situation.

The talmudic era comprises 970 years and is divided into four minor sections or epochs:

1. The epoch of the Tanaim, from the fall of the state and the institution of the Sanhedrin in Yavneh to the close of the Mishnah (70–200).

2. The epoch of the Amoraim, from the close of the Mishnah and the founding of the Amora academies in Babylonia to the close of the whole Talmud (200–500).

3. The epoch of the Saboraim, from the close of the Talmud to the development of the Gaonate under the dominion of the Arabs (500–650).

4. The epoch of the Geonim, from the beginning of the Gaonate to the extinction of the same (650–1040).

3

Introduction to Volume Five
of the *History of the Jews*

The Jewish nation expired amid the bloody and smoldering ruins of Jerusalem and Betar; the Jewish community formed itself from the fragmented remains, and was held together and strengthened by insightful, dedicated leaders. The Jewish state collapsed under the repeated blows of the Roman legions; new centers emerged for the Jewish diaspora in the schools of Yavneh, Usha, Sepphoris, and finally on the beautiful shores of Lake Tiberias. And as triumphant Christianity, armed with the fasces of the Roman lictors, shattered the last center on Jewish soil and doomed the Patriarchate which stood at its head to oblivion, new foci arose for the dispersed communities on the banks of the Euphrates in the academies of Nehardea, Sura, and Pumbedita. But then the fanaticism of the Magi incited the usually moderate neo-Persian (Sassanian) kings against Jews and Judaism, and a new era of persecution opened. The strength to resist appeared smashed. With the dissolution of the communities into atoms without a center, the demise of Torah was at hand. How did Jewish history manage to continue winding its way through the long centuries? Since the close of the Talmud, has it been merely a cluster of accidental events, persecutions, and acts of martyrdom? Or has it assumed the character of a dry literary history in which books and authors play the key role? Is the sequence of post-talmudic history devoid of all cohesion or focus? Does it follow a single, concentric path or does it disintegrate into more or less uninteresting details? Is it governed by the chaos of the accidental or by the ordering hand of an inner law?

The historian and reader for whom an answer to these questions is vital must constantly bear in mind when considering the post-talmudic era that Jewish history, the Israelitic history of the pre-exilic period as well as the Jewish history of the post-exilic period, consists of two essential factors. On the one hand, the apparently eternal Jewish people as the body; on the other, the seemingly no less permanent teaching of Judaism as the soul. Out of the interaction of this national body and national soul unfold the threads of history in the era of the diaspora.

The following are all part of the physical dimension of post-talmudic history: the fate of the Jews among the nations to which they were driven by their persecutors or carried by their own wanderings; the manner in which individuals combined to form communities as atoms are moved to crystallize; how these communities sought and made contact with all or a part of the people, often over great distances; the fate of the center itself, the circumstances under which it arose, the nature of its attraction, the way it was transferred from one place to another, assuming at times the form of a community, at others that of a great personality.

The spiritual dimension of Jewish history in the diaspora consists of the following: the structure and development of a Judaism, stamped by Bible and Talmud, slowly working its way up from the mist of the letter and the law to the brilliance of thought and self-consciousness; the opposition and encouragement it encountered through intimate contact with the ever-changing course of world history; the intellectual purification it experienced as a result of the friction produced by the sects and movements that sprang forth from its own midst; the learning and poetry to which it gave rise and which, in turn, beautified and ennobled it; the personalities of its leaders who, as the living embodiment of its essence, set forth new directions and objectives; and the organic interaction of these two dimensions—as when the national body, pulled down by the dead weight of a hostile environment, dragged along its soul into the depth and darkness, and how the latter, when it began to reflect on its divine origins, freed itself from depression and rose in flight thereby hastening the recovery of its body—all of this must be portrayed by an empirically based history.

The history of the post-talmudic era, therefore, still manifests a national character. It is by no means merely a religious or ecclesiastical history, for its subject is, not only the evolution of a teaching, but also the story of a people who, admittedly, live without soil, fatherland, geographic definition, or a political state, but who do manage to replace these physical requirements with spiritual powers. Despite its dispersion over the civilized corners of the earth and its firm attachment to those lands hospitable to them, the members of the Jewish tribe do not cease to regard themselves as a single people by virtue of their common beliefs, historical memories, customs, and hopes. As a history of a people, therefore, Jewish history is far from being merely a history of literature and sages to which the uninformed and narrowminded reduce it; rather the literature and religious development as well as the tragic acts of martyrdom which have been exemplified in this people or society are only individual moments in the course of its history, and do not exhaust its character. Indeed, this history is as unique as the people which has endured it, a unique phenomenon which has no analogue in world history. As a mighty stream flowing through and coming into close contact with a large body of water maintains its course and preserves its color, so have the Jewish people and Jewish history in the diaspora preserved their style and character unaltered amid the rushing flood of nations. The Jewish people felt, thought, spoke, and sang in all the languages of the nations that offered them hospitality, either warmly or reluctantly. But it never unlearned its own language. On the contrary, the people continued to love, enrich, and refine it according to the cultural standards it attained along with the rest of humanity. They participated, more or less, in the intellectual labor of the nations among which they settled without ceasing to cultivate their own literature and to shape it into a new instrument by which to help keep the dispersed members together as a single group.

To be sure, the history of this people contains neither victories with their bloody trophies, nor battles won or lost on fields strewn with corpses, nor conquests of additional territory, nor the enslavement of subjugated nations, but rather spiritual victories and achievements in abundance. While swords clashed outside and nations, incited or at least backed by their teachers of religion, tried to annihilate each other, the house of Jacob was concerned solely to maintain the light of the spirit, feeding it with the oil of scholarship and poetry to make it burn more brightly and banishing when possible the specters of darkness that had invoked ignorance and superstition. In the midst of a world of moral depravity and barbarism, the house of Jacob struggled to attain genuine religious feeling, a high level of morality, and a sanctification of daily life. It even provided the elements of a new religious view which soon won enthusiastic acclaim from the inhabitants of three countries and thereby laid one of the foundations for a significant international movement that created new alignments and cultural forms.[1] Crude men may regard such bloodless, noiseless laurels with contempt; the finer sort will not withhold their admiration.

History still has not produced another case of a nation which has laid aside its weapons of war to devote itself entirely to the peaceful pursuits of study and poetry, which has freed itself from the bonds of narrow self-interest and let its thoughts soar to fathom its own nature and its mysterious relationship to the universe and God. Indeed, Jewish history in the so-called Middle Ages does offer such a case in the Jewish people. Enslaved a thousand times, this people still knew how to preserve its intellectual freedom; humiliated and degraded, it still did not become a horde of gypsies nor lose its sense for the lofty and holy; expelled and homeless, it built for itself a spiritual fatherland. All this, post-talmudic Jewish history depicts in bold strokes. It knows no Middle Ages, in the pejorative sense of the word, which is afflicted with the symptoms of intellectual stupor, brutishness, and religious madness. On the contrary, precisely during this period and in this hostile environment it repeatedly brings forth the most brilliant examples of intellectual greatness, ethical idealism, and religious purity. If a religion be judged on the basis of the conduct of its major figures and leaders, then Judaism as it emerged in the period from the tenth through the thirteenth centuries would deserve to take the prize. Insofar as the quest for truth and moral greatness is valued, many of the Babylonian Geonim and most of the Spanish and French rabbis can serve for all time as models of attainable human perfection. The rabbis of this period were not merely one-sided talmudists but also genuine personalities with a high degree of intellectual nobility; they were patrons of learning, themselves often doctors, and not infrequently advisers and leaders of princes. However, this great period was also not free of errors and weaknesses which tarnished its leaders and communities—and the non-partisan historian must not conceal them—but in comparison to its great virtues they recede into oblivion.

If we wish to characterize the history of the Jews in the diaspora more precisely, then we are forced to say that it is predominantly a cultural history whose bearers are not a few extraordinary spirits but an entire people. Spiritual movements that somehow emerge from its midst interest and grip the entire Jewish people, even in the remotest communities. The prayers in poetic form which Jewish bards compose in Judea or Babylonia, along the Rhine or the Guadalquivir soon become the common property of nearly all communities and are incorporated into the liturgy, all without official pressure, without the rules and edicts of a hierarchy. Written works of substance from the hands of a gifted personality were copied in all parts of the diaspora; they were read, studied, and made part of life. If, someday, the words of the Jewish prophets should ever be fulfilled that no nation will again take up arms against another, if olive leaves, rather than laurel wreaths, should ever adorn the heads of great men, and the work of noble spirits gain entry to huts and palaces, then the history of the nations will approximate that of the Jews. Their pages will not be filled with military actions, victories, and diplomatic coups, but rather with the advances of culture and their realization in life.

Despite the disorganized and fragmented external appearance of post-talmudic history, in which the Jewish nation seemed to disintegrate into as many groups as there were communities, one must not be misled into believing that it lacked an orderly progressive course or central direction. On the contrary, it did establish significant and prominent centers from which historical life poured forth to the distant periphery. An ancient Jewish preacher observed: "If the members of the house of Israel should be persecuted in all parts of the world, from north to south, from south to north, from east to west, and from west to east, they would still remain in the center."[2] The scepter had indeed departed from Judah, but not the lawgiver from his people. And what is worth noting is that this lawgiver, who constituted the center and bond of the communities, felt no need to maintain unity through punishment and chastisement; instead, the local groups strove somehow toward the unifying center for counsel and direction. At first, Jewish Babylonia, the successor to Judea, as it became the seat of the Gaonate rose to serve as the unifying center of the far-flung diaspora. From the banks of the Oxus, the Volga, the Danube, and the Rhine to the islands and shores of the Mediterranean, the gaze of the Jewish communities was fixed on Babylonia, that is, on the Gaonate which was located there. No king enjoys more obedience and love than that granted to the academic heads of Sura and Pumbedita by the millions who were not their subjects but their brothers. From them, the communities received not only religious and ethical instructions but also scientific and poetic stimulation. And even before the Geonic center was broken up by the disintegrating forces of history, a new center of gravity in Spain of more substance and greater productivity emerged, one might say, in a miraculous fashion. Alongside this one, another center slowly constituted itself, first in southern France and then in Lorraine, and both centers related to each other as two foci. Severe trials, coming from two different sides and confronting both the communities under Islam and Christianity, nearly smashed both foci and weakened Jewish unity. At that moment, a richly endowed, powerful personality arose who embodied the concept of unity and became himself a center, thereby representing a new turning point in Jewish history. It began with Maimonides, who brings to a close the great cultural period of diaspora history.

This era from the close of the Talmud to the end of the Maimonidean period, or from the death of Rabina to the death of Moses ben Maimon falls into three epochs:

1. The transition from the talmudic period to the Geonic or the Saboraic epoch (500 to 640)
2. The Geonic epoch (640 to 1040)
3. The cultural peak or the scientific-rabbinic epoch (1040 to 1204)

The major arena of history in this era, next to Palestine, is the land of Babylonia which the Arabs call Iraq, for a time North Africa, then southern and in part, northern Spain, northern and southern France, and also western Germany.

4

The Rejuvenation
of the Jewish Race[1]

Are nations really only geographic concepts? Are they but a soft substance from which the heavy or skilled hand of a ruler molds unshapely or attractive figures to have them march forth or to encase them depending on the needs of the hour? Are they originally but a white sheet of paper on which the cartographer of chance paints either one color or another? In our day, when the burning nationality question threatens to set every corner of Europe afire, Metternich himself, the creator of the "geographical concept" and of the secret police, would have had second thoughts about answering this question affirmatively and without reservation. The violent facts now surfacing also would have startled him and forced him to weigh politically the secret or manifest stirrings of the different nationalities.

But, on the other hand, is every national type a separate nationality? Is every large or small group of people, simply because it differs ever so much from its surroundings in speech and customs thereby justified to claim to be a nation, to boast of independence, and to thrust its quills out in every direction? Could we not call out in this case, along with the prophet: "Can a land arise in a single day or a nation be born in an instant?" What legal title is there to justify its effort to be recognized as a legitimate nation? The crude, uncivilized racial type is not capable of achieving by itself the higher form of a national political body. Isn't history full of examples in which different racial types merged into a single nation? A distinct language does not confer this claim either. Otherwise, neither Switzerland with its three linguistic areas nor Austria with its polyglot population could constitute an organically integrated state whose inhabitants could not be torn asunder without pain and bloodshed. France and England in the Middle Ages, despite the linguistic unity of their rulers, were enemies, an antagonism that still reverberates faintly in our day. The soil, the dead earth, no matter how much it binds the natives and permeates their feelings is by no means a durable factor upon which to build a national body. How often have historical forces converted the sons of the same earthy bosom into brothers who were bitter enemies!

Great historical memories, shared experiences of joy and suffering, of victory and defeat, certainly provide an important unifying force for a nation. However, then the civilized peoples of Europe themselves still represent very young nations. For how long has it been since the people themselves, the broad, firm foundation of the European states, vigorously participated in public life, in the battles, triumphs, and conquests into which the rulers either forced the masses or for which they hired mercenaries? As long as serfdom obtained in Europe—and this covers the long period from the barbarian invasions to the French Revolution and, in some places, beyond—and as long as the citizenry itself was split into patricians and peasants, European history was made by a small but powerful coterie of men with sword and steed, while the people remained merely dull, inert spectators or the stakes for which dynasties threw dice. Also the higher forms of existence, the ideal possessions of culture, literature, and art cannot make a nationality. For they, too, are of recent vintage, since nations first learned to write and read, and how many still lack them today? Regardless of the way we may turn and twist the question concerning the legitimacy of a nationality, the basic component remains a mystery which eludes the eye of the scholar much like the individual essence which so decisively distinguishes and separates one man from another.

But who would deny that there are mortal and immortal nations? Even nationalities with a highly distinctive individuality, weakened by the powerful and lasting blows of historical events, have returned to the grave or been absorbed as atoms by other national bodies. From the once so vigorous and so richly gifted ancient Latins and Greeks who ruled the world in their day, there is scarcely a microscopic trace left. Immortal in the true sense of the word—and not merely in terms of deeds and ideas which are handed down from one generation to the next—are those nations which defy the chemical decomposition of history, which do not succumb to catastrophes, which have the elasticity to pull themselves together and rise again. The first test which a nationality has to pass to establish its durability and its right to undiminished development is to give evidence of a capacity for rejuvenation after having lived through the frailties of old age. If but once it has proven its ability to rise from the slumber of the grave then it will have attested its immortality. It must, when flung to the ground, be able to spring up; it must have preserved under the most adverse conditions a latent life-power, like an unextinguished spark beneath the ash heap. The Talmud contains a thoughtful parable about bodily resurrection. When death and decay have scattered the atoms of the human body to the winds, there is still left a tiny bone from the spine that withstands all destruction, that cannot be smashed even on the anvil. From this indestructible core, resurrection unfolds. If a nation has such a diamond core, then neither iron nor fire can harm it, and even less so corrosive acids. On the contrary, it will begin to expand again, even if extensive pressure has squeezed it into a tiny spot.

The Jewish people is heading before our very eyes toward a process of rejuvenation which previously was scarcely imagined. The enemies of the Jews observe it in bitter rage, the cosmopolitan Jews shake their heads at it pensively and silently, the rigid fundamentalists connect it with illusory hopes, everyone is amazed by this phenomenon. Is this apparently incredible stirring a true heartbeat or the galvanized twitch of a corpse? Can deceased and scattered bones live again? A Jewish seer once tossed out this question in exactly those words at a time when the Jewish people resembled a corpse perhaps even more than it does today. And the spirit which came over him showed him how bone approached bone, how they were covered with flesh and veins, how skin was spread over them, and how then finally the spirit of life imbued them and raised them as living beings [Ezekiel 37]. In fact, the Jewish race in the Babylonian exile experienced precisely such a resurrection from the dead, and the story of this astounding phenomenon which derived from the most inconspicuous origins affords us the most fruitful kind of instruction. From many sides, this rejuvenation of the national body offers an interesting analogue and deserves to be properly understood.

Of the five to six million inhabitants in ancient Israel, nearly two-thirds were transplanted some 150 years before the Babylonian exile to Media, Bactria, and the area around the Caspian Sea. They disappeared completely into the native population. The most diligent research has been unable to uncover even the slightest trace of the Ten Tribes. As long as 1700 years ago the level-headed R. Akiba had already observed: "As the day which has passed will never return, so will the Ten Tribes no longer return." Whatever has been fabricated in our century about this withered branch is merely a learned joke or humbug. The core of the remaining third, "the tribe of Judah," was shipped to the left bank of the Euphrates. Small groups were also driven into Egypt or dumped by the Ionian and Phoenician slave traders on the islands and along the coast of the Mediterranean. Slavery came with dispersion. "To be dispersed to the four corners of the globe"—the prophets had already familiarized the Jewish people with this painful prospect while the state was still standing in undiminished vigor.

The Babylonian exiles represented the core and heart of a national body weakened on every side. In their midst lived the Jewish aristocracy, insofar as it had not fallen defending the fatherland and the capital against the Chaldean conquerors. There were still a few descendants of the royal family, including one who had worn the Davidic crown for a hundred days only to move from the throne into prison from which he was only released toward the end of his life for a short time. There were the priestly Levites from the house of Aaron, who, after the temple was reduced to ashes, turned their attention to the portable sanctuary, the book of the Law. Those who had already lived there for more than half a century, acquiring land, flocks, and slaves, felt at home in Babylonia and forgot the fatherland which had been lost, Jerusalem which had been leveled, and the temple which had been burned. Every period has its sober, well-meaning, and unidealistic men. And this isn't all bad, for blunt realism serves to counterbalance high-flying idealism.

These people, then, quickly adopted the idolatry of Babylonia, since in their homeland they were already used to idolatry with an Israelite coloring: ". . . those forsakers of God who forgot the holy mountain, prepared a table for the god of fortune (Gad) and filled a cup of wine for fate (Meni)" [Isaiah 65:11]

Alongside these pragmatic and fashionable groups, there were also among the Babylonian exiles not a few, who despite their attachment to the traditions of their fathers sadly despaired of the possibility of restoring the Jewish state and rebuilding the Jewish sanctuary. They exclaimed: ". . . We are withered, our hope is gone, we are destined to disappear" [Ezekiel 37:11]. They believed that God Himself, who brought so much misery to His people, had delivered His temple to the enemy, that God Himself had left, abandoned, and forgotten Israel. In the ancient world this idea that nation, soil, and deity belong together was ineradicable. A nation severed from the umbilical cord of its mother earth has no footing, and even God, regardless of how exalted the Israelites conceived Him to be, stood in a certain relationship to the land that He had promised the patriarchs and had given their sons. With the expulsion of this holy nation and the alienation of the Holy Land, the bond that attached the temple to heaven was broken forever. This kind of self-surrender by those who certainly did not worship the gods then fashionable but who had no confidence in their own cause, always tends to crop up in a time of defection and in consequence thereof.

Indeed, the situation of the exiles in Babylonia, precisely in the last years before the redemption, was designed to crush the spirit and to show up the hope for a return as nonsense. At that time the Jewish nation acquired for the first time that terrible slave image, which not only rendered it the object of ridicule for the thoughtless masses who looked only at externals, but also provoked self-deprecation. Israel was already compelled in the Babylonian exile to offer "its body for blows and its beard for plucking." The overpowering victor said to it already then: "Bend over we want to step on you"; and it already had learned the patience and numbness required to turn "its body into a street" for insolent footsteps. Already then spectators said of the Jewish nation: "It has no form, no stature, no beauty that we should love it; it is despised, rejected by men, saddled with pain and familiar with suffering" [Isaiah 53:2-3]. Already then "it was beaten and tortured without opening its mouth. Like a lamb it was led to slaughter and like a sheep to be shorn, it remained silent and did not open its mouth" [Isaiah 53:7]. The school of suffering with its hatred, contempt, ridicule, fists, kicks, mistreatment, and misunderstanding, which in other periods was to take the Jewish race long, long centuries to pass through and which stamped its face with a tragic mien, had already begun in the Babylonian exile.

Nevertheless, precisely in the midst of these unspeakable agonies, with defection on one side and despair and loss of courage on the other, there emerged a circle of zealots who clung to the God of Israel and did not give up the hope for a better future. They were the "sufferers" who submitted to everything, men of broken heart and morbid mood, who in their inner dedication, humility, and self-sacrifice gave everything to God. These were the men who "mourned for Zion," who sat weeping along the rivers of Babylonia as often as they thought of the desolate temple, who hung their harps on the willows in order not to sing of Zion in a foreign land. The passionate poet who sang: "May I forget my right hand, may my tongue cleave to my palate, if I should forget you, Jerusalem, if I should not treasure your memory more than all joys," this poet belonged to that circle [Psalms 137:5–6]. To it belonged also a few Jewish servants at court, "the eunuchs who observed the Sabbath and held on firmly to Israel's covenant" [Isaiah 56:4]. This was the diamond core of that "indestructible little bone" from which resurrection and rejuvenation proceeded.

How did this miraculous and consequential fact, whose influence is still operative today, come about? Not by virtue of the return from the Babylonian exile. For this event was already the result of prior causes and would not have fructified very much if something had not previously awakened the Jewish nation to new life. From whom did this awakening proceed? From a single man, to be sure a man of God, who knew how to read the signs of the time and was able to strike the right note in order to arouse the echoes that slumbered in the hearts of the people. A man whose powerful, inspiring, sometimes consoling, sometimes admonishing voice transformed depression into courage, despair into hope, timidity into confidence, indifference into personal involvement, and apathy into activity. The stylus of history failed to preserve the name of this prophet. We are thus forced to call him the exilic or the Babylonian Isaiah. In any event, he deserves this name, for in terms of the loftiness, mellowness, and impact of his prophetic poetry he is certainly the equal of Amoz's son, while in terms of sheer vision he is far greater.[2]

The exilic Isaiah rang forth with the magical word of Zion at a time when a new, historic situation began to emerge through the bold and yet mild conqueror, Cyrus, who led the might of Medea and Persia against the dominant Chaldean empire in order to smash it, and found a new empire. He infused that term with such an inimitable ring, sometimes a sad and mournful tone, sometimes a joyous, exuberant explosion, that it reverberated deep in the hearts of the exiles. He pictured Jerusalem as an unfortunate widow, deep in mourning, who had emptied the goblet of strong drink down to the dregs, who had no one left of all her sons to lead her or support her. "She is the unfortunate, ravaged, and unconsoled woman who has borne so long the shame of her widowhood and the disgrace of her childlessness" [Isaiah 54:11, 4]. But he calls to her "to shake off the dust of her lowliness, to spread out her tents afar; for her dwelling place will be too small for the overflowing crowds of her own and foreign admirers, so that she herself will be amazed at who bore all these for her since she had been childless, ostracized, banished, and shunned" [Isaiah 54:2, 49:19, 21]. In the face of the unbelievers, the scoffers and denigrators, he prophesied speedy redemption for her through "Koresh" (Cyrus), the annointed of God, the victor summoned and fortified by God. No other prophet poured consolation into the hearts of the suffering and hope into the souls of the wearied as he did. The balm of his words still has the power to heal the wounds of the soul in our day.

But Israel was not to enter the imminent redemption in its defiled state, but rather to earn it through self-purification and by ennobling its character. It was to seek God, for His grace was nigh: it was to open the knots of wickedness, to loosen the straps of the yoke, to free the oppressed from slavery, to offer bread to the hungry, to bring home the lamenting poor, to clothe the naked, and not to turn its eyes away from its languishing brethren. Then Israel's light would rise like the dawn and its salvation would come speedily [Isaiah 58:6–8].

The great prophet of the exile viewed Israel's deep suffering from a higher vantage point. The enormously painful martyrdom was part of its salvation. Not only it, but the sinful world of paganism was to be reconciled thereby. God Himself desired Israel's humiliation to the point of enfeeblement. "If it regard itself as a guilt offering, then it will see a long-lasting posterity and God's purpose will be furthered through its hand. Because it dedicates itself to death and is numbered among the transgressors, it bears the sins of many and serves as intermediary for the sinners" [Isaiah 53:10, 12].

No one has comprehended and presented Israel's ideal vocation as deeply as the exilic Isaiah. The Jewish people is the apostle whom God sends to a morally depraved world in which idols are worshipped and God is forgotten. It is to be a light unto the nations, so that God's salvation might reach the ends of the earth. Israel, "the servant of God," has a mouth like a sharp sword and is destined to be a chosen arrow. God has poured His spirit over this nation that it might bring justice and righteousness to the nations. But "it should not shout, be overweening, or let its voice resound loudly in the street. He is not to work by force, never to break a bent reed, never to extinguish a flickering wick, but rather in gentleness to bring justice to truth" [Isaiah 42:2–3]. Israel is the Messiah-nation, that is the great idea of this prophet; it alone is the redeemer of the world who is to utter the redemptive word in the night of our prison. The royal progeny of David, to whom most of the prophets had transferred all splendor, recedes for this prophet before the ideal greatness of all Israel. The stunted, despised, spat-upon, downtrodden slave is summoned for great things precisely because of its state of suffering. The crown of thorns which this Messiah-nation bears patiently makes it worthy of a royal diadem. A nation which is to be resurrected through suffering and death, to be revived at the gates of the grave, represents an interpretation which makes good sense; to interpret it as a single personality makes it a caricature and leads to romantic excesses.

The great exilic prophet reassured his contemporaries also in regard to another worry, enlarging their vision also in another direction. The enemies of Israel themselves would become its friends and associates. Many prophets have, indeed, in their inspired moments envisioned the participation of the nations in the future salvation of Israel, but none proclaimed the universalism of Judaism so purely and clearly as this prophet. "The outsiders, the strangers, the sons of paganism should not say the Lord will exclude us from His people. . . . On the contrary, the strangers who will cleave to Him, who will serve Him, who will love Him and who will become His servants, . . . He will bring to His holy mountain, for His temple will become a house of prayer for all nations" [Isaiah 56:3, 6, 7].

These lofty thoughts, gushing forth from the innermost heart, and the deepest conviction, eloquently articulated and attractively clothed, would have nevertheless reverberated in empty air if in that tiny remnant of the Jewish exiles did not exist the inclination to work at its own rejuvenation. And the nation let itself be resurrected by this inspiration. The apparently dry bones moved toward each other, clothed themselves with flesh and skin, and received the breath of life. The circle of those "zealous for the word of God" became steadily larger. The closer Cyrus pressed to the Chaldean capital, the stronger became their hope for recovery of their lost independence and nationhood. The "eunuchs" from the tribe of Judah, the descendants of the house of David, Zerubbabel, "the strangers," who joined the Judeans out of love for God, all undertook efforts to realize the words of the prophet. The process of self-purification went ahead quickly, the seemingly ineradicable tendency toward idolatry, from which many of the exiles still suffered, was fully and permanently excised. It was the work of burning enthusiasm which completed the miracle that the older prophets thought impossible. And when, finally, Cyrus finished off the Babylonian-Chaldean empire and miraculously fulfilled the hopes of the exiles by proclaiming that "Whoever wishes to return to Jerusalem may do so," more than 40,000 families decided to return home with a royal son from the Davidic house and a high priest from the house of Aaron at their head.[3] This small band rebuilt the state, again produced heroes from its midst, heroes of the sword and the mind, who filled mankind with their names and their deeds. This small band poured its healthy sap into the veins of mankind.[4]

5

The Stages in the Evolution
of the Messianic Belief[1]

The lovely Greek myth of Pandora's box, which visited
mankind with suffering while preserving its hope, doesn't
begin to exhaust the blessings which lie in the nature of hope.
It is the element that first gives meaning to the life of the
individual. Without hope the treasures of the rich would be a
burden and his pleasures insipid; the ambitious would regard
their prizes with indifference; and even the efforts of the wise,
the virtuous, and the moral would be blunted without the
feeling that they could realize their inner ideal or the hope of
striving to achieve a moral world order. Life without hope
induces melancholy and, along with it, thoughts of suicide.
But hope is even more important for nations and states than
for individuals. Nations and empires which have become
satiated with nothing left to strive for, if that were
conceivable, would be heading straight for disaster. Thus
they require all the more the impulse to attain some good.
Hope is the oil that keeps the gears of a national or state
machine moving, providing it with energy, mobility, and
tension. Should this fluid vanish, rust and stagnation would
quickly set in with total disintegration not far behind. In
contrast, a national group that feeds on a specific hope, no
matter how difficult to achieve or how fantastic it seems, will
remain eternally young despite the failure to effect its fondest
dream. The need to hope and strive for better things is so
deeply ingrained in man that he may be able to conceive of

progress, but certainly not a state of absolute perfection or the attainment of his highest goal. The messianic idea, that constant hope for a better and more beautiful future, is the elixir of life which has granted the Jewish people its remarkable tenacity.

When did the messianic hope or idea first appear in Judaism? Certainly not later than its basic document, the Torah, the Pentateuch. The oldest Sinaitic legal document already confronts the Jewish people with the prospect of misfortune, misery, and banishment to foreign lands. Born in suffering, Israel is already told, while still in the cradle, of the full measure of suffering that will serve to cleanse it of the dross that remains. As for an end to the suffering, a bright future is promised. "Even when they will be in the land of their enemies, I will not despise and reject them, by destroying them and breaking My covenant with them, for I am their God; instead I will always remember the covenant with their forefathers in order to be a protecting God for them" [Leviticus 26:44–45]. The second legal document from the plains of Moab, gentle and warm like a mother's blessing, depicts in even more tragic terms the wretchedness that awaits the Jewish people for breaking the covenant, but it does not fail to add words of comfort: "If you (people of Israel) would take my warnings to heart, then your God would once again bring your captives home, love and gather you from among all the nations where He dispersed you. And should your exiles be at the end of the horizon, the Lord would return you from there to the inheritance of your fathers and would even circumcise (calm) your heart, so that you might love Him with all your heart and all your being" [Deuteronomy 30:2–6].

The messianic hope, which is only casually alluded to here, went through a number of different stages of development, being conceived, either narrowly or broadly, nationally or universally, in conjunction with the general rise of mankind, soberly or ecstatically and mystically. Just consider the chasm that separates the messianism of the prophet Isaiah from that of the pseudo-messiah Sabbatai Zevi!

Once David, "a king after God's heart," had been chosen as the leader of the Israelite nation securing national independence, and Solomon had added a good deal of splendor and a central sanctuary, the messianic hope attached itself permanently to a scion from the house of David, without whom the glory of the future could no longer be imagined. The poets and psalmists sang: "May David's descendants endure forever, and his throne be always before God as the sun, established as the moon forever, a reliable witness in the sky" [Psalms 89:37–38]. The early prophets had the thankless task of working on a people that seemed beyond repair, a people misled by degenerate rulers who divided it into two tiny, weak, and hostile states. As they confronted it with threats of catastrophe and daily and tirelessly painted its untenable position, they mixed into their gloomy cup of chastisement the balmy drops of consolation, and always pointed to a Davidide as the man who would fulfill their promises. One of the earliest literary prophets, the shepherd Amos, concludes his grim speech with a glance into the future: "I will (says God) erect again the tabernacle of David which is fallen, will repair the breaches, and rebuild it as in days of old. I will bring back the captives of My people Israel: they will again build and populate desolate cities, they will plant vineyards and gardens and enjoy their fruit, and they will not again be driven from their land" [Amos 9:11, 14–15]. The somewhat younger Hosea foresees this future in terms of the harmony that will reign between the divided kingdoms of Judah and Israel, "who both will submit to a single ruler, seek the Lord and King David, and tremblingly approach God and His blessing" [Hosea 3:5]. "Then God will be for Israel as the dew so that it will blossom as the lily and strike roots as the Lebanon" [Hosea 14:6].

The prophet Joel portrays this future in terms of God in His anger waging a war of annihilation in the valley of Jehoshafat against the nations that hate His people. "Sun and moon are turning black, the stars withdraw their light, heaven and earth tremble, but the Lord will remain a refuge for His people, Jerusalem will be eternally holy, conquerors will no longer pass through the city, a fountain will go forth from the temple and fertilize the valley of Shittim" [Joel 4:15–18].

The prophets at the time of Hezekiah made an advance in this messianic portrayal of the future. They did not limit the messianic proclamation to the people of Israel alone but included all nations, even the bitterly hostile neighbors of Israel, the Edomites, the Philistines and the Amorites. In general, they conceived this messianic time more ideally and purely.

"At the end of days the mountain of the Lord will tower over all other mountains and all nations will stream toward it. They will invite each other: 'Come, let us go to the temple of the God of Jacob, that He may teach us and we may walk in His paths.' Then from Zion instruction will go forth and the word of God from Jerusalem. They will turn their swords into plowshares and their spears into pruning knives. No nation will take up arms against another and indeed there will no longer be any training for war" [Isaiah 2:2–4; Mic. 4:1–3]. There can be no doubt that the honor for this incomparably splendid description of eternal freedom among men guided by Israel's teaching, a prophecy attributed to both Isaiah and Micah, goes to the great Isaiah. In the younger prophet Micah from Morash, the thought sounds borrowed and stands alone, while in Isaiah it is repeated several times in other connections. This great idea of universalism, of all nations belonging to God, of the brotherhood of all men, is the beautiful fruit of Judaism. The prophets of Hezekiah's day brought it to full fruition, although at that time the Israelite nation was already becoming the bone of contention between the mighty powers Egypt and Assyria, being hard pressed and tyrannized by both. "One day Israel will be a third in alliance with Egypt and Assyria, a blessing on earth, for God will say: 'Blessed be My people Egypt, My handiwork Assyria, My inheritance Israel" [Isaiah 19:24–25]. What spiritual greatness is manifest here to conceive this idea and to present it as self-evident, in the midst of universal barbarism, when the concepts of humanity, brotherhood, and civilization were not even known by name! The same universal messianic idea was articulated also by the contemporary prophet Zechariah b. Berechiah, but ponderously, without Isaiah's poetic lilt and charm. "In the land of Hadrach and Damascus will be God's resting place, for He has put His eye on mankind as on all the tribes of Israel. I will tear the bloody prey of Ashdod from his mouth and the abominations from between his teeth, and he will also be a remnant for our God and will be just as important as Aluf (a town) in Judah and Ekron will be equal to Jebusi (as holy as Jerusalem)" [Zechariah 9:1, 7].

If people criticize the Judaism of an earlier age or ancient Israelite religion of national particularism, they do it an outrageous injustice. In the dryly presented but deeply humane law of the Torah, the stranger among you is equal to the native; this profound idea which classical paganism did not know and the Middle Ages refused to take to heart and modern society still fails to implement universally, the prophets of that age cast into a promise for the messianic era.

The last prophets, Zephaniah, Jeremiah, and Ezekiel, who not only had to prophesy the complete loss of independence, but also had to witness it, were unable to allot much space in the grim pictures of their prophetic judgments to the hope for a better future. However, the messianic strain is not entirely missing, though it is introduced only in very general terms, through a reference to the descendants of the Davidic house. The prophet Zephaniah envisions a divine court in judgment against Israel's enemies as preceding the messianic era, though not to destroy them but rather to educate them. "God will bring the nations a purified language, that they will call Him and serve Him as if with one shoulder (unanimously). From beyond the rivers of Ethiopia the daughter of Put will bring God incense as an offering [Zephaniah 3:9–10].

Jeremiah, the prophet of the deepest pain and sorrow, clung to the idea that Israel was as likely to disappear as were the laws of nature, or as the prospect of heaven being spanned, or the foundations of the earth measured. Even the two families in Israel which God had specially chosen, despite their present degeneration, would never be spurned by Him again. The immoral nation would someday possess an undivided heart to honor God; the knowledge of God would spread, great and small would be permeated with the exaltedness of God, and then God would lavish the fullness of His blessings upon His people.

The prophet at the beginning of the exile, Ezekiel, thought of the messianic era in terms of the unification of the long-divided kingdoms under one king from the house of David, who would bring them peace. He did not, however, see the core of the people in the masses fighting for survival in Judah or in the capital, but in the nobility of the Babylonian exiles who were capable of improvement. He labored to help turn their heart of stone into a heart of flesh, to revive, and rejuvenate them despite their present state of death. According to this prophet, the messianic era would be preceded by a crushing attack by a mighty people called Gog from the land of Magog (Caucasia), accompanied by an enormous multitude of allies. But God would protect Israel.

Thus, when the Jewish people was forced into exile, the messianic idea had already taken definite shape: the return from exile to the fatherland, which would bless its inhabitants abundantly; the unification of the divided branches of the house of Jacob into one nation; the participation of the pagan nations in this peaceful kingdom of God; a long, happy, and peaceful era free of enemies; the elevation of the people by means of an altered disposition and the fear and knowledge of God; a scion from the house of David, filled with the fear of God and the love of justice, as its leader and the founder of a new dynasty.

The voice of the prophets, which during the existence of the Israelite state the people listened to with but one ear or not at all, now permeated the remnant in the Babylonian exile with the full warmth of passionate faith. What previously was only the ideal of a few now became the common possession of the greatly reduced remnant of the Jewish people. Each member carried with him the vision of an inevitably better future. The

Babylonian exile was the smelting oven which consumed the dross of the nation and let its noble elements come to the fore. As the last prophets had proclaimed, the Babylonian exile led to a process of purification which markedly bettered the adherents of Judaism and impressed them with a stamp that made them quite unrecognizable, the very people who formerly could not desist from idolatry and immorality. It matured them in preparation for carrying out their assigned mission. There were also in the exile inspired men who confronted them steadily with their greatness, and one of them vividly preached the great idea that Israel has the vocation to spread truth and justice among the nations. As a result, Jewish eunuchs in the court worked energetically to bring about at least the beginning of this glorious future, the return to the fields of Judah.

But the new state of Judah, which was founded again with the permission of Cyrus, in no way corresponded to that painted by the prophets. Tiny and dependent, exposed to the harassment of old enemies like the Philistines and Edomites and new ones like the Samaritans, battling privation and crop failures, this new Jewish community seemed to bear within it the seeds of death. In addition, there surfaced at the very beginning a good deal of jealousy between the two houses which felt called upon to lead the community, between Zerubbabel representing the Davidic house and Jeshua b. Jozadak representing the house of Aaron. The disconsolation reached such a point that the building of the temple which had begun was interrupted for fifteen years while the morale of the people plummeted. Only the prophets did not let loose of the hope for a better future. Haggai and Zechariah, the son of Iddo, one already old and the other still young, together proclaimed the imminent arrival of messianic conditions, the former in the dark colors of terrible catastrophe, the latter in the soft colors of better days: "The streets of Jerusalem will be filled with boys and girls playing. Many peoples and powerful nations will pilgrimage to the Jewish capital to seek the Lord. Ten men from among all the tongues of the nations will take hold of the skirt of a Jew and say: 'We would like to accompany you, for we have seen that God is with you'" [Zechariah 8:5, 22–23].

But things did not improve so quickly. A new generation arose which in despair nearly gave up its Jewish identity through unions and mixed marriages with the neighboring nations. The children born of these mixed marriages were no longer able to speak a pure Judaic. The priests from the Aaronide house led the way in this improper example of denationalization. But since at that time the voice of God's heralds had not yet been fully silenced, the despair of the people was again assuaged by the messianic message. The last of the prophets, Malachi (about 500–460 before the Christian era), announced the imminent approach of that frightful day on which the sun of salvation would rise for the pious. Elijah, who was so zealous for the purity of the Torah, would appear and unite the hearts of fathers with those of their children. This motif of the last prophets of the coming of Elijah before the great day, of Elijah's preceding the messianic era remained ever since as a part of the messianic picture. The writer of aphorisms, Jeshua ben Sirach (about 300 B.C.E.), already firmly held this belief: "Elijah is inscribed to come in rebuke at the appointed time, to quiet anger, to turn the heart of the fathers to that of the sons and to reestablish the tribes of Jacob. Fortunate are those who will see you" [*The Wisdom of Sirach* 48:10–11].

In the turbulent years before the Hasmoneans, a half-crazy tyrant had a statue of Zeus placed on the altar of the Jerusalem Temple and, with fire and sword, he tried to impose an already degenerate paganism on the Jewish people. Even Jewish priests were willing to assist him. In those days, as the blood of martyrs flowed to preserve Judaism for the first time, a passionate prophet foretold of the imminent coming of messianic redemption in a peculiar, murky, and mysterious language which affected the mood of the people the more deeply precisely because of its enigmatic character. According to the symbolism of several metaphors, "Four kingdoms

would rule over the world and subjugate Judea: the
Babylonian, the Persian-Medean, the Greek-Macedonian, and
the Syrian-Macedonian; but in the end the Jewish kingdom
would be established 'not by human hands' and would outlast
all these kingdoms, surviving for eternity." According to
another metaphor, "Whereas the four pagan kingdoms are like
animals having hearts of stone, the fifth messianic kingdom
will be like a human being; it will be granted dominion,
honor, and dignity; and peoples, nations, and tongues will
serve it; its dominion will endure forever." To partially avoid
misunderstanding and misinterpretation, the enigmatic metaphor, "With the clouds of heaven came one like a son of man
and attained to the Ancient of days" [Daniel 7:13], was quite
clearly explained. "Kingdom, dominion, and greatness of
kingdoms under the whole heaven will be given to the people
of saints and all will serve and obey it" [Daniel 7:27]. The
date of that divine kingdom of a holy people is calculated in
this artistic, messianic vision according to weeks of years,
years, and days. As a result of this vision, the messianic
picture took on a mystical coloration which it had lacked till
then.

To be sure, redemption followed soon thereafter, though
not by means of mystical and supernatural events, but rather
by that marvel which slumbered in the depths of the soul,
religious enthusiasm and the heroism of the Hasmoneans.
Judea was not merely rescued but also transformed into a
magnificent community in which the law of God, the
commitment of the people to it, a willingness to sacrifice, and
powerful enthusiasm reigned and new hymns to the Lord of
heaven resounded.

When the Hasmoneans, having founded an independent
Jewish state, gained control of the government, the people
conferred upon them the right to rule, but this mandate to rule
was granted them only provisionally, "until the true prophet
(Elijah) would appear," as the forerunner of the scion from
the Davidic dynasty, who alone had the right to the throne
and crown of the Jews.

But times came and went without the fulfillment of the hope so long yearned for. The happy days of Hasmonean rule were all too brief. They were followed by deep divisions between Pharisees and Sadducees, between the religious-minded and the worldly, between a lofty striving for freedom and absolutism. The outcome was civil war, self-laceration, and exhaustion. Besides all this, there now came to power the Idumean, half-Jewish dynasty of the Herodians, which relied heavily on the strong arm and cold heart of Rome, betraying and delivering the fatherland to it. But Herod's anti-national tyranny did have the virtue that it powerfully stimulated the longing for redemption in the hearts of the pious and provoked efforts to realize it. But just as Jewish life had ceased to be naive, shaping itself now to a much greater extent according to the model of the Law and its interpretation, so likewise the idea of the Messiah no longer lived in the breasts of those who yearned for it in its original, naive form. They immersed themselves much more in the Bible and searched collectively for the traits which the future messianic king would manifest. Reflective and synthetic interpretation replaced spontaneous creativity, Aggada replaced prophecy. The question about the personality of the Messiah came to the fore. Should he be less than a prophet? Should he not be equal to the great prophet Moses or even outlive him? With this kind of meditation, this poring over every puzzling word in the Bible, the future Messiah was outfitted with supernatural traits. But the devout disagreed in their views about the Messiah and, accordingly, their means of effecting any improvement in the conditions of Jewish life also differed. The Messiah would appear as redeemer (*goel*) to bring the redemption (*geulah*). Some felt he would be a political figure who would free the people from the yoke of Herodian despotism and Roman arrogance; others felt him to be an inner redeemer from the yoke of sin, from the evil inclination (*yeṣer ha-ra*). Both sides could bring biblical support.

On the one side, there developed a patriotic party that scorned any contact with the authorities, recognized no king other than God and no law other than the Torah, and with the wrath of Elijah, sword in hand, and contempt for death, hoped to drive the Herodians and the Romans from the land and to found a kingdom based on God's law in Judah. They were to a certain extent the disciples of the zeal of Elijah who had put the priests of Baal to the sword. On the other side, the excessively pious, the descendants of the Hasidim, those who ritually immersed themselves each morning, the Essenes, meditated on the nature of the Messiah in the Bible. They became mystics and arrived at the conviction that the kingdom of God, the kingdom of heaven, the messianic era, could only be hastened through repentance, penances, asceticism, and purity of body and soul. They were to a certain extent the disciples of the priestly zeal of Pinchas, who halted the plague by offering incense. Two contemporaries from different circles come forth one after the other as the men who would realize the messianic hope: Judah from Golan representing political messianism and John the Baptist (the Essene) representing inner messianism. The one called on the people to resist the Roman census, the other urged them to immerse in the Jordan and to repent. The one succeeded in inspiring nearly the whole nation to acts of heroism. It threw itself against the Romans and mounted a resounding, glorious martyrdom for its political independence and religious freedom and, thereby, went under as a nation. The other paved the way for that great messianic phenomenon by which the messianic idea through a chain of a thousand miraculous events was brought to the nations of the earth, the non-Israelite world.

Since that time when people took the messianic hope more seriously and struggled more energetically to realize it, messiahs arose at different times only to disappear in most cases without a trace. Only a few of them enjoyed a success for which they hadn't even aimed. In the last three decades before the second demise of the Jewish state, several men emerged as messiahs: Theudas, Simon of Cyprus, and a nameless figure from Egypt who all found some adherents and believers, but who died in disgrace without having accomplished anything. Their lack of success branded them as false messiahs.

After three years of war, with Jewish soil trampled by the Roman legions, the capital reduced to shambles and the temple to ashes, hundreds of thousands of glory-bedecked warriors strewn on the battlefields, the entire nation at home smashed despite the most heroic exertions, and the captured Judeans dragged from the slave markets to southern and western Europe, all hope for better times certainly appeared gone and messianic expectations sheer idiocy.

But since when does a people with a thousand-year history so rich in experiences lose hope? The second generation after the destruction of the Temple—a mere half-century later —again took up arms wherever Jews lived in sizable numbers, in Babylonia, Egypt, Cyprus, and even in the homeland, in order to shake off the Roman yoke and again found an independent state with its center in the Temple. And the patriots, although slain here by Lucius Quintus and there by Martius Turbo, Trajan's generals, instilled the weak Roman emperor with such respect that he was forced to grant the Jews concessions. Seventeen years later (135), without the Romans getting wind of it, a Jewish army of several hundred thousands stood ready to face sinful Rome, and at its head a hero who combined courage with military skill. Bar Kosiba, the terror of Hadrian and the Roman legions, revolted with such force and aroused so many hopes that the most respected teacher of the day, the great Rabbi Akiba, who did so much to preserve and develop Judaism, acknowledged him to be the Messiah, applying to him the verse, "A star has gone forth from Jacob" [Num. 24:17], and gave him the by-name Bar-Kokhba (son of the star). It is worth noting that R. Akiba did not ask about the genealogy of the Messiah-king Bar-Kokhba! But even Bar-Kokhba could not produce. In no way did he fulfill the messianic hopes, bringing, on the contrary, much new misery to a nation scarcely healed from its previous wounds. Behind the walls of Betar, he and thousands of his warriors met their death. It took a long time before the remnant could pull itself together and reorganize.

Again centuries passed without a messianic effort. Only calculations were made, on the basis of Daniel's prediction of weeks of years, to determine the coming of the messianic era. Some claimed the messianic era would begin with the end of the fourth millenium (i.e., 240 C.E.). When that year failed the test, it was said that the Messiah would appear at the end of the fourth century after the destruction of the temple, or the year 4231 after creation (468–471), or that history would extend until the year 4291 after creation (531). Others denounced such speculations as undermining the will of the people to survive. Still others, like Hillel (probably the Patriarch Hillel around 360 favored by the Emperor Julian), insisted that the prophecy of Isaiah about the Messiah referred to Hezekiah. The people of Israel had already witnessed these predictions. Not even the rebuilding of the Jerusalem temple so energetically sought by the Emperor Julian stirred any messianic ferment.

Meanwhile, the talmudic era developed its own messianic doctrines which ran the gamut from sober rationalism to mystical glorification.

The Babylonian amoraic sage, Samuel (200–258), openly stated that in the messianic era there would be neither miracles nor supernatural events, but only the redemption of Israel from its state of political servitude among the nations. In contrast, his contemporary, Joshua b. Levi, portrayed the Messiah as existing since creation. Afflicted with leprosy and residing among the lepers in Rome, he waited for the call any minute to fulfill his mission. Others refused to accept this mystical preexistence of the Messiah and contended that God would only create him when the need arose. To be sure, this excessive glorification of the Messiah rested on faulty biblical exegesis. While one preacher made him equal to Moses another placed him not only above Abraham and Moses but also above the angels. But the more the Messiah was glorified and exalted, the less did other biblical descriptions fit him, for example, he would head an army, be defeated, and be pierced by a sword. But the fantasy-rich, mythic mentality was not fazed by this at all. It gave birth to a second Messiah, a Messiah from the tribe of Joseph or Ephraim, who would wage war, clear the path for redemption, and then succumb to death. And then the Messiah from the house of David would appear in the clouds in exalted majesty. He would complete the work of peace and even resurrect the slain Messiah from the dead.

There is considerable doubt as to the originality of a number of these motifs. They may well be the imitations of Christian messianic beliefs. If the messianic era is to come, the great enemy of Judaism, wicked Rome (whether in its birthplace along the Tiber or in the land of its Byzantine successor) must first be vanquished. This assignment was given to the Messiah from the tribe of Joseph. Furthermore, Rome was personified by aggadic messianism and presented as the anti-messiah, either under the name of Armilaos or more correctly Eremelaos (the pernicious Balaam)[2] or in the figure of the Emperor Latinus, the main representative of the despotic Caesars of the Latin line. With this anti-messiah (who was appropriated by the poetic and aggadic fantasy and portrayed as a frightful figure with the blackest of souls, the son of Satan and a block of marble) the Ephraimitic Messiah was to wage war, only to be beaten and killed by him. In general, much of this subject appealed directly to the wildest imagination. The outline of this portrait was already sketched in the talmudic era, but only in the later gaonic period did it acquire precision, content, and color.

During the entire talmudic period after Bar-Kokhba, only a single messianic enthusiast arose, and then only toward the end of the era and far from the center of Jewry. He promised to lead the Jews from the island of Crete through the Mediterranean Sea on dry land back to Jerusalem (about 400). Not until the first century after the rise of Islam (720–750) did messianic enthusiasts bestir themselves again, provoked by the recognition that the Roman Empire, which appeared impregnable, was beginning to totter all over, in Rome, Byzantium, and the provinces, and was destined to end up as booty for the Arab conquerors. This sense of triumph at the total collapse of the Roman Empire, at the demise of the wicked Edom, is clearly reflected in the number of messianic-apocalyptic texts from that period.

In the second decade of the eighth century and again in the middle, two messiahs arose, one in Syria, called Severus, who even attracted Jews from Spain and France, and the other in Persia, called Obadiah Abu Issa from Isfahan. Both had programs they wished to implement. In Jewish circles it was firmly assumed that in the messianic era the law with its religious prescriptions would end, no longer being obligatory. Both messiahs, Severus and Abu Issa, hoped to bring in this era. However, they did not go so far as to abrogate the laws of the Pentateuch. They merely modernized talmudic legislation, thereby becoming the precursors of antitalmudic Karaism. Anan, the founder of the Karaite schism, was already a mature young man in the days of the widespread agitation precipitated by Abu Issa. Karaism, which paved the way for sectarian disintegration, gave rise to yet another messianic enthusiast in Persia at the beginning of the ninth century: Yehuda Yudghan from Hamadan, who abrogated the entire body of Pentateuchal law while also introducing an ascetic life-style for his followers.

But again messianism subsided until about the end of the eleventh century when a messiah allegedly arose in France. However, we have only one unreliable source about him. He may have been connected with the apocalyptic-messianic book of Zerubbabel. The twelfth century produced in different regions of the Islamic world four messiahs: one in Cordova (about 1117), a second in Fez (about 1127), a third in Persia, named David Alroy (about 1160), a military figure, and a fourth in Arabia (1172) whose unholy adventure Maimonides was forced to counter.

With the rise of the Kabbalah as a counterforce to the philosophic school of Maimonides (about 1200), the messian-

ic idea entered a new stage of development. Although
Maimonides raised the messianic hope to a dogmatic article of
faith, he also gave expression in his majestic wisdom to the
rationalist idea: "Not to believe that someday the Messiah
would prove himself through miracles or that in the messianic
era the laws of nature and the present world order would
cease to exist." Rather, the course of things would remain
unchanged; only the animosity toward Israel would cease.
The supernatural sounding prophecies of the prophets are to
be regarded only as allegories. But that was too much for the
mystics who tended to view the idea as heresy.

According to the Kabbalah, messianism is the pinnacle of
Judaism. The Messiah would not only bring about the earthly
freedom of the Jewish people, but also the redemption of the
soul of mankind. The soul of the Messiah, which existed from
eternity in its own sanctuary of souls, the nest of a bird, would
at last enter the ranks of those born in the world of flesh and
blood. Then the great jubilee would start and the reincarna-
tion of those human souls who in their earthly life did not
attain their goal or failed entirely would be terminated. The
Messiah, though present since creation, would be the last one
born.

Simultaneously, kabbalistic-messianic enthusiasts made
their appearance: in Sicily, the Spaniard Abraham Abulafia
(1285–1290) who also entertained a critical view of talmudic-
rabbinic Judaism; another in Avila and a third in Ayllon
(Spain). Then came Moses de Leon, the author of the *Zohar,*
who gave the development of kabbalistic mysticism a
tremendous boost. He brought back into vogue the attempt to
calculate the coming of the Messiah and even saw himself as
functioning in some messianic capacity. Generally, the very
years predicted by the kabbalists as heralding the messianic
era witnessed persecutions of Jews.

It is entirely likely that the messiah from Cisneros (about
1400), whom the brilliant Hasdai Crescas supported, was
connected with the Kabbalah. The latter had fully appropriated the messianic idea as its own, and like every extreme

movement which is based on the principle of *credo quia absurdum* (I believe because it is absurd), this one, too, presumptuously and bitterly decried every thinker as a heretic. This policy provoked the philosophically trained Spanish preacher Joseph Albo (1432) to argue that the messianic belief was definitely not a basic article or dogma of Judaism, that it was merely a tradition, and that a disbelief in the coming of the Messiah could never be labeled heresy since even some talmudic sages had repudiated it. That amounted to a pretty daring position in Albo's day.

Indeed, Joseph Albo was accused of heresy, not by his contemporaries, but rather by a later believer, by the famous Isaac Abravanel. This brilliant statesman, well-informed finance minister, and prolific writer lived through the horrible misery of the expulsion of the Jews from Spain and Portugal and the indescribable suffering which the survivors experienced in their wanderings. He and his family were themselves hard hit. He observed the despair of the survivors who, although they disdained to create for themselves a comfortable life through betrayal and conversion and despite all deprivation remained faithful, had still given up all hope for the future of the Jewish people. In order to raise the depressed spirits of his contemporaries, Abravanel occupied himself thoroughly with the problem of messianism and wrote three tracts to demonstrate, on the basis of Bible and Talmud, the great importance of the messianic belief and to defend it against any attack. He also relied on messianic calculations and concluded that the messianic era would dawn in the year 1503. This date was no doubt inspired by Asher Lämmlein (or Lämmlin), a messianic enthusiast from Istria. He summoned the communities from near and far to repent and give charity in order to prepare themselves for the great day which was imminent. The German and Italian Jews who yearned for redemption believed in this new proclaimer of the Messiah. In Prague they believed so fervently that they dropped all worldly concerns. If acts of penance and charity alone could produce the Messiah, then he should have appeared at that time, for no era ever witnessed as much fasting, prayer, and charity as took place in the days of Lämmlein. But he also proved to be a false messiah and produced only the conversion of learned Jews in Germany, Italy, and even in Poland to Christianity. Furthermore, he gave to the wicked apostate and bitter enemy Johann Pfefferkorn the weapons with which to wage a war of annihilation against his former coreligionists, which failed only because of Reuchlin's intervention.

In the meantime the Kabbalah chalked up enormous gains as a result of the publication of its basic book, the *Zohar,* a book denounced by pious Jews but promoted all the more by mystics. It continues to this day to spread ruin among Jews. The mystery of the Messiah was the goal of all its speculations and hallucinations. Kabbalistic enthusiasm ensnared a gifted youth, the Portuguese Marrano Solomon Molcho, formerly the private secretary of the king of Portugal, later the astrologer of Pope Clemens VII.

The historian can't help identifying with this twenty-four-year-old enthusiast, as he is led astray by David Reubeni. Reubeni presented himself as the prince of a Jewish royal house, he related glorious tales to the Jewish victims of the Inquisition, and he incited the Marranos in Spain and Portugal to rattle their chains. Solomon Molcho proclaimed, likewise by means of kabbalistic calculations, the imminent arrival of the Messiah in the year 1540, and he aroused great hope among the Jews. In all of Turkey from Jerusalem to Salonica the Jewish communities awaited redemption. Letters came and went in 1531 through Ofen to Cracow and as far as Frankfurt am Main. But in the very next year the messianic precursor Solomon Molcho at the age of thirty-one was burned in Mantua at the command of the German emperor and king of Spain and America. But the Kabbalah persisted in its messianic proclamations, disseminated by two important men, Joseph Caro and Isaac Luria, who both lived in Palestine. The first, in fact, longed for a martyr's death like that of Solomon Molcho, but it never went that far.

The last messianic enthusiast, the extraordinarily handsome but intellectually limited Sabbatai Zevi from Smyrna, who disseminated a highly sensuous mysticism in the East at the very time that Spinoza was teaching a unique form of pantheism in the West which was not uninfluenced by the Kabbalah, aroused enormous interest in Jewish, Christian, and Moslem circles. He or his followers contended, with an unshakable conviction worthy of a better cause, that the world of divine order (*Olam ha-Tikkun*) began with him, that the laws of Judaism, including those dealing with marriage, were abrogated and no longer obligatory. He evoked such a blind faith among the Jews of Asia, Africa, and even Europe that even after he abandoned Judaism and took the turban (1666), his followers continued to hope for his victory and messianic redemption. Madness is as blind as love. It scarcely recognizes failings, or tries to apologize for them if it does not actually regard them as virtues. So also in the case of Sabbatai Zevi; his believers justified every trait typologically, even his repudiation of Judaism. All this had to take place in order to fulfill this or that passage in the Bible or the *Zohar*. His adherents, the Sabbatians, or Shebs, maintained themselves long after his death as a sect which professed a motley faith consisting of elements drawn from Judaism, Christianity, and Islam. The last crony of kabbalistic-messianic enthusiasm was the brilliant young poet Moses Hayim Luzzatto from Padua (beginning of eighteenth century).

Such were the aberrations produced by the messianic belief. And we have no guarantee that in our own day in the bosom of the modern adherents of the *Zohar*, among the Hasidim in Poland, Galicia, Hungary, and Walachia, whose propaganda becomes increasingly more intensive, a false messiah will not burst forth some fine morning and sow new confusion. There would be no shortage of mindless, believing masses, not even of standard-bearers for any hasidic rebi who could bring them to believe in him and occasionally perform a miracle.

Is the messianic belief therefore condemned, and are the

critics of Judaism right in declaring it to be a lamentable and self-evident delusion? By no means! A vision nurtured by thousands of years, foretold by divinely inspired prophets, and entertained by the wisest men of Israel cannot be sheer idiocy or remain a dream. Examined soberly, world history points unmistakably toward a messianic kingdom of peace, brotherhood, and the pure knowledge of God. Even a contemporary ruler, armed to the teeth and eager for trade and conquest, is compelled to play the patron of peace, and this pretense is likewise a tribute exacted by the spirit of the age. We Israelites can be proud that Judaism was the first to plant in the world the messianic longing "to turn swords into plowshares," which in our age is shared by the noblest men of all nations. There is also no need for us to despair that the messianic bearer of peace who will silence the "ultimate argument of kings" will come forth from the bosom of Judaism. For thousands of years the people of Israel has proven to be energetically creative in the area of religious and moral truths for the benefit of mankind. It may also boast another unique quality, namely the strength to die as martyrs, the willingness to sacrifice.

This religious capacity, this partially innate faculty which has been such a pioneering force in world history, which inspired Moses with his tablets of law, David with his psalms, Isaiah with his penetrating vision into the future, the Maccabees with their flaming courage and trust in God, which produced Paul of Tarsus who brought the message of salvation to the non-Israelite nations, R. Akiba and R. Meir with their spiritually refreshing dialectics, Judah ha-Levi with his profound and poetic disposition, Moses Maimonides with his determination to exorcise the phantoms of the mind, and Moses Mendelssohn with his ability to rejuvenate; this morally rooted, creative religious capacity is still not exhausted, but rather with the increasing level and clarity of knowledge becomes visibly greater. Israel's ability to suffer has also not declined; it is maintained by constant practice as a result of prejudices which have not yet died and which continue to be directed against this people whose weakness is its strength. A people which combines such rare qualities—to which also belongs indefatigable activity—can certainly count on a future.

To be sure, without self-purification, self-ennoblement, and self-knowledge, without immersing itself in its basic element of religiosity and the sanctification of life, Israel will be unable to complete its, so to speak, assigned mission. Everything points to the future so clearly depicted by Isaiah: "Israel will become a light unto the nations, and the earth will be filled with the knowledge of God as water covers the floor of the ocean" [Isaiah 42:6; 11:9]. Indeed, the messianic hope does not appear so fantastic and illusory in the light of a thorough study of the past and a proper understanding of the present. But is it, therefore, a dogma of faith, so that the man who ignores it because of the pressure of his work, or simply knows nothing about it, or pessimistically rejects it is guilty of heresy and deserving of excommunication? The man who takes this position wholly misunderstands Judaism and is unable to appreciate the fact that the strength of Judaism does not derive from binding dogmas. In fact, it would be relatively simple to suggest the circumstances to which Judaism owes the concepts of heretic and heresy (*min, minut, epiqorsut*) which are so alien to it. Let us hope that just as they clung to us for historical reasons and are not innate, so will we be able to discard them, and that the unification and reconciliation of our people which is the basic prerequisite for the fulfillment of the messianic vision, will begin with the end of fanatical heresy hunting.

6

Introduction to Volume One of the *History of the Jews*

We are about to narrate the story of a people's birth, a people that stems from ancient times, endowed with stubborn perseverance, that, since its entrance on to the stage of history more than 3000 years ago, has never departed. This people is therefore both old and young. While from its countenance the lines of hoary antiquity cannot be effaced, the face is as fresh and youthful as if born yesterday. Should there exist such a people toughened by age in some remote corner of the world, which has preserved itself through an unbroken chain of generations down to the present, and should it have managed in its isolation to tear itself loose from its barbaric origins, though accomplishing little else thereafter nor exerting any influence on the rest of the world, this people would still be sought out and studied as a remarkable rarity. A fragment of antiquity from time immemorial, which once witnessed the founding and decay of the most ancient empires and today is still prominent certainly deserves careful attention. Now the Hebrew or Israelite people, whose ancient history is to be narrated here, did not spend its days in protected loneliness and contemplative flight from the world but was repeatedly swept into the maelstrom of history. In its more than 3000-year history it fought and suffered, being driven from place to place and severely injured. It bears countless scars of honor and no one would deny it the crown of martyrdom. But above all, it is still alive. It has, moreover, made its

173

contributions, a record which only a few skeptical or malicious observers would challenge. Even if it had cured only the civilized sector of mankind from the delusion of unrestrained idolatry with its inevitable ethical and social depravity, it would still deserve special attention. Yet it has done so much more for mankind.

What are the origins of the lofty culture in which the civilized nations of our day take such pride? They themselves are not its creators but merely the lucky heirs who have successfully speculated with their ancient legacy. Two creative nations were the progenitors of the lofty culture which raised mankind above the barbaric and savage conditions of its birth: the Greeks and the Israelites. There was no other. The Romans merely developed and transmitted a rigidly controlled social structure and a sophisticated art of warfare. Only at the end, in their old age, did they in addition perform the service of the beetle which bears the waiting pollen to the receptive stigma. The creators and founders of higher culture were none other than the Greeks and the Hebrews.

If you take away from the Latin, German, and Slavic nations of our day on both sides of the ocean that which they owe to the peoples of Greece and Israel, a great deal would be gone. But we can't even finish this line of argument; it is simply impossible to deprive these nations of that which was borrowed and to separate it from their very being. It has so permeated their blood and sap, that it constitutes part of the organism itself, which in turn has become its carrier and transmitter. It was the ladder by which these nations ascended to the top, or even better: it was the electrical current which unleashed the slumbering forces within them. Hellenism and Hebraism or—to speak without affectation —Judaism, have together created an atmosphere of ideas without which civilized nations would be unthinkable. No matter how small the dosage of the rich idealism of these two sources which the barbarians received through the Romans after the demise of the so-called old world, no matter how poor the vessels which delivered to them this life-giving humor, the modest intake did wonders and slowly effected a thorough transformation of character. During the violent Crusades, these same nations received from those same sources, by now diluted and weakened, new vigor. Only when these sources, which were buried by monks, dervishes, and recluses of all kinds who wished to keep them buried, were tapped anew and brought to the surface, did the modern era begin. Neither Loyola, nor the Inquisition, nor petrified fundamentalism, nor self-deifying despotism were able to stem the blessings which the Greek and Hebraic humanists first brought to Europe.

The part played by Hellenism in the rebirth of civilization is acknowledged freely and without envy. It dispersed the flowers of art and the fruits of knowledge. It unveiled the realm of beauty and illuminated it with an Olympian clarity of thought. And a regenerative power continues to pour forth from this literature and the legacy of its artistic ideal. The classical Greeks are dead, and toward the deceased posterity behaves properly. Envy and hatred are silent at the grave of the dead; their contributions are, in fact, usually exaggerated. It is quite different with that other creative nation, the Hebrews. Precisely because they're still alive their contributions to culture are not generally acknowledged; they are criticized, or given another name to partially conceal their authorship or to dislodge them entirely. Even if the fair-minded concede that they introduced the monotheistic idea and a higher morality into the life of nations, very few appreciate the great significance of these admissions. They fail to consider why one creative nation with its rich talents perished, whereas the other, so often on the brink of death, still wanders over the earth having rejuvenated itself several times.

No matter how pleasant their polytheistic message, nor how envigorating their wisdom, nor how lovely their works of art, the Greeks could not stand the test of crisis, when the Macedonian phalanxes and the Roman legions confronted them with the serious rather than the joyful side of life. They despaired of help from bright Olympus and their wisdom turned to folly; at most it gave them the courage for suicide. Like an individual man, a nation also proves itself only in misfortune. But the Greeks did not possess the tenacity to endure misfortune while remaining true to themselves. Neither the Olympic games nor the memories of greatness provided them with a common bond; their wisdom also failed to engender any hope or solace in their hearts. As soon as exile was inflicted upon them, either in a foreign land or in their own, they became estranged from each other and disappeared in a mixture of barbarian nations. What caused this total demise? That the Romans, the most powerful nation of antiquity, succumbed to death exactly like the powerful nations which preceded them resulted from their reliance on the sword, for the law of retribution applies equally to nations: "He who trusts in the sword, will fall by the sword." But why did death also sweep away the Greeks, who besides their military handiwork also pursued idealistic goals? They lacked a definite and self-conscious life's task.

The Hebrews, however, possessed a life's task, which united, strengthened, and preserved them amidst the most terrible misfortune. Moreover, a nation which realizes its mission, because it does not spend its life dreaming and groping, is rooted and strong. The task of the nation of Israel was directed toward working on itself, toward overcoming and controlling its selfishness and animal desires, toward acquiring a capacity for sacrifice, or to use the language of the prophets: "to circumcise the foreskin of the heart," in one word: to become holy. Holiness meant for this nation, first of all, to refrain from animal-like behavior and sexual perversion. Holiness imposed upon it self-restraint and duties, while preserving body and soul in good health. History provided the test. The nations which defiled themselves through immorality and grew callous through the use of force succumbed to death. We may call this life's task of Israel a higher morality—the term doesn't really cover the concept, but it helps us to convey our idea. Still more important is the fact that Israel recognized this to be its task, namely to take this higher morality seriously. Set in the midst of a wicked and debauched world, it was intended to provide a counterpoise and to raise the banner of moral purity.

The philosophy of life of ancient nations, however, was intimately connected with their polytheism; they determined each other. Was their perverse morality the daughter of their perverse theology or the mother? Whatever the causal nexus may have been, it changes nothing in regard to the pernicious results. The multiplicity of gods, no matter how poetically transfigured, cultivates divisiveness, passion, and hate. In a council of many gods, controversy is never lacking; their conflicting opinions were bound to make enemies. Even when the number of deities worshipped by man is reduced to two, hostile opposition still develops between them: a god of creation and a god of destruction or a god of light and a god of darkness. Furthermore, the creative deity is divided into two sexes and thereby acquires all the frailties of sex. It is said, in fact, that men cast gods in their own image. But once the mythology had crystallized, it determined the moral behavior of the believers who soon became as wicked as the models they revered. Then the people of Israel appeared with a counterproposal and proclaimed a God who is one and unchanging, a holy God who expects man to be holy, a creator of heaven and earth, of light and darkness, who, to be sure, is sublime and exalted but who is still close to man and shows special concern for the poor and oppressed. They proclaimed a God of zeal (not a God of vengeance) who is not indifferent to the moral behavior of man, but also a God of compassion who embraces all men with love because they are his handiwork, a God who abhors evil, a God of justice, a father to the orphan, a protector of the widow. That was a proclamation of universal significance which penetrated deep into the hearts of men, eventually driving the beautiful and mighty gods into the dust.

This intellectual core assumed universal significance first

by virtue of the ethical posture which was derived from it. It is certainly not irrelevant to the moral behavior of man whether he believes the world, the platform of his actions, governed by a single unified power or by several antagonistic powers. The former view assured men of universal harmony and peace and civilized them; the other offered universal disintegration and discord and brutalized them. The concept of man made in the image of God, in contrast to the nefarious notion that God resembles man, impregnates man with respect for himself as well as for his fellowman and places even the lowliest life under a religious and ethical canopy. Is the abandoning of a newborn baby by his parents a crime? Among the nations of antiquity, even among the Greeks, it certainly was not. Mountains often reverberated with the screams of little girls and rivers bore away the bodies of children whom parents had abandoned without any pangs of conscience the moment they became a nuisance. People in antiquity felt no pain at the sight of such infanticide and even less did the courts punish the perpetrator. To kill a slave roused as little attention as slaying a wild beast. Why is it that today civilized men shudder at the mere thought of such barbaric acts? Because the Israelite nation proclaimed to the world the law: "You shall not murder, for man is created in the image of God." You shall not murder even a child or a slave. It has been argued that man's intellect has made enormous strides, but his moral conscience has lagged far behind, giving evidence of only the slightest advance since primordial times. But we must not forget that man's savagery began to wane much later than his ignorance. The dormant conscience, the instinctive horror in the face of evil was aroused very late, and the people of Israel was one of those responsible for awakening it. The idea and conviction that all men are as equal before the law as they are before God, that the stranger ought to be treated no differently than the native likewise derives from the belief in man's divine image, and Israel adopted it as a basic national law. It was the first recognition of at least some of the rights of man. In contrast, the nations of antiquity, even those in the forefront of civilization, failed entirely to recognize this right, which today is accepted as self-evident. If strangers, restricted to their region, were no longer slaughtered, they were still saddled with oppressive disabilities, putting them only a notch above slaves. This lack of love toward the stranger remained a universal disgrace long after the demise of the ancient world. Kindness toward the slave and even the first move toward his emancipation stemmed from the people of Israel.

The nations of antiquity paid even less attention to sanctifying themselves through chastity. They were sunk in lewdness and sexual aberrations. The Jewish Sybilline poets had warned the nations of antiquity often and emphatically, when they stood at the height of their power, that as a result of their unnatural forms of self-defilement, their hard-heartedness, their perverse theology and its related ethics, they were courting disaster. But they ridiculed these admonishing voices, continued to weaken themselves, and finally went under. Neither their art nor their philosophy were able to rescue them from death. Thus the people of Israel delivered the message of salvation single-handedly when it proclaimed the virtue of self-sanctification, the equality of the stranger with the native, and the concept which is called humanity. It's not superfluous to recall that the cornerstone of morality: "You shall love your neighbor as yourself" was laid by this nation. Who raised the poor out of the dust, the needy, the orphans, and the helpless from the ash-heap? The people of Israel. Who proclaimed eternal freedom, "that one nation will no longer draw its sword against another, that neither will learn the art of war anymore" as the holy ideal for the future? The prophets of Israel. This people has been called a wandering mystery; it would be more appropriate to call it a wandering revelation. It revealed the secret of how to live, it taught the art of all arts. It taught how a nation could guard itself against death.

It is simply not true that this people introduced the ideals of renunciation and self-mortification, and a melancholy, mournful view of life, or paved the way for monastic asceticism, or bedecked a blossoming life with shrouds. Just the opposite. All the nations of antiquity, with the exception of Israel, were preoccupied with death. They offered sacrifices for the dead and succumbed to a mood of devout gloom. These were their mysteries which, like every exaggeration, turned into the exact opposite, into licentious orgies. The gods themselves were not beyond death; they could not save man from it but were, in fact, themselves subject to it. They too had to undertake a journey of death, and here and there they would be shown the coffin, grave or Calvary of some god. The Israelite character, which revered God as "the source of life," emphasized life to such an extent that it sought to expunge from the realm of the sacred everything which reminded of death, and beyond that it brooded so little over what would happen in the grave and beyond, that it opened itself to the charge that it toiled only for earthly interests. And it's true. Its prophets knew no higher ideal than that "the earth should be filled with the pure knowledge of God as the ocean covers its bed." It valued life highly, though, to be sure, a moral, noble, and holy life. Only after a long and unhappy history did a grim and ascetic view of life infiltrate into its midst from outside. A grim, life-hating style emerged which gradually stamped even simple joys as sinful, regarding the world as a vale of tears and partially rendering it one. No, the people of Israel have nothing in common with their kindred, known as Semites, neither with the self-lacerating frenzy by which they pay homage to one god, nor with the sexual ecstasy by which they honor another. Israel separated itself from them and through rigorous discipline weaned itself from their perversions. People entirely misunderstand Israel when they cleverly attempt to derive its character from the nature of the Semites, just as they do when they judge it by the conduct of the two daughters born from its bosom. The latter entered mixed marriages and lost much of their inherited character.

To be sure, the people of Israel also has its great faults. It sinned frequently and was punished harshly enough. History must likewise uncover these failings, their origins, the resulting chain of events, and the errors which derived from them. Some faults of course were acquired, at least partially dragged in from the outside, but there were also indigenous sins and structural defects in character. Why should Israel be more perfect than all other national organisms, none of which has yet manifested perfection, on every side? Those who zealously try to seek out the faults and defects of the people of Israel unwittingly pay it great honor by demanding more from it than from any other nation.

Many of its alleged defects are simply unwarranted. Some accuse it for having failed to develop a good political constitution. But the criticism is the product of confused thinking. A political constitution can actually be evaluated only according to the success or length of time which it confers on the state. Now the fact is that the Israelite state maintained itself as long as most of the large states of antiquity, certainly longer than the Babylonian, Persian, Greek, and Macedonian states, roughly more than 600 years in its first try, excluding the second. Only two or three states maintained themselves longer, the Egyptians, the Romans, and the Byzantines. If one subtracts the centuries of senility, infirmity, and gradual disintegration, then their life span is considerably reduced. Is the Israelite state to be condemned for the fact that it was unable to maintain the peak it reached under David and Solomon, thereafter being often subjugated? It shared this fate with many large states. Or is it to be considered a defect that Israel split into two kingdoms and could never regain its unity? Greece never achieved a unified state, but was from start to finish divided into at least two hostile sections, and even the Roman Empire split into two antagonistic states.

However, the sharpest criticism is actually directed against the political theory of the people of Israel. It is described as visionary, chimerical, utopian. In truth, the political constitution which the national code of law prescribes is really utopian like every ideal which, because it expects to be realized only in a better future, appears unfeasible as long as that time has not yet come. Thus people are condemning the ideal when they belittle the theory of the Israelite constitution. For it was the first, as we have seen, which defined the rights of man, which set the structure of the state on a democratic foundation, which made not only all native-born but also the foreign-born equal, and which eradicated caste and class differences. It even undertook to protect slaves against the whims and harshness of their masters. It declared as a national principle that "there were to be no poor in the land" and labored against the accumulation of wealth and the vice of luxury on the one hand and against the proliferation of misery and the vice of poverty on the other. Through a system of sabbatical and jubilee years it sought to prevent acts that entailed the forfeiture of freedom or the sale of land from becoming permanent. In short, this constitutional theory strove for the ideal, not to succumb to the evil from which the civilized states of today still suffer. People may ridicule the ideal if they wish, but they should consider that it is the salt which guards society against decay.

To be sure, the people of Israel did manifest a certain deficiency in failing to leave behind any gigantic structures of architectural wonders. It probably lacked any architectural skill; but this deficiency may also have derived from Israel's ideal of equality: it simply did not value its kings sufficiently to build them palaces and pyramids. The huts of the poor were more highly valued. Likewise it did not build temples for its God—the Solomonic temple was built by Phoenicians —because the goal was to transform the heart of man into God's temple. Israel neither sculpted nor painted gods, for it considered the deity as an object of solemn and devout reverence and not as a subject of frivolous play.

Nor did the people of Israel excel in artistic epics and still less in tragedy and comedy. This again may be a character defect, but it certainly is also related to a decided aversion against mythologies on the birth and lives of the gods as well as against the levity and theatrics of the stage. In its place, Israel created two other poetic genres which reflected the full richness of its idealistic life: the psalms and the poetically wrought eloquence of the prophets. Both are marked by the essential trait of truth rather than fiction, whereby poetry is elevated from an instrument which merely entertains and charms our fantasy to one that can be used for moral edification. Although drama and comic irony do not predominate in this literature, dramatic vitality and that kind of irony which proudly looks down from its idealistic heights on everything unreal do. The prophets and psalmists of Israel in addition achieved a poetic form of great beauty, but they never sacrificed content and truth for the sake of form. The people of Israel likewise created its own historical genre which was exceptional in not passing over in silence, concealing, or touching up the unworthy and immoral acts of heroes, kings, and nations but always recounting them truthfully.

This unique Hebraic literature, which no nation on earth has matched, and at best merely imitated, achieved moral conquests precisely because of its superiority. Civilized nations could not withstand the sincerity and truthfulness which permeated it. If Greek literature illuminated the realm of art and knowledge, Hebraic literature idealized the realm of the sacred and the moral. The latter had the additional advantage that a living people always sustained and cultivated it, even under the most trying conditions.

Viewed externally and superficially, the course of history from the entry of the Israelites into Canaan until well into the period of the kings can easily be misleading. For the visible events have merely a political character. Invasions, raids, wars, and victories occupy the entire foreground of history. Onstage are national leaders, heroes, kings, and generals. Alliances are made and broken. Any kind of spiritual activity in the background is scarcely noticeable. The Judges who provide the earliest historical matter, heroes like Ehud, Gideon, his son Abimelech, and especially Jephthah and

Samson, manifest so few Israelite traits that one could easily mistake them for Canaanites, Philistines, or Moabites. Some have thus contended that Samson was modeled after the Tyrian Hercules. Most of the kings, their sons, and courts behaved without restraint, as if there were no laws which set limits for their despotic will, as if they had never heard of the Ten Commandments of Sinai. The people itself was mired for centuries in dissolute idolatry and was fairly indistinguishable from the surrounding pagan world. Was it really, therefore, from the outset no different? Did it merely keep step with its Semitic kin for the longest time and only later, much later, did it in a given period develop its own uniqueness and opposition to the surrounding world? Was Mt. Sinai not aflame at its cradle but only read back into history at a later time? Skeptics have so contended, but the remnants of Israelite poetry from hoary antiquity contravene them. Several centuries before the establishment of the kingdom, in the early days of the Judges, the days of Deborah, "the mother in Israel," a poet already intoned the great event of the revelation at Sinai, already depicted the "people of God" as essentially different from its surroundings, and already attributed its weakness to the fact that it had chosen strange gods and fallen away from its unique origins. Although many are unwilling to trust the historical narrative, they must surely believe the poetry. It is an infallible eyewitness. It is beyond doubt that the spiritual birth of the people of Israel occurred simultaneously with its physical birth, that Sinai was the location of the former as Egypt was of the latter, and that the Ark of the Covenant with the sacred Ten Commandments was its steady companion since childhood.

The essence of Israel's antithetical conviction in God and its own ethical mission, namely the fundamental teaching which was engraved in stone tablets, is not only ancient but as old as its bearer. Selected representatives of the people who have nothing to do with the daily hustle and bustle of the masses built the cherubim to protect the spiritual and holy legacy received at Sinai. This sacred legacy has only an apparent religious form and is only apparently theocratic; its essence is the moral law. God is the source of the teaching but not its goal. This goal is rather the individual human being and the community with its legitimate demands. God is the sacred will in this teaching who determines the ethical and the good, the sacred model who shows the way, but He is not the goal for whose sake the action is to be done so that He might derive some benefit therefrom. The teaching of Israel, therefore, can in no way be defined as a creedal faith, but rather as a teaching of duty in regard to moral acts and moral dispositions; it is also a teaching of holiness, but without any mystical overtones. It has been called the "religion of the spirit"; it is, insofar as it presents the divine in a purely spiritual form, freeing it of all moral limitation and attributing to it only power and a sacred will.

However, this religion or teaching of holiness was too lofty to be grasped by the entire people in its youth. The ideal, which was to assure it significance and survival, remained for the longest time an enigma. The prophets had first to unravel the enigma for the people. A good deal of time passed, even after the prophets had spoken with such burning passion, before the people became the guardian of the teaching heard at Sinai and built a temple for it in its heart. However, as soon as this level of maturity was reached, as soon as its "heart of stone" was transformed "into a heart of flesh," as soon as prophecy had rendered the intermediary function of the priesthood useless, the prophets could exit from the stage, for they had become superfluous. The people itself had achieved a full understanding of its character and its vocation.

History reveals how this twofold transformation occurred, how the tiny family of a sheikh acquired the mentality of a people, how this miniature people was reduced to a horde, and how this horde was then educated to become a divine people by being imbued with a soul that consisted of a teaching of self-sanctification and self-control in conjunction with a lofty concept of God. This national soul grew just like the national body, developing itself and assuming a legal garb. And even though it did not succumb to changing times it did accommodate itself. The transformation was completed amid some hard struggles. Internal and external obstacles had to be overcome, mistakes corrected, and relapses healed before the national body became a malleable organ for the national soul. The concealed had to be brought into the open, the obscure illuminated, and the vague presentiment raised to the clarity of consciousness so that the Israel envisioned by the prophets in the distant future (which they emphatically distinguished from the Israel of reality with its defects) could become "a light unto the nations." Indeed, there is no other nation on earth or in the flux of time which, like Israel, carried with it a definite teaching.

But this nation did not only possess that teaching, it was also fully conscious that it survives only for its sake, that the nation itself is merely a means and instrument for the teaching, that its significance derives solely from its vocation to disseminate that teaching as a sacred truth, and that it should disseminate this sacred truth not by power and force but by the example of its own practice and the realization of its declared ideal. As far as the Greeks are concerned, penetrating historical research first demonstrated that they had the task to render the ideal life of art and learning visually; they themselves were unconscious of it. (The Greek nation thus lived only for the present, not the future, and lived only for itself, not for others. Not so the Israelite nation. It not only sensed its mission, but also clearly realized that this was its mission, that it had meaning only by virtue of it and that without it, Israel would be but "a drop in the bucket, a fleck of dust on the scale." Its men of God designated it as the chosen people for this reason alone. In no way did they thereby wish to arouse and nurture in Israel a sense of conceit. Did they view it as a better or superior or more noble people? No! The same men of God repeatedly and all too harshly reprimanded Israel for its unyielding, stiff-necked, and base character.[1] Its chosenness was intended only to subject it to a greater and more onerous responsibility, a fuller complement of duties. Israel was to consider itself as the "servant of God," as the executor of His teaching, as the holy messenger of a higher moral world order; in return, it was to endure martyrdom, which it did gloriously and consciously. From the moment Israel came to a clear realization of its task as the bearer of its own religious-moral world view, it treasured this above all else, above fatherland and nationality, above life itself. And because it offered itself as sacrifice, it achieved longevity and immortality. Israel was the first nation that had the courage of its convictions and renounced the pleasures of life for its beliefs. It was the first nation that showed that a beneficial truth could be sealed only by the blood of martyrs. Its faithfulness granted it tenacity and perseverance. Since it succeeded in defying the disintegrating forces of nearly 4000 years and a world full of enemies, its essence cannot have been too inferior.

The history of the Israelite nation manifests, therefore, at the beginning a thoroughly irregular pattern. Two factors determine its rise and fall, a physical and spiritual one, or a political and a religious-ethical one. At first, the national leaders, the Judges and kings, generally represent one, and the Levites and prophets the other. But as the faith in the unique teaching becomes the common property of the masses, these two currents steadily converge until finally they flow together. At the outset the political current is stronger and conceals the other to such an extent that only small, weak traces of it are visible, and then only to the trained eye. Deep into the period of the kings only the political character of Israelite history is prominent. Hence, the deceptive appearance that this is its exclusive nature. Suddenly the spiritual current gushes forth with vigor and lots of foam, like a mountain spring which has slowly collected out of sight beneath the earth, but whose existence does not date from the moment it broke out of its rocky womb. The appearance of the literary prophets and the psalmists from Amos till Isaiah is fully comparable to the bursting forth of a mountain stream in their ability and power to fructify. The prophets and psalmists, who always delivered their great and truthful thoughts in artistically gripping form and who constituted the noblest blossom of the Israelite nation, could never have arisen and worked if favorable prior conditions did not exist. They arose out of a soil that had already been spiritually fertilized, and they were understood only because they told the people nothing new or strange when they spoke of their lofty ethical view of life. On the contrary, they merely clarified in an uplifting and poetic manner the old and familiar, preaching passionately, courageously, and in a mood of self-sacrifice. Their mighty strength seems to have diminished after Isaiah, but again only like the mountain stream, which becomes clearer, more transparent, and more useful as it levels off on the plain.

Even those who don't believe in miracles must acknowledge the seemingly miraculous element in the course of Israel's history. It offers not only the pattern of growth, flowering, and decay which characterizes the history of other nations as well, but also the extraordinary phenomenon that decay is followed by a new process of greening and flowering and that this rise and decline has occurred three times. The history of the crystallization of the Israelite family group into a nation and its entry into Canaan till the rise of the monarchy constitutes the first period, that of growth. The second period, that of flowering, covers the reigns of David and Solomon, who raised Israel to the level of a great power. The period of flowering was brief and was followed by a gradual decline in power which ended in the destruction of the nation. But it rose again, growing slowly under Persian and Greek rule; under the Maccabees it experienced again a glorious prime only to sink back once more into the hands of the Romans. But it declined apparently only to experience a revival again in another form. However, this transformation no longer belongs to the ancient history of Israel. No less miraculous is the phenomenon that this nation twice launched its period of growth on alien soil in an apparent state of lifelessness: the first time in Egypt, the second in Babylonia, and, if you wish, the third time in the Roman and Parthian empires. One of Israel's prophets portrays the growth of Israel in Egypt with the picture of a young girl covered with blood and dirt and abandoned in the fields, who despite her misery and abandonment develops into a beautiful young woman.[2] Another prophet portrays its growth in Babylonia with the picture of a distraught, lamenting widow robbed of all her children, who is comforted and rejuvenated by the sudden streaming back of all her children from the ends and corners of the earth.[3] Admittedly, analogies are lame, but they do offer a better perception of a phenomenon that transcends everyday occurrences. In any event, this people, which stems from hoary antiquity and still exhibits the freshness of youth, which has endured many changes and still remains true to itself, is an extraordinary phenomenon.

7

The Correspondence of an English Lady on Judaism and Semitism[1]

FIRST LETTER

Dear friend,

You will be astonished to find in my present letter a subject other than the one we have been bickering and wrangling over until now. Not a word about Wagner's highly romantic music or E. Caro's elegant metaphysics or Schopenhauer's philosophy of the grave; nothing about the upsurge of recent Italian literature or the decline of French literature. I want to talk with you about a religious theme. Why do you make such a face? Well, the content of my letter will not be exactly religious, but rather quasi-religious or better, anti-religious. Our modern way of speaking has produced its own nomenclature so that we use a word for a concept which expresses precisely the opposite. We make use then of a *lucus a non lucendo*.[2] How do I come to occupy myself with a subject that deals with religion? Listen.

I spent an evening recently with some very elegant company representing high society. In the demeanor and language of these men and women, one could detect no trace of Jewish or Semitic descent. Only someone familiar with the sounds of society might have guessed where these people came from by the liveliness of the conversation and the

191

sarcastic, witty punchlines, or even more, by the subject of the conversation. Two men withdrew to a windowsill to talk. "Now what?" one of them asked. An attractive, intelligent-looking, spry woman, upon hearing this question, immediately chimed in with the remark: "What kind of a question is that? First of all, we baptize our children. Should we expose them to the ridicule of their classmates and to the spiteful allusions of teachers who fancy themselves comic with their Jewish intonation? Should our sons be barked at in the army by some coarse sergeant or some insolent boor of a second lieutenant simply because they are Jews? Should they fulfill their military service conscientiously only to be discriminated against? Should our daughters who attend a public ball, even if graced with physical and spiritual charm and impeccably and modestly dressed, be scorned by geese with crosses on their breasts, avoided by the men and forced into a gloomy corner? No, I will not tolerate that! Should my children and grandchildren tremble when somewhere in Egypt, Russia, or Hungary a Christian child disappears or is whisked away in some theatrical fashion and the culprits delight in exploiting it by inciting drunken *katzaps*[3] or fanatical Magyars against us? Of what concern to me is the Talmud? Do I have any idea whether it's filled with stupidities or gems of wisdom? And yet I and my children should be held responsible for it! No, no a thousand times! Therefore my husband and I have definitely decided to bring our children into the Church at the first opportunity. I also feel that we should be baptized at the same time. In regard to a fatal jump, a little more or less makes no difference. Personally, we would gain nothing thereby; for the Christian clubs would still exclude us even with the drops of baptismal water on our foreheads and the cross worn conspicuously on the lapel. On this point Christian society behaves entirely in the spirit of the Old Testament: it requites the sins of the fathers down to the third and fourth generations. However, the likely conflict facing our own Christian children would thus be avoided. Only my husband is against this wholesale conversion out of some silly consideration for, I don't know what, an old grandmother or an orthodox friend."

These were some of the ideas expressed with real fervor by this attractive and intelligent woman. The men at the windowsill listened carefully to every word and conveyed their agreement by nodding repeatedly. At that moment a thought occurred to me which you may again consider as a specimen of feminine logic. Nevertheless, you have accustomed me to pour out to you everything that goes through my head. I am, you know, my dear friend, no longer nervous, even though a lady is permitted to be. I can listen to and bear many paradoxical things; also a dose of characterlessness, as long as it is not plain egotism or meanness, does not cause me now to faint so quickly. And Judaism—well of course I was born and raised in England and therefore initiated into that which is called "Jewish." But I have lived too long in skeptical Germany and lighthearted Austria for it to be the center of my intellectual life. An attack against it does not affect me greatly. But I must confess that this jumping from one religion to another, this frivolous treatment which entails less seriousness than one shows when one changes clothes enraged me somewhat. And I had already whetted my tongue for an acid retort which would not have pleased that woman whose past I knew quite well.

But a second thought reduced the first to silence. I pondered the fact that the woman who spoke so frivolously of conversion and had no idea that it is always bound up with the stain of apostasy was not alone, but rather represents a type to which Judaism and Christianity alike mean equally little. This group would accept Islam or Buddhism with the same indifference in order to escape social disabilities and not to be hindered in its pursuit of pleasure. To this group belong especially idle rich Jewish youth who despite their superior refinement and athletic ability are constantly reminded of their pariah status by Christian rogues. Also middle-class Jewish youth, including well-paid Jewish buyers and salesmen, and especially the average Jewish member of the bureaucracy: lawyers, judges, university instructors, as soon as their Jewish birth inconveniences them careerwise or socially, they crawl to the cross as if it were their last resort.

I find this large group still somewhat less harmful than another which raves in nasal tones about "Christian culture." Like apostate theologians who have jumped from liturgy to the feuilleton, these people turn up their noses at Judaism and speak of it in the same terms as that enlightened creature of Heine's phantasy, Hirsch Hyacinth, the assistant collector of lottery tickets, who defines Judaism as "not a religion but a misfortune," as if it were improper for them to speak more fully on the subject.[4] To this category belong Jewish professors of history and experts in political science. These people with all their learning know nothing of Friedrich David Strauss's incisive comment, which blurted out the secret of thousands: "Are we still Christians? Is there still a Christianity in spirit and truth?"[5] This was the thought which caused me to hold my tongue and kept me from giving that lady seeking baptism my answer to the question "now what?" But this wise thought saddened me, as does every experience drawn from life. I asked myself "now what?" with a different meaning. If both these groups treat Judaism with indifference or even with disdain—and they do actually constitute the cream of the Jewish community—what will become of Judaism? Will it be preserved only by the poor and uneducated among our people? And when they too will achieve wealth and education and also turn their backs on Judaism, then will the rabbis, cantors, and sextons remain its only adherents, and not even all of them?

With such sober thoughts I left that group. For the longest time I could not get rid of a scene which once had impressed itself upon me. In a hospital, the body of a person whom I knew in better days was put in a coffin; its cortège consisted of two people: a cripple and an old woman. Is this the way Judaism will be brought to the grave? Will culture become its gravedigger? In order to rid myself of this sadness, I write to you. To relate the anguish of my heart already provides some alleviation. Perhaps you will be able to restore the disrupted equilibrium of my soul. I would be grateful to you.

Your friend,
Edith

SECOND LETTER

Dear friend,

Your letter interests me greatly, not because of its contents but rather because it reflects a new and—let me be honest—very becoming side of you. I have never known you to be sentimental, least of all over Judaism. Our conversations and correspondence, therefore, never went along these lines. And now your morbid views concerning the future of Judaism show me that you do sense, I won't say pain, but a certain discomfort at the prospect that it is sinking like the heathen world to the level of paganism, that only the coarse rural masses remain loyal while the educated world turns away to join a triumphant Christianity. I am delighted about your seizure of sadness and—forgive me—I see also in you a definite type just as you did in the lady of your soirée who was seeking baptism. You also are not alone in your ambivalence but share it with many respectable men and women of your religion and race. You still have a small, and I would add, warm spot in your heart for Judaism; you still regard it as a lovely family idyll, a precious relic. On the other hand, you are overwhelmed by the enormous cultural ferment of our century and are thrilled by the achievements which ensue. In comparison, Judaism appears to you like a remnant without culture. An idyll can survive only in a quiet corner; how can it possibly assert itself in the raucous, strident life of the present? All will inevitably be submerged as a soft song is drowned out by a thunderstorm. You are anxious that your reverential feelings toward Judaism might be driven from your heart. Is my analysis of your mood correct?

Now let me try to free you from your emotional dilemma. Permit me to shed a little light on the ideal on which your heart lavishes most of its affection. In addition to the cultural ferment, our century is also distinguished by the free exercise of criticism, the merciless exposure of all half-truths and confused emotions. Criticism does not destroy the genuine ideals but only those that are spurious, which essentially are no more than idols. Criticism hurts, but it also heals.

You, culture enthusiast, do you have any idea how sick our highly civilized Europe really is? I do not mean metaphorically, like a feverish patient whose sleep is disturbed because he is consumed by anxiety, first over the nihilists in the East, who could commit yet another atrocity rendering the chaos there still more chaotic, then over the anarchists in the West, who might someday gain the upper hand making bloody anarchy the order of the day with possible intervention by neighboring states ensuing in both cases, and, finally, over the partition of Turkey, which is only a matter of time and which could toss the apple of Eris into the midst of Europe and readily precipitate a conflagration. One could also declare the condition of Europe as ailing in the sense that these eventualities undermine the sense of security in the financial sector, and from there the disquiet is transmitted to the most sensitive areas of the social organism. However, the sickness from which the civilized world suffers is not metaphoric but physical and tangible, much more destructive than war, fire or plague. If this disease continues to rage, as doctors and statisticians believe it almost surely will, then this highly civilized Europe will soon look like a deathbed patient on whom there is literally nothing healthy left from the crown of his head to the soles of his feet. Today, there is already no class or age group that is spared, though perhaps the tattered proletariat, bent with worry, more so than the decorated citizen who struts about putting on airs or the gifted artist or the preacher of morality.

You must forgive me my esteemed friend, for discussing this unmentionable, suppressed disease with a lady, for this evidence will support my thesis that not all that glitters is gold and not everyone is civilized who presumes himself to be.

You can hide this letter from your small daughter. Have you ever heard of Professor Alexander von Oettingen?[6] Probably not, nor is it likely that you know his highly interesting book *Die Moralstatistik in ihrer Bedeutung für die Socialethik* (The Significance of Moral Statistics for Social Ethics). It is a very interesting but shattering book to read. Oettingen says about the disease to which I alluded that as a result of a moral breakdown it clearly threatens to ruin the social fabric of the civilized world. This scrupulous statistician of morality derived his unexpected and depressing conclusion from a variety of sources which throw a drastic light in terms of statistics on the standard of morality or immorality in all the enlightened countries of Europe. The main cause of the different manifestations of the disease is carnal lust. One of them is syphilis.

The actual extent of this contagious disease cannot be determined statistically, of course, for the simple reason that important and prominent people conceal it behind a veil of secrecy. But the number of those who seek medical help is shocking enough. In the hospitals of Vienna alone, during a four-year period, some 24,000 afflicted with this disease were treated, including some 16,000 men and 8,000 women, mostly girls. And now the constant increase in the number of cases! Whereas in 1860 only 3030 men and 1440 girls were stricken, in 1863 the figures were 5800 men and 2224 girls, that is, nearly double. According to this same statistician (Hügel), there are annually some 14,600 cases in England alone. The increase in this disease is all the more destructive because the bacilli are transmitted to the embryo. In London alone some 78 percent are stricken with the disease during the first year of life, while in all of England some 75 percent come down with it at some point during their first five years. And this occurs with good lumber in England, where a deeper religious spirit provides some kind of a dam against inundation by that secret sin. If anywhere, then it is certainly here that the truth of the biblical declaration is confirmed: God requites the sins of the fathers down to the third and fourth generations.

I still can't let you go, dear friend. In order to thoroughly recognize the full achievements of European culture, I must also take you along the sewers, no matter how indelicate that may be. I am compelled to offend your sense of propriety by pointing out a number of widely practiced sins which will make you shudder. One of these sins, the source of the plague, is the abysmal decline of the female sex. Have you any idea of the large number of unfortunate girls who earn a living at the expense of their self-respect? In London there are some 4,500 houses of ill repute with more than 20,000 registered boarders, and besides them another 40,000 who are not supervised by the police. In Paris and all of France, for that matter, the size of the demimonde can't even be estimated. And this despicable vice assumes ever greater proportions. In Berlin, in 1859, there were only 6,380 such unclean creatures but their number rose steadily until in 1871 it reached about 15,000. Maxime du Camp says in his description of Paris:

> We stand today in front of the Augean stables, where men of every type and station have been dumping their dung. What Hercules will have the courage and strength to clean out this cesspool? The only remedy lies in a moral reformation: but then who is willing to listen to this word without smiling.[7]

London, Vienna, Berlin, Rome, Munich, and all the other centers of civilization compete with Paris. The number of Sodoms and Gomorrahs has increased phenomenally.

The depravity of the demimonde with all its immoral consequences is known fully only to the police and statistician who keep tabs on it. But it has a still more repulsive sister who brings its shame out into the light of day. I am referring to the bastards born of illicit love affairs. It has been estimated that during the short period of five years from 1847 to 1851 in France and Germany not less than a million bastards were born, rising in France from 69,000 to 76,000 annually, and in Prussia where the total in the five years from 1860 to 1864 was nearly 315,000, from 60,500 to 68,000 per annum. In Catholic cities such as Graz, Munich, Vienna,

Prague, and Rome half the new-born babies are bastards. The rural population constitutes no exception, in fact it displays a still more precipitous decline of moral standards. In Mecklenburg there are some 300 places with the same ratio and 80 where, at one time, all the children born were illegitimate. The statistics have shown that in this regard the Germanic nations sin still more than do the Romance-speaking nations. These bastards, poorly educated and provided with a defective inheritance, transmit the sin of their elders like a hereditary poison to the very fabric of society, thereby either implanting or advancing the disease. In particular the foundlings' and children's homes are the ones who numerically record the fateful fruits of that collective moral guilt of an enervated and depraved society.

This is then the state of Europe's lofty culture. Sexual depravity and carnal lust continue to spread. The results are the increase of illegitimate births and overall degeneration. There is little hope that from decay will come regeneration. Doctors whom I know assure me on the basis of their own experience with patients that only a few are not afflicted with this hidden disease and that not even the most modest women are beyond suspicion.

I bid you farewell and wish you much pleasure in your passion for culture.

Your friend,
Caspi

THIRD LETTER

Dear friend,

I can hardly be grateful to you for making me gaze into the midst of a dizzying abyss. You have robbed me of my gilded illusion, which is about the same as robbing me of my valuables and leaving me a beggar. As we zip through these cultured lands on the railroads or a steamship or seek out the popular rural landmarks, with what pleasure does the eye feast on the creations of modern architecture, on the arrangements of cities, gardens and parks, on the most charming and alluring views. Public buildings, railroad stations, parliamentary buildings for those who represent the rights and welfare of the people, halls of scholarship, temples for the art of Thespis and Melpomene, and even houses of worship by their very size induce amazement and by their symmetry please our still very demanding aesthetic sense. The wondrous works of which antiquity boasted are surpassed even in smaller cities. And now to discover that all these marvels are only hospitals in which tenants, builders, and visitors alike suffer from secret, ravaging diseases! You are really cruel to have opened my eyes and destroyed my world of fantasy. Your merciless statistics were chilling. Is it not an oppressive thought to be forced to believe that civilized men equipped with all the means of science stand far, far beneath other living creatures? Plants and animals are steadily perfected by breeding while mankind should head toward destruction?

I am really quite angry with you and sullenly bid you good-bye.

Your friend,
Edith

FOURTH LETTER

Dear friend,

I had hoped to earn not only your pardon but even more your thanks for having prescribed for you a moral drug for vomiting. Are you going to disappoint me? You, such a good daughter of our people, suffer like so many from indigestion due to eating too many delicacies. You must again learn to find pleasure and satisfaction in eating simpler fare. High society, with all its glitter and color in which the frivolous world with its hosts of ladies is mirrored, must be stripped of its spell and shown in its true form to save those healthy souls who are deceived by it from falling into an intoxicated sleep and reeling in bright daylight. Perhaps I can replace the disillusionment I caused you with something that has less glitter but more substance.

The gifted Thomas Carlyle has struck a powerful chord of the human keyboard: man's need for hero-worship. He accounts for the great achievements of world history on the basis of this human inclination according to which men are readily amazed by and willing to submit to a figure who towers over the ordinary and mediocre. When such a figure appears it naturally exerts an attractive force and the duly rendered homage transforms him into a historical world hero. His admirers overlook his faults and exaggerate still more his outstanding qualities.[8]

This inclination to hero-worship is rooted in the clearly noble side of human nature, in the need to wonder. The oft-invoked sardonic comment that "the world longs to be deceived," misses precisely that which distinguishes man, namely speech and an aesthetic sense, and the drive to be brought forth and uprooted from the tediously dull and ordinary. It is the same inclination which, in poetry, gives rise to a sensitivity for the exalted. To be sure, in the history of religion this drive gave birth to the foolish belief in miracles, this degeneration of hero-worship which has caused so much heartrending sorrow in the history of mankind. But there is a countervailing force against the exaggeration of this inclination of human nature, namely skeptical criticism which examines the deeds and fame of individual heroes or a heoric group to determine if they really deserve to be admired. It takes a long time, sometimes thousands of years, before such criticism can be openly articulated. As a result, figures like Peregrinus Proteus,[9] Apollonius of Tyana,[10] and Cagliostro[11] could long attract admiration and exercise considerable influence. In the wake of countless frauds perpetrated by great pretenders, modern man, that is, the upper ten thousand, has grown very sober about the miraculous. The critical faculty has gained the upper hand over the inclination to wonder; it belittles everything and entirely rejects whatever smacks of the miraculous.

Thus we can now pose the question: are there really miracles or, indeed, were there ever any?

For the mature and well-educated man of culture, there are, of course, no miracles. Rationalism has severely underminded and nullified the miracles of religion, those of the Old Testament as well as of the New. The miracles of nature have been entirely set aside by empirical science. Only the science of physiology is still bewildered; it has been unable to discover the bridges from physical movement to mental activity, how the cruder or more delicate senses can instantaneously produce sensations of pleasure or aversion, arouse thoughts, inspire truths, and determine knowledge and consciousness. But physiology marvels at this influence of the crudely physical on the ethereally spiritual and vice versa only in terms of a riddle. Someday, perhaps, it will find a satisfying solution for this riddle according to the laws of nature. Thus it is embarrassed to regard them as miraculous events which might point to a higher being who could have fixed the preestablished harmony between matter and spirit, between the senses and the soul. In turn, moral philosophy and theology bemoan this assault on the miraculous because in its wake will come the decline of morality. Should the structure and tissue of the cell really be the last word on the actions of man as they are for animals? Must man then submit to the desires of the eye and heart? These are the complaints of the moral theologians and they show with moral statistics, or rather criminal statistics, the extent to which immorality has increased as a result of the decline of religion.

But of what avail are complaints and laments? Wailing has never revived the dead. And religion is dead if that which gave it birth, the miracle, no longer sustains and bears it. In this regard, Protestantism finds itself in the worst predicament. It has combined morality with religion and acknowledged only the miracles of the past. Then along come Strauss and Colenso[12] and dissolve the miracles of the Gospels into types and myths with the result that the helper falters and the recipient stumbles. The Catholic and Orthodox Churches are much wiser. They have never let the occurrence of miracles cease. Saint Januarius[13] continues to bleed year in and year out, the holy fire still shoots forth every Easter in the Church of the Holy Sepulcher while the faithful behold the miracle with their own eyes and kindle their hearts thereby. Besides the saints of the Church, the votive offerings prove the continual healing power of the respective relics. This policy yields results. Without miracles there can be no religion, and miracles are rendered believable, not only by written texts, but by continuing to be visible and effective down to the present day.

"And Judaism?" I hear you ask. Relax!

There is a miracle which is visible even to the weakest eyes and which is not explicable in terms of the laws of physics, physiology or ethnology; in fact, it defies them. Would you like to know what it is, dear friend? Look at yourself once in the mirror, not in order to see how your new suit fits but rather to reflect on yourself. And if you reflect deeply then you must eventually ask yourself: how can I as a Jew be still physically alive? The thousands of years which have passed over the head of my people have bombarded it with cyclopean blows but have not succeeded in smashing it. Just think: three thousand years, at least a hundred generations! Consider what disintegrating processes a century unleashes and then multiply this overwhelming destructive force by the large number of generations, in fact you must infinitely square it, because thousands of living factors have united with the destructive elements of time to completely exterminate the Jewish race; malice, illusion, religious simplicity have all worked to annihilate it from among the nations "so that the name of Israel would no longer be recalled." And how often has this war of annihilation been planned secretly and implemented openly with fire and sword!

> Here they beat him with heavy whips,
> There he fell beneath the weight of the cross,
> Here they spit disdainfully into his face,

There they crowned his temples with thorns,
Here they nailed him to the cross, with a sharp spear
They pierced his loins—blood, blood, blood—

And the presence of a single Jew, a single Jewess is not a miracle?

Just don't come with the ridiculous fable of the eternal Jew who, exhausted by persecution, yearns for the grave. Ask the Jews in France, England, and Italy, where they stand at the pinnacle of society, ask the Jewish statesmen, legislators, and kings of the stock markets in these lands if they are praying for the tranquility of the grave. How did the Jewish race manage to persevere through these many generations? For the hostile attitude toward this race does not date from the triumph of Christianity when Constantine and his successors decreed: "If you do not accept the faith of the Church, you will be banished and become sons of death." The war of annihilation against the sons of Judaism is ancient. At least five hundred years before the emergence of Christianity a psalmist was already complaining: "'From my youth on they have attacked me many times'; thus can Israel say:—'many times have they attacked me and still they could not get near me'" [Psalms 129:1–2]!

Some profound thinkers have been amazed by this in-comprehensible fact of the indestructibleness of the Jewish race. Even Voltaire, the terrible enemy of all miracles and, for this reason as well as others, a terrible enemy of the Jews says: "One is astonished that this people still exists and is today more numerous than in antiquity." A few have tried to account for this phenomenon. This people's tenacity, its isolation, its peculiar religion which is so intimately bound up with its national life—all these should have produced this phenomenon. But this is no way explains the basic problem. In what way are the Jews more tenacious than the Egyptians, Phoenicians, Babylonians, Medes, Persians, Greeks, and Romans who all dominated the world for a period of time and were still devoured by the Hades of history? How did the vanquished manage to outlast the victors? Why does the law of the effect of greater bodies upon smaller ones, which also obtains in the historical process, suffer an exception precisely in the case of this inconspicuous, tiny nationality? "Religion constitutes in this case a countervailing force." Thus you are actually admitting more than you intended, that in the religion of this minority there is something which endows it with extraordinary powers of resistance.

Thinkers who have freed themselves from their prejudices and biases toward this race have not been afraid to acknowledge that the continuity and indestructibility or eternity of this race is truly a miracle. A French Catholic preacher has formulated the miracle thus: "You may dig a grave for this race, seal it with your strongest cement, surround it with guards, it will merely laugh at you and arise to prove once again that it has a spirit which you lack and that matter cannot control the spirit."

Your
Caspi

FIFTH LETTER

Dear friend,

The French language has the knack of giving an idea its proper garb, of rendering it perfectly clear by casting it pointedly. *Vous prouvant une fois de plus, que la matière ne peut rien contre l'esprit.*[14] Now that's certainly a fine phrase. But fancy phrases are somewhat like proverbs that are coined out of a one-sided view of the events of experience and are often less than half-true. To what extent does the nicely formulated idea of Father Lacordaire[15] about the indestructibleness and eternity of the Jewish race imply the philosophic corollary that matter has no power over the spirit? Does the Jewish race represent the spirit? You yourself must regard that as quite an exaggeration. Also, our George Eliot in her equally superb literary and philosophic novel *Daniel Deronda* has the half-prophetic, half-deluded, restless Mordecai propound

something similar.[16] But this is not only grist for the mill of
the anti-Semites but also for well-meaning religious and
irreligious Christians who accuse us of being possessed by an
incorrigible arrogance stemming from the superiority of our
religion. The miracle of the continued existence of the Jewish
race despite the war of extermination against it can in any case
be accounted for physiologically in terms of race. That is the
hobbyhorse of our Disraeli who even as Prime Minister was
proud of his Jewish descent and in several of his novels
intoned the vigor of the Jews.[17] But that is a dangerous
precipice. We approach the point of materialism, which is
inherently exclusive and intolerant. In the material world the
law of the stranger governs, and since we are unable to assure
our survival by force of arms the powerful races of Europe are
entirely justified in devouring us in one way or another if our
race should block their path. In short, I do not understand
what you wish to establish, prove, or refute with what you call
the miraculous, tenacious survival of the Jews.

Your only partially reconciled
Edith

SIXTH LETTER

Dear friend,
    In order to make clear to you what I intend to do with this
miracle I must approach it from yet another side. Is it not
remarkable, to say the least, that we Jews, of today as well as
of the past, have always been the object not only of hatred but
also of contempt? The cry of hep-hep against us does not date
from yesterday or from the beginning of the century but is
extremely old. I will skip over the biblical period, in which,
according to the biblical sources the complaint was often
aired that Israel has been mocked and derided by nations
politically and numerically far inferior. You as a student of
the Bible know the words of the prophets regarding the tiny
Ammonites and Moabites and other mini-nations which
abused and slandered Israel. This phenomenon is repeated

from century to century down to our own day and just in those periods when the Jewish race appears to have emerged from an unfavorable situation. What did the motley rabble of the Samaritans not throw up against the Judeans as they took possession of their land a second time and prepared themselves to found a state! Scarcely had the Samaritans departed from the scene when depraved Grecophiles began yelping. In poisonous literary denunciations they defamed the Jewish race and Judaism with wholly invented defects which, no matter how groundless, are still searched out and refurbished by the enemies of the Jews to this day. These defamations passed from the Greeks to the Romans. The Jews were also compelled to suffer insult added to injury. It was not enough that the brutal sons of the wolf first crushed and then destroyed the Jewish state, but as the vanquished began their journey through the wilderness of nations they branded them, as if with burning metal, with ridicule and humiliation. Cicero, Tacitus, and the Roman satirists transformed the Jews into a caricature.

Finally the outwardly attractive but inwardly rotten heathenism of the Greco-Roman world was conquered by a son of Judaism. In the temples of Rome, Alexandria, Athens, and Byzantium, where till then sacrifices had been offered to heathen gods, psalms now rang forth, and from the pulpits the holy books of the Jews were quoted and interpreted. Now at last the Jews, who certainly constitute the foundation of Christianity, will find peace. For "out of Zion goes forth the law and the word of God from Jerusalem." [Micah 4:2] How wrong! Now the hostile defamation against them became only more intensive, bitter, and more poisonous. The entire Christian world was consumed with hatred for Judaism. It contested every right to physical and spiritual existence enjoyed by the Jews. Christianity called itself "the true, authentic Israel" just as today the Popes and Protestant fundamentalists in theological terms still refer to the Church as Israel and Zion. And every Jew was considered not only as free game but as contemptuous and worthy of being spit upon, for every Jew was abhorred as God's murderer, the murderer of that God whose crucifixion according to the Church was indeed a necessity to effect salvation. Is that not an amazing story?

Is it entirely accidental that the Greeks accused the Jews of fattening a Greek in their temple in order to slaughter and consume him,[18] and that the Christians, as soon as they had broken the umbilical cord to Judaism, raised these and other equally believable accusations against the Jews? Is it entirely accidental that Islam, which owes the core of its religion and its political organization to Judaism, should come to despise Judaism after a brief period of energetically wooing the Jews? I have no exact information as to whether there were many Jews in India and how the Brahmins, when they were still politically independent, behaved toward them. But the Christian and Mohammedan nations that dominated the old world were filled with the same antipathy toward this weakest of races.

Then the shadows of the terrible Middle Ages began to disappear; Christianity lost many of its most gifted adherents. Those who set the tone of the educated world in the previous century ridiculed the teachings of Christianity, not only Voltaire and the Encyclopedists but also the matadors of German literature, Goethe and Schiller, and the philosopher on the Prussian throne. At last the brainless stupidities about the depravity of those who denied Christ and murdered God were silenced. In vain. The same voices that called *"Écrasez l'infâme"* also screamed hep-hep against the Jews, namely Voltaire, Fichte, and third-rate philosophers. A Jew-hatred suffused with contempt survived and exerted still greater energy to delay the manumission and liberation of the Jews, a step which merely signified the healing of their countless wounds. In France the Broglies, the representatives of clericalism, opposed the extension of equality to the Jews; and in Germany, who didn't?[19] Even in your England there were bullheaded opponents, and it required great effort to toss out the disabilities of English Jewry. And the fight is not over.

In all parts of the civilized world a Jew-hatred long thought dead raises its Hydra-like head, organizes an international league against the Jews, and deliberates in congresses on how to effect their humiliation.[20] Some use the pretext of race, others religion, and still others the rise and alleged power of the Jews in journalism and the money market. The enemies of the Jews are as unlikely to die out as the Jews, and they seem to renew themselves along with the Jews from generation to generation. Doesn't this tenacious, indestructible, unnatural hatred and contempt provoke reflection? If it be a riddle, it is worth seeking the solution. Furthermore, it's not so far away. And with it the survival of the Jews would be rendered all the more obvious and striking, recognizable even by those with the poorest eyesight. The crown of thorns which is repeatedly placed upon the Jews should only increase its glory; the cup of suffering actually belongs to the fate of this race and demonstrates the vital energy with which it responds.

Had we traveled the road taken by other peoples, we would have represented a common phenomenon not worth any special consideration. Just suppose that the glorious Solomonic empire, lead by victorious generals and maintained through shipping and international trade, would have managed to survive and build a world empire along the lines of Assyria and Egypt—an achievement that was entirely within the realm of possibility. Or suppose that the heroism and political sagacity of the early Maccabees had been inherited by their descendants who might then have succeeded in annexing the disintegrating empire of the Seleucids—a development which the Romans would not have regarded unfavorably. Or what if the fearless zealots led by the heroic Bar-Giora and John of Gishala had been able to inflict a few more defeats on the Romans thus forcing them to permit the Kingdom of Judea to survive—an effort which would have required only national unity? Or what if that hero Bar Kokhba, the terror of the Romans, had continued to win, compelling the trembling Emperor Aelius Trajanus [sic] Hadrianus [Hadrian] to withdraw his legions and to permit the rebuilding of Jerusalem—an effort which nearly succeeded? Or suppose that in the Middle Ages the bellicose Kazar kings in southern Russia and Crimea, who had genuinely adopted and seriously practiced Judaism, could have maintained their control over the Russians and founded a Jewish empire on the borders of the Califate and the Byzantine shadow-emperor—an achievement likewise within the realm of possibility. On what if other favorable opportunities to establish an independent Jewish community had actually materialized? In short, if the Jews had managed to preserve somewhere a modicum of political independence down to our own day, would their existence still represent something extraordinary? Certainly not! They had to be harassed, humiliated, and spat upon; they had to become serfs of the royal chamber, pariahs, and almost gypsies in order to be viewed as a miraculous phenomenon defying the natural laws of national development and arouse the amazement of those who have eyes to see, that they themselves might say of the Jewish race:

> Who would have believed the reports and to whom was the revelation revealed? He rose as a sapling before us and as a root out of dry ground. He had no form nor beauty that we should look upon him, no unusual appearance that we should inquire about him. Despised and foresaken by men, burdened with pain and familiar with suffering; in his unsightly condition we scorned him and rejected him entirely. . . . He was tortured and abused but did not open his mouth. As a lamb is led to the slaughter and as a sheep is silent when sheared, he did not open his mouth. [Isaiah 53: 1–3, 7]

Since this picture of the servant of God was sketched by that masterful prophetic orator, 2400 years have roared by and the description still fits today to the last detail. You clearly realize now, dear friend, why Israel's existence had to be threatened from century to century; why nations and sovereigns continually agreed: "Let us annihilate the Jews so that the name of Israel will no longer be mentioned" [Psalms

83:5]; why, periodically, the most stupid tales and the most unbelievable accusations were directed against them. All these stations of suffering in Israel's history were and are as necessary for its significance as are the plutonic eruptions and upheavals for the formation of mountains. The sacrificial offerings which were brought to the altar of madness in the wake of accusations that Jews desecrate the host, poison wells, and use the blood of Christian children for ritual purposes; the hecatombs which the Inquisition in Spain and Portugal dedicated to the torture chamber and auto-da-fé; the still larger number of those who, while wandering from city to city, from country to country, languished on the roads—all these should serve to open at some time the eyes of a thinking generation and impress it with the realization that even if thousands upon thousands of its members are rubbed out, death enjoys no power over this race. I say thousands? Millions have been slain on this road of suffering; but the race as a whole cannot be liquidated.

Will this realization with its implicit ramifications ever dawn upon the civilized nations of the world? Will they ever admit, like the inspired Independents of Cromwell's day, that they owe the Jews if not reparations for the anguish of the past at least consolation and the right fully to develop their particular nature?[21] It's not important. The main thing is that we ourselves take to heart this miraculous fact and gain the conviction that our continued existence has a meaning.

Unfortunately this letter has become much too long, but I must still add one observation. Are you familiar with Darwin's theory about the significance of the earthworm? We owe these ugly creeping creatures no less than our physical existence. They loosen the hard crust of the earth with their bodies, they fertilize the soil with their slime and thus ensure the fertility of the humus. The same function is served by the archenemies of the Jews down through the ages. When Jew-hatred stagnates or is about to vanish, then the Hamans, the Apions,[22] the fanatical preachers of the Crusades, the Capistranos,[23] the Torquemadas,[24] the Thomas Paines, the

Istoczys and Önodys[25] root it up anew and render it fertile with their nauseous slime. You surely know the words of the eloquent prophet: "Every weapon forged against you will rebound, every tongue intending to accuse you, you will silence" [Isaiah 54:17].

Heinrich Ewald,[26] the profound student of Hebrew sources who admired ancient Israel no less than he hated and despised contemporary Israel, summarized quite strikingly the aforementioned prophet's trend of thought regarding Israel's significance: "Israel remains as a totality indestructible and unconquerable, for it is no longer a tangible thing, a mortal human being or nation. It is just like an idea, an immortal being, which men may passionately despise and furiously persecute but which cannot be destroyed." Ewald correctly understood the mission, but its fulfillment he could not recognize. He was a pious Protestant.

But now it is high time to bid you adieu.

Your
Caspi

SEVENTH LETTER

Dear friend,

From the conclusion of your last letter, I detect that you are inclined to offer a vote of thanks to the Jew-burners. Certainly the Hamans never dreamed that with their poisonous tongues they would earn the gratitude of the Jews. We must be careful, therefore, not to betray to them the secret that in their nobly intended agitation to destroy or at least to humiliate and suppress the sons of Jacob, they have actually contributed to bringing the miracle of this people's continued existence out into the light of day. For otherwise they might cease their war of annihilation in order not to increase the glorious martyrology of the Jews still further. But, alas, there is no danger. The enemies of the Jews are the last to find or admit something miraculous in a Jew. Indeed, we, ourselves, are, I won't say, blind, but certainly too diffident in evaluating historical events to detect in ourselves something that transcends the ordinary. To the extent that I know my coreligionists, and especially the women, I believe they give little thought to historical miracles and have even less knowledge about them, even here in England. They read the Bible diligently, generally believe in the miracles reported therein, the passage through the Red Sea, the rain of manna, and the revival of the dead by the prophet Elijah. Many also believe in the tales told in the Talmud. But that they themselves should be a part of the mirror which when they look at themselves would reflect an ongoing miracle, this lies entirely beyond their mental horizon. Our George Eliot remarks strikingly about this self-ignorance of contemporary Jews: "The holy spirit could reside here, but people would merely smile and say: 'a poor Jew!' and the main scoffers would be my own people." But why do I accuse others, for I myself am guilty of the same sin! The miraculous quality of our history, precisely because of its tragic dimension, was also entirely strange to me. Admittedly, in England we, at least, don't share the pessimistic view George Eliot put into the mouth of an enlightened Jew: "I do not wish to recognize any difference between me and the pagans; I do not wish to preserve the prophetic vision of our nationality. If only the Hebrews would cease to exist and all the old memories would become for us mere antiquarian facts, dead like the frescoes of a race not yet identified by scholarship." To repeat, even if we don't regard our race in such disparaging terms we still lack the leisure and motivation to ponder over it. Our educated classes are so European that, like the Christians, they are more inclined to literature, art, politics, and the finer pleasures of life than they are to the past and future of our people. Can you de-Europeanize us? It may be disastrous, but it is nevertheless a harsh fact that for the educated person of Jewish descent European interests fully occupy his field of vision while Jewish matters appear only in a remote corner of the background in pale light. And then we are only too glad to close our eyes to the horrible, oppressing, and heartrending scenes of the past, and we are relieved to be able to forget them like a bad dream. Why rip open the wounds that have healed in order to inflame them again? I shudder just to think about it. I will admit that every Jew is a wandering miracle, and I am quite convinced that if there were only a single Jew left on earth dressed in some ancient garb and striking an exotic pose people would pay the most outrageous prices to see him. One would exclaim to the next: "Look, a Jew, a descendant of Abraham, a son of the tribes of Israel from whom the Lord came, a single remnant of the people dispersed and persecuted for centuries." But should you clothe this miracle in a European outfit and have it speak a modern language, then even if, like the prophet Isaiah, it should proclaim the message of a new heaven and earth in the soft tones of a gentle breeze or blast it forth like the trumpet of the day of judgment, the spectators would surely concede: "It is wonderful," but never "It is a miracle." And indeed the thousands and millions of Jews, be they dressed in the stylish clothes of the latest fashion or in Polish caftans or in Turkish turbans, carrying a ministerial portfolio under the arm or a peddler's pack on the back, leafing through a Zola novel or a Hebrew prayer book—how can you possibly imagine them to be an astounding phenomenon deserving of admiration? I come back again to our beloved Hamans. Their honest or hypocritical complaint is that there are too many Jews. They speak like Pharaoh: "Behold, the people of Israel's sons become too numerous, so let us contrive that they will not multiply" [Exodus 1:9–10]. The fools! If there were fewer, their respect and admiration would rise infinitely. Therefore they should work that the Jews multiply like sand at the beach so that they will not suddenly loom as an exception.—I see that I have lumped all sorts of things together with little connection between them. So perhaps it's better that I close.

I remain

Your friend,
Edith

EIGHTH LETTER

Dear friend,

You would make a lousy nurse in a hospital for incurables. If the wounds I have described make you shudder, how could you bear the sight of a revolting disease? And then too I must chide you for your short memory. You refuse to glance back into the past in order to avoid the torment of your ancestors. How much time has elapsed since the medieval scenes of plundering, vilifying, and maiming Jews broke out once more in southern Russia?[27] Are you so sure that the same might not occur elsewhere, be it only in Eastern Europe?[28] The actress Sarah Bernhard, despite her success in erasing every trace of Jewishness, barely escaped being manhandled. If you are so fearful, I would not advise you to stay for any length of time in an anti-Semitic city. Your English papers would not protect you in the midst of an angry outburst.

But you beseech me to spare you from the heroic wounds of the Jews. So let me show you the miracle from another side, the most glorious side of all. You certainly are familiar with the droll description in Heine's piece on Börne of the minute beginnings of the House of Rothschild on the Jewish street in Frankfurt am Main, and of the enormous significance it has acquired as a financial power. We don't really know whether the description stems from Börne or Heine.[29] In any event, the contrast between the tiny house in Frankfurt and the long row of houses on the rue Lafitte in Paris wherefrom Europe's financial world is dominated by means of branches in London, Frankfurt, Vienna, and elsewhere—this contrast is radical enough. Also, the analysis by one or the other of these satirists of the revolution—that it was by means of national paper currencies that the Rothschilds obtained the property not only to demolish the granite-like stones of feudalism but also to a certain extent to devalue the price of silver and gold—this analysis is as radical as it is true. Through the creation of paper money which forced out other currencies, money became more fluid than water and lighter than air. Money became in actuality merely a chimera, for, ultimately, it rested only on a colored piece of paper and on the confidence in its usability. The enormity, or if you permit me the expression, the colossality of the wealth of individuals or the banking associations at the present time can by no means be covered any longer by precious metals. All the minted money in circulation today could not conceivably suffice to compensate for the value of the railroads. Our wealth which runs into the billions rests, therefore, entirely on the guarantee of bank notes. If this certainty is shattered, the millionaire can become a beggar overnight. The recent years of crisis offer enough examples.

Thus one can say without exaggeration that the Rothschilds are the arbiters in questions of war and peace. For to wage war today more than three times as much money is needed, because modern warfare wastes sums which all the gold mines of California and Australia could not cover. Hence every war increases the national debt still further. But a war loan can scarcely be contracted without or in opposition to the Rothschilds. If the Rothschilds should devalue the bank notes only slightly, a war would be almost impossible or it would have to be waged by means of brutal war levies à la Wallenstein, and this kind of war policy would ruin more thoroughly than did the Thirty Years War not only the warring factions but also the neutrals, wreaking a havoc like that of Sodom and Gomorrah or provoking a coalition of the affected neutral states. Just imagine, dear friend, if the Rothschilds would join the League of the Friends of Peace, whose messianic horn of peace till now has been blaring in the wilderness, then the passions for war could no longer keep Europe in constant turmoil, and a conflagration for which so much tinder is available would be averted.

Now tell me, dear friend, is it not miraculous that this great financial power rests in the hands of Jews? Is it entirely accidental that it is the sons of Jacob who dominate the European money market? For the male members of this house, with very few exceptions, remain faithful to their religion and, in critical situations, firmly refuse to deny their solidarity with their coreligionists.

Do you recall how, a few years ago, at the wedding of one of the English Rothschilds which was performed in a synagogue the English aristocracy headed by the Prince of Wales, the future king, participated? The same spectacle was recently repeated at the wedding of the daughter of the head of the Paris branch. There, too, the cream of French society was represented, a prince from the House of Orléans and many ambassadors and envoys from the courts of Europe. This event signifies two things: the loyalty of this house to its religion and the great respect it enjoys in the highest circles. In France at the present time high society considers it bad taste to be married in a religious ceremony. But unperturbed, Alphonse de Rothschild had the rabbis with their Hebrew blessings officiate at his wedding. Let me add, tangentially, that the envoy of the Spanish crown, a state which till the end of the last century knew Jews only as candidates for the stake, represented his king at the Rothschild wedding. What a remarkable turn of events![30]

Thus a family, whose ancestors a century ago in Frankfurt were still subjected to the most humiliating treatment and to whom every shabby Christian burgher could call, "Clear out, Jew!" if he was caught walking at the wrong time near the town hall or on the pavement, can now mingle on equal terms with the most powerful men in the world. However, among ourselves we can admit that the huge sums of money accumulated in the hands of Jewish bankers in Paris, London, Vienna, Berlin, Frankfurt and probably also in St. Petersburg are still basically only illusions of paper which, like the dragons of children, can rise as readily as they can fall.

But this phenomenon has its noteworthy origins. If you are interested, I'll explain it to you briefly. Christianity, which confiscated the heavens, and feudalism, which confiscated the earth, both deprived Jews of the right to own land. Forced into trade, and suited for the import-export business by virtue of the connections they maintained with their far-flung coreligionists, the Jews became the major holders of liquid capital. The unbelievably stupid legislation of the Middle Ages forced the Jewish capitalists to lend money on the basis of pledges and to charge high rates of interest. Of course, both the large and small rulers, the actual legislators, acted here to their own advantage, for liquid capital which lies in the possession of only a few men can be more easily and effectively confiscated than that which is dispersed among many. As a result of this compulsion, the Jews acquired the skill of manipulation, to make still better use of their liquid assets. With the discovery of America the gold treasures of Peru came to Spain, a development which coincided with the expulsion and forced conversion of the Jews on the Iberian peninsula, and great Jewish banking houses sprang up. Spain became impoverished by the discovery of America, but the Jews garnered millions. To be sure they were ex-Jews, the so-called Marranos, but in two respects they remained Jews: in their inner disposition—they could never come to recognize Christianity as a higher form of religion—and in their livelihood—they knew how to handle money frugally. In the sixteenth century, the Mendes Nasi family with its branches already consituted a kind of House of Rothschild. Kings and states were indebted to them. The same rank was later attained by Suasso in Amsterdam and Texeira in Hamburg. Jewish capitalists helped found the Giro bank in Hamburg. Some credit the Jews with the doubtful service of having invented bills of exchange.[31] Perhaps. But at least it is certain that they did provide the system of exchange with a wide area of operation and considerable impetus. The ex-Jews or pseudo-Christians in Spain, Portugal, and America, whose lives and wealth were by no means secure under the watchful eyes of the Inquisition, transferred their liquid cash, their silver and gold bullion from America to their fellow Jews in Italy, Amsterdam, Hamburg, and London, taking in return bills of exchange whose value was guaranteed and which were passed from hand to hand. This was the beginning of the circulation of paper money. Thus capital accumulated in the hands of Jews and increased to millions, making their possessors indispensable. Princes employed them as agents for their courts and financial advisers. The intolerance of the Christians transformed the Jews into the kings of finance. Renan expressed this strikingly in the lecture he delivered on the 27th of May: "This is one of the punishments of the proscribers, namely the advantage they grant to the proscribed."[32]

Doesn't this remind you of the words of the Bible: "They will enslave and afflict you for many hundreds of years and then the afflicted will depart with great wealth" [Genesis 15:13–14]. To be sure, if the frenzy of the Crusades, the delusions during the Black Death, and the bloody fanaticism of the Inquisition had succeeded in wiping out the Jews root and branch, then of course they never would have reached this period of prosperity. We can thus observe the indestructibility of the Jews also from this angle. After the Black Death, German cities which had ravaged the Jews most cruelly and had passed legislation sealed with an oath never to readmit Jews, again invited them to come and settle. Spain, after its successful expulsion of Jews yearned for Jewish doctors, jurists, and artisans. From the seventeenth century on, as the experience of Holland, Hamburg, Bordeaux, and the Italian cities attested that the wealth and business acumen of the Jews was creating a flourishing prosperity, a veritable rivalry arose among nations bidding for the despised sons of Jacob. Can't you see in this the finger of God or, if you wish, the rectifying justice of history?

However, the Jews possessed still other assets besides capital and means of exchange. The hardships of life or, as they say today, the struggle for existence steadily sharpened their spirit from generation to generation enabling them to devise the means for self-preservation. The Jewish religion in no way restricts the development of intelligence and never demands the sacrifice of intellect. On the contrary, the Talmud, which since the demise of political independence

has surrounded Judaism to a certain extent with a Chinese
wall and distanced it from any contact with the outside world
and from general intellectual currents, provided the Jews with
sufficient intellectual nourishment, honed them, and rendered
them clear-sighted and astute. The passion to learn and the
drive to study became habitual and led from the onesidedness
of talmudic studies to other, so to speak, worldly studies such
as medicine, science, philosophy, and especially to the art of
criticism, which meant never to be satisfied with the given but
to analyze it in terms of ideas and to extract the truth. Spinoza
did not become the critic of pure reason by virtue of his
classical, philosophical training, but through his talmudic
studies.

In the days during which the leading classes of Christendom could not read or write and were forced to make use of a
churchman (cleric), an *homme de lettre,* that is, a man who
knew how to spell and thereby was considered a scholar, the
Jews in the main were to a certain extent literati. The
consequences of this familiarity with books were startling. As
the wall of separation was slowly breached and ultimately
fell, as Jewish youth was granted entry into the higher schools
of learning, it literally plunged into the humanities and the
academic fields even without the prospect of getting an
official position. At the outset, it was the purest drive to study.
Compulsory school attendance did not have to be introduced
for the Jews. Jewish youth streamed to the schools. In Russia
edicts were issued against the hordes of Jewish students.

And now, dear friend, take a look at what the Jews have
achieved in less than one century. They perform well in all
branches of science and literature and in some they are the
leaders. Let me only mention that the young science which
intends to solve the riddle of the future and eradicate poverty
is led by Jews; David Ricardo, Karl Marx, and Ferdinand
Lassalle, the three saints of socialism, were of Jewish descent.
Of course, I regard this theory of happiness, according to
which every worker could have a chicken in his pot, as a sad
illusion. As long as the majority of mankind is not ethically

raised to a higher level, wickedness and crime will not cease, and they are the main cause of poverty. But, still, the insight is a good one. The social-economic system, if you please, stems from Jewish soil. It manifests strong powers of observation, careful reckoning or, put another way, logical talmudic analysis plus critical ingenuity.[33]

Now what did I really want to say? I have lost the thread and jumped from subject to subject. Actually I wanted to show you that the Jews attained their prominence in financial as well as intellectual matters quite innocently. Endless struggle has awakened in them the energy of the intellect, and since the circumstances that produced this result still obtain in some countries, the consequences also occur which evoke the bitter complaints of old women. The Jews in Germany, to a certain extent in Austria, and in the barbaric lands of Eastern Europe are still excluded from many careers. Therefore they must devote themselves to the cultivation of the intellect, to the acquisition and utilization of knowledge.

The most recent product of this intellectual activity, a child of the French Revolution, is particularly cultivated by Jewish paladins of the intellect; I am referring to journalism, the organ of public opinion, the second great unofficial power next to money. The major prerequisites are a critical bent and careful observation, both of which are part of their natural endowment; the intricacies of form and style they quickly learned. All the talk about the Jewish press rests on ignorance or intentional deception. There is no Jewish press in the sense that the editors of newspapers with wide circulation represent the interests of Jews or Judaism. On the contrary, many of the leading journalists, on the basis of terrible ignorance, speak of Judaism as disparagingly as do the alleged Christian apologists of the Jews, treating it as the product of a thousand-year more or less harmful illusion. In the feuilleton of the *Neue Freie Presse* or in the *Journal des Débats* you can often read brilliant articles by Jewish authors, which could easily have been written by Jew-haters, if they were only decent stylists. However, although the existence of a Jewish

press is about as true as a special Jewish order or the blood
libel, it is still correct insofar as the Jews generally play a large
role in determining the newspaper's direction either as the
writers of bad articles, political correspondents, or feuille-
tonists. Is it really nothing to belong to the upper ten thousand
who constitute public opinion or the "world"? And are you
not amazed at the long road and morphological process from
Joshua and Saul, who slew the Amalekites with the edge of
the sword, down to Belinfanti and Schlesinger, who slew the
Philistines in the *Times* and *Revue des deux mondes* with the
tip of the feather?

Since this letter also has come out too long, I will break off
and leave it to your logical ability to make the application.

Your

Caspi

NINTH LETTER

Dear friend,

I can't quite follow your deduction; perhaps my female
logic to which you alluded so nastily at the end is simply
inadequate. Are you trying to prove that it is the vocation of
Jews to accumulate a lot of money and to write good or bad
articles for the upper or lower half of the newspaper page? A
good friend of mine has summarized your long-winded
address with its simple message in three small words, in fact
in three letters. The Jews need three G's in order to survive:
Geld (money), *Geist* (intellect) and *Geduld* (patience). This
service should not be valued too highly. To translate from the
language of the salon into that of the common man, a Monte
Cristo is a Midas, a journalist is a Catiline[34] and long-suffer-
ing victims are called in Italian *poverini* (poor guys). Is this
why the Jews have tormented themselves for three or four
thousand years, so that a few banks could extend huge loans
and form companies for major undertakings or that poorly or
well-paid journalists could write for or against something or
someone? You remind me of an Irish girl I know, a passionate

enemy of England, who once insisted that the mission of her people was to destroy England, Scotland, and Wales as Joshua destroyed the people of Canaan. For this purpose God had the gold mines of California discovered so that the Irish could 'dig out the treasures and use them to gain the upper hand against England. Admittedly my analogy is weaker than most. But I find just as little logical connection between the continued existence, goal, and vocation of the sons of Jacob and the gold barons and top journalists among them as I do between the hostile aspirations of the Irish against the English and the discovery of gold in California. You must enlighten me a bit further with your masculine logic and show me the connecting links which you have incorporated in your theory.

Your friend,
Edith

TENTH LETTER

Dear friend,

One should not admit to a woman that she is right, because she will detect therein the concession that she is never wrong. Nevertheless, I will grant you that your objections are in order. I began at the wrong end and you correctly perceived gaps in my reasoning or illogical statements. But I had no idea that our correspondence on the subject of Jews and Judaism would become so extensive. Otherwise I would have started from the beginning and determined the necessary point of departure. So let me now fill in the missing pieces, though I will have to strain your patience and understanding somewhat, for I must broach the fields of theology and Bible. However, since you are English and therefore know your Bible, I will be spared the need of extensive commentary.

Indeed, we Jews do have a vocation and in fact one of the most attractive there is. This vocation or mission was depicted for our ancestors at the very beginning; it is clear, comprehensible and needs no commentary. You know the verse in Genesis in which God speaks to Abraham: "I have called him so that he would command his sons and his house after him that they follow the way of the Lord, to practice justice and mercy" [Genesis 18:19]. How long has it been since this verse and what goes with it have been written down? According to the usual assumption, some sixteen hundred years before the Christian era; that would make it more than 3000 years ago. Do you wish to be critical and subtract something from this time span? I'll grant you five hundred years, but still an inspired biblical author has established the premise that the descendants of Abraham have a vocation and that it consists in the practice of virtue. You shrug your shoulders as you think of the shouting Jewish peddlers in London's Pettycoat Lane or the Jewish porters in Amsterdam or the sorry-looking Russian refugees of recent years, for in these stunted figures you can't find a trace of Abraham's testament to his posterity. And even if you juxtapose the ideal and reality in such a glaring contrast you cannot portray it more graphically than did the eloquent prophet some 2400 years ago when he spoke sarcastically of the apostolic office of the Jewish race.

> Hear, you deaf,
> And look, you blind, that you may see.
> Who is blind, if not my servant,
> And deaf, if not the messenger whom I send?
> Who is as blind as my emissary
> And as deaf as the servant of God?
> You have seen many things but retain none,
> You keep your ears open yet hear nothing.
> The Lord intended for His holiness' sake
> To make the teaching great and glorious,
> But this is a people robbed and plundered,
> All of them are crouched in holes
> And hidden in prison-houses,
> They serve as prey
> And no one comes to rescue,
> As spoil and no one says: "Restore."

> Who abandoned Jacob to plundering,
> And Israel to the robbers?   [Isaiah 42:18–22, 24]

Here you have the contrast between the ideal and its caricature sharply juxtaposed. The apostle is deaf and blind, an object of derision. In spite of this, the very same prophet never despaired of the mission assigned the Jewish people. On the contrary, he preached incessantly and with great poignancy to his "deaf" audience of its holy mission, and for the "blind" he held aloft the vision of a majestic future.

What a pity that his name is unknown; we merely call him the "great anonym" or the Second Isaiah. This prophet spoke of our mission both in exuberant and logically sober terms, delineating it comprehensibly. Precisely in the role of the slave, in which Israel appears openly with its bodily wounds, that is, in the deepest humiliation, he perceived in an extraordinary fashion a vehicle of its apostolic glory. At the outset of his description of the contrast between the brilliant ideal and the repulsive reality he depicts the role of this apostolic people:

> Behold, My servant, on whom I rely,
> The chosen one, in whom I have pleasure,
> On him have I given My spirit,
> That he might reveal righteousness to
>   the nations.
> He shall not cry or fume,
> Nor let his voice be heard in the streets.
> A bruised reed he shall never break,
> A flickering wick he shall not quench,
> For the sake of truth he shall reveal the
>   right.
> He shall not quench nor crush,
> Until right is established on earth,
> And the islands will heed his teaching.   [Isaiah 42:1–4]

Are you not struck by this poetic yet at the same time comprehensible, almost modern language? The designated

missionary to the nations should not preach death and
destruction in the stentorian voice of a Capistrano, nor even
push aside that which has decayed, but rather he is to
accomplish his Messianic work by means of his extraordinary
suffering. He is to dedicate himself as a sacrificial offering and
to be brought like a lamb to the slaughter, never opening his
mouth. The bringer of good tidings is to be both a priest and a
sacrifice. Whenever I look at the Jews of the present and at the
tragic history of this race and begin to question our fate, I
need only leaf through the book of this richly consolatory
prophet to find reassurance and to hope for the improvement
of the deaf and the blind. Let me quote you just one more
passage that expands his view greatly.

> Listen to me, O islands, and hearken,
>   you nations from afar,
> The Lord has called me from the womb,
> From the bosom he has used my name,
> He made my mouth like a sharp sword,
> With the shadow of His hand He hid me,
> He made me a chosen arrow
> And hid me in His quiver.
> He spoke to me: "You are my servant, Israel,
> In whom I glory."
> But I thought that I have labored in vain,
> For nought and a puff of air have I spent
>   my strength.
> Still my justice is with the Lord and my reward
>   with God.
> Now, however, spoke the Lord, who formed me from
>   the womb to be His servant,
> To bring Jacob back to Him and to gather Israel,
> So that I am honored in the eyes of the Lord,
> And my God has become my strength.
> He said: "It is a small task to raise up
>   the tribes of Jacob,
> And to restore the offspring of Israel.
> I have made you the light of the nations,
> That My Salvation might reach the end
>   of the earth."   [Isaiah 49:1–6]

If this passionate language does not convince you that we Jews have had a mission from the very beginning and that we should fulfill it as servants and despite the role of servant, then I will not waste another word on the subject.

Your
Caspi

ELEVENTH LETTER

Dear friend,

The rationalistic theologians call the words of wisdom of the Old Testament prophets oracles, and oracles require interpretation. You interpret the eloquent address of the Second Isaiah, as you call him, as referring to the messianic people. Christian theology, as you well know, explains it as referring to a messianic personality and finds in the fifty-third chapter of this book, which you regarded as foretelling the suffering of the sons of Jacob, a clear allusion to the lamb of God, the crucifixion, and salvation.

Does this oracle refer to this man or that people? I am also somewhat familiar with the field of biblical exegesis. I also know that the Reverend Pusey, the head of the pro-Catholic party in the Anglican Church and Regius Professor of Hebrew at Oxford has collected for edification the various interpretations of this passage; there are no less than fifty-four different interpretations.[35] An orthodox Protestant commentator explains it as a kind of oratorio and even some Jewish commentators refer it to the Messiah and not to the apostolic nation. For mysticism is contagious like miasma and Jewish lore also appropriated a type of suffering Messiah. But I am wandering. I merely wanted to take my revenge, to repay your bantering in kind. Let's stick to the facts. For the proof from Scripture you don't really offer seriously. The elliptic pronouncements of the prophets are not very cogent if they are not confirmed by facts. Therefore you correctly emphasize the latter in your proof. Let me summarize your factual argument. On the one hand, the amazing tenacious survival of the Jews over hundreds of years of pain and suffering; on the other, their intellectual energy by which they have in a short time raised themselves to a major unofficial power. The latter is an achievement that deeply perturbs the narrow-minded, though, as far as we can see, they are unable to change it provided we remain true to ourselves. From this you conclude that we are called upon in this new age of nations, beginning with the French Revolution which transformed the world from top to bottom and helped achieve equality for the Jews partially as a completed fact and partially as a commanding principle, I mean to say that in this new age we are called upon to count as an active force and thus the fulfillment of our mission is now more evident. Have I interpreted your trend of thought correctly?

But you must allow me one objection. Your arguments rest on facts of a secular nature, and that corresponds, by and large, quite nicely with the present state of the Jews who have likewise become fully secularized. But it corresponds very little with the ideal task assigned us, to become the teacher of the nations in matters of justice and truth, in short, to found the kingdom of heaven on earth. Moreover, the term "Jewish mission" or "the mission of Judaism" strikes me as a worn-out phrase. Of what does it really consist or of what should it consist? Berthold Auerbach, the victim of recent anti-Semitic agitation, expressed before his death in a letter to Döllinger the following noteworthy sentence: "The mission designated for the Jews by virtue of their amazing preservation during an incomparable history of martyrdom will be fulfilled."[36] But death prevented him from answering my request for an explanation of what actually should be fulfilled. Usually the dissemination of monotheism is invoked as their vocation. That strikes me as very problematic. Castelar's statement in a letter that "only the tenacity of such a people could preserve the idea of God's unity untarnished" sounds hollow to me.[37] If the atheists, who, with few exceptions, are among the leading intellectuals of our age, if the scientists from Tyndall to Haeckel[38] empty the heavens of God, then the service of the

Jewish race in disseminating and popularizing the unity of God would not be valued so highly. Monotheism would then be as much of an illusion as polytheism, the former the product of a hastily drawn conclusion, the latter an exercise in fantasy. You're still not rid of me! Let me be a little long-winded in this letter, a privilege to which as a woman I am really entitled. Is it really the case that Jehovah originally belonged only to Judaism? An Egyptologist once whispered to me that he had read somewhere about Jehovah in an Egyptian papyrus, that monotheism was in fact the invention of the priests of the Egyptian god Amen-Ra. Others insist that the unity of God was taught in the esoteric Greek mystery cults in contrast to that which was represented exoterically in the official polytheistic religion. Nevertheless, I place no great worth on this objection, for unlike the field of inventions, in matters of faith the question of who is first is unimportant. What counts is the strength of the commitment. No nation acknowledges with such fervor the verse "Hear, O Israel, our God is one," and what is still more significant, no nation has sacrificed its happiness and life itself for this belief as we have done.

If, however, the mission of the Jewish people rests solely in disseminating the idea of monotheism, then it has already been fulfilled. For indeed it brought first Christianity and then Islam into the world and through these daughter religions the civilized nations have become monotheistic. It could thus depart from the stage and leave to the Christian missionaries the further work of spreading this truth. Or do you believe that these adherents are not true monotheists, because in addition to God they have adopted an intermediary, and the Moslems also get pretty close to deifying Mohammed? If so, then Judaism would really have achieved very little in its 3000 years of labor. At best it overcame in the civilized countries the crudest forms of idolatry, and even this not fully. Still unanswered is the question whether the religions stemming from Judaism have made men better and happier. Not a few poets and thinkers mourn the demise of a paganism bursting with life, of an Olympian serenity in whose stead has come a nervous churchliness which through its constant awareness of death no longer lets one imbibe the foamy cup of joy.

The above is not an example of female logic. I am not interested in adorning myself with strange ideas. I have learned these things from serious and intelligent men. Thus you must answer me seriously.

Your friend,
Edith

TWELFTH LETTER

Dear friend,

This time you, or the man who said these things first, are partially right. The history of nations and religions has by and large established the fact that religious feeling and worship were utterly unable to achieve a satisfactory level of morality, neither Judaism nor Christianity nor polytheism. The most fervent prayer at home or in the cathedral to the accompaniment of the organ and the singing of Te Deum along with all the religious pageantry were unable to break the power of man's evil inclination, his egotism and bestiality, let alone to arouse a lasting virtuous behavior if it did not strike deep roots in his soul. The belief in one God or many gods or in the Trinity, and the fear of punishment in heaven or hell have rarely if ever changed a corrupt man. At best they have channeled his energies in another direction, namely to commit atrocities approved by public opinion for the sake of God's greater glory and to generate religious fanaticism: in behalf of paganism to give Socrates a cup of poison because he repudiated the gods; in behalf of Judaism to slaughter the priests of Baal; and in behalf of Christianity to declare heretics free game, to build stakes for Jews and Moslems, and to burn witches. On the other hand, men who are intoxicated with genuine religious feeling and devote their entire life to religion sink into lethargy and are absolutely incapable of

performing an energetic act. Man's inherent animal nature—
for all I care Darwin's animal atavism—or his congenital
sinfulness—for all I care original sin—cannot be cured or
moderated by religion alone. To do so requires long centuries
of constant practice and habituation. But your lofty culture,
dear friend, is as incapable as religion of driving out desires
and lusts that are only intensified by refinement. It only
conceals them beneath a beautiful exterior. You remember
what I wrote you once regarding Europe as a hospital for
incurables. This horror developed right under the eyes of a
cultured and religious world.

Still, people talk of a moral theology, decidedly accentuat-
ing the word moral. Since faith has lost its power of appeal,
morality becomes the tugboat to pull theology. Or it is said
that theology gave birth to morality and, for the sake of its
lovely daughter, we should continue to respect the mother,
even if she is somewhat old-fashioned. This widely shared
opinion is entirely false. Émile Burnouf, the incisive critic of
the history of religion, observes quite correctly: "In itself
religion has no connection with morality. Only later did the
churches claim to impose on their adherents rules of conduct
and commandments; thus only in the course of time was
morality introduced into the different religions."[39] This
historical critique is quite relevant and appropriate to the
examination of the various forms of the Aryan religion.
Neither the Indian nor Greco-Roman cults had anything to do
with morality. Abominations that outrage the sentiments of
ethical man were precisely among the commandments of
these religions. Just as little did Christianity adopt morality as
its starting point. Its point of departure was rather redemption; it set its sights on the world beyond to free the faithful
from the power of Satan and to assure their resurrection or
immortality. However, this entire distinction is an academic
question. In actual fact, morality as the twin or adopted sister
of religion has not exerted the kind of influence in the history
of nations to make jails and jailers, doctors, and hospitals for
venereal diseases unnecessary. On the contrary, the latter

continue to increase at a startling rate, as I showed you once in figures. Will this malady eventually lead to death or is a cure still possible?

If you remember, I have referred previously to the comprehensive statistical study of morals by Alexander von Oettingen who has exposed the festering wounds of the civilized world in all their repulsive hideousness for the single purpose of proposing a cure. What is his prescription? "The recognition of the moral law as stemming from God, as being a vital factor in social life and operating in the guise of conscience in every man." This miracle is to happen "through the royal law of love, whose root is faith and whose crown hope."[40] In another place, this moral theologian who wants to base theology on statistics asserts that organized religion is a necessary condition, a system of healthy religious-ethical realism. But not just any organized religion or Christianity in general, not love "nor the pietistic reformed version, nor the orthodox Roman version, i.e., Catholicism, nor the "idea of the protestors" (as the author calls the Association of Protestants), can heal this abscess of immorality, but only the Lutheran version.[41] In that case, ailing mankind would have to wait a long time for this remedy merely to begin to take effect. Lutheranism or Protestantism, but only the correct version, must first absorb or convert the false views on the right and left, then the countless denominations in England and America, and then it must still assimilate the not-so-easy-to-digest Catholicism, the Uniat and Greek Churches, etc. And, furthermore, if faith, love and hope, or organized religion, were actually a talisman against vice and crime, then the current frightening state of the civilized world could scarcely have arisen. The long period from the Church's victory over polytheism under the Constantines till the Reformation and, later, contained faith and hope in superabundance (but dreadfully little love) but still contributed to the ethical elevation of nations much less than Humanism, which was unaffiliated with the Church. A sick world cries for health and they offer it grace and rosaries.

Tell me, dear friend, which of the two human inclinations, egotism or the one they cover with the fig leaf and call love, which of these two effects the most irreparable harm, not only on the individual but on the entire social complex, for nations and states? Mylitta brought about the disintegration of the Asiatic states, Aphrodite that of the Greeks, and Venus that of the Roman state of iron. A Greco-Jewish sage succinctly characterized polytheism and its ethical effect thus: "The introduction of idols was the beginning of lewdness and their invention, the degeneration of life." The abominable symbol of all the ancient religions was the lingam, a term whose meaning you can find in the dictionary. The goddess of infamy still continues to ravage the marrow of the spinal cord of the civilized world. Antiquity was little more than a huge public house of infamy, and modern civilization has merely transformed it into private houses. The showing of nudes in all art exhibitions whether in the form of Venus or that of the repentant Magdalena, the rush to Makart's sensual colors of flesh, and the intense interest in so-called academies that destroy any sense of shame and against which the police have moved in vain, prove sufficiently that the cult of Aphrodite still has enthusiastic adherents in our civilized world. And now, in addition, the filthy novels à la Zola.

Can you guess the secret now as to why the smallest and weakest of nations has overcome the great and powerful ones? Because from the very beginning its teaching has most decisively abhorred the cult of Aphrodite. Its fundamental law, I mean the Ten Commandments on the stone tablets whose antiquity no one disputes, includes as its sixth injunction: "You shall not be lewd." It is not directed exactly at an individual, but at the entire people and, like the fourth commandment, it could also have been provided with the rationale "That you may live long upon the earth." This basic book of Judaism reveals clearly and unmistakably the simple though seldom accepted insight that the survival or demise of nations is determined by the observance or violation of the laws of sexual morality. The chapter dealing with incest and the animal passions of man is introduced with the following words: "You should not behave according to the practices of the land of Egypt, where you lived, nor according to those of the land of Canaan, where I am taking you, nor walk in their ways, but keep My law by which man can live" [Leviticus 18:3,5]. And after the enumeration of what constitutes sexual immorality, the Bible adds: "For the nations have defiled themselves with all these abominations and the land itself has become defiled and vomited out its inhabitants and the land will also vomit you out if you defile it, as it vomited out the people before you" [Leviticus 18:27–28]. The pagan style of life cannot be more briefly characterized than the way in which it has been done by Döllinger. But I must render it in French translation, because the German sounds too indecent. "Sexual gratification was a component of the religious cult." If you are interested in appreciating the opposite of this, then read Döllinger's basic study which rests firmly on primary sources, *Heidenthum und Judenthum, Vorhalle zur Geschichte des Christentums* (Paganism and Judaism, Anteroom to the History of Christianity).

Can one fail to appreciate, even for a moment, that the fundamental law of Judaism sets up sexual restraint as the elixir of life not only for the individual but also for the entire national body to insure the survival of the community?

And these repeated warnings against debilitating carnal pleasures did not remain a mere dead letter for the Jewish people but inculcated noble and moral patterns of behavior. The sons of Jacob took bloody revenge against the violation of their sister, and when their father condemned the act fearing reprisal, they refuted his criticism with the words: "Should we let our sister be treated like a prostitute?" [Genesis 34:31]. Are you not struck by the story of Joseph? His seducer tries daily to ensnare him but he remains chaste and answers her: "How could I commit this great evil? I would surely be sinning against God" [Genesis 39:9]. Can you find in the history of ancient nations and religions, no matter what race, even the smallest counterpart to the self-control of this youth?

Both Aryan and Semitic tribes would have regarded such imperviousness to an offer whose acceptance guaranteed satisfaction but whose rejection entailed the most unpleasant consequences, as unbelievable stupidity. I could cite for you still many other examples from the ancient history of Israel which all prove the same thing: that sexual modesty became an inviolable moral pattern of the Jewish people and that disregarding it carried social opprobrium. When Amnon trapped his half-sister Tamar, she defended her purity with the touching words: "Such an act must not happen in Israel; don't commit such an abomination, where shall I carry my shame? You would become one of the most abhorred men in Israel" [II Samuel 13:12–13]. The popular King David was overcome by passion at the beauty of a married woman. And the prophet did not spare him, but threw the crime in his face: "You are the man in the fable" [II Samuel 12:7].

Through the force of religion and a standard of morality acquired over centuries, sexual modesty became in Israel a basic life-preserving factor. Tacitus believed to have saddled the Jews with a blemish, but instead delivered an encomium for their self-control in a period when the Roman Empire was ravaged by the most shameful depravity. He pictures them as refusing to eat with and to marry non-Jews, adding: *projectissima ad libidinem gens alienarum concubitu abstinet.* Since I cannot assume that you will understand Tacitus's elliptic Latin style, let me translate it for you into the language which best provides a decent veil for matters of the flesh: "Although strongly inclined to sexual gratification, this people abstains from love affairs with strangers."[42] What a favorable piece of evidence did this Roman historian submit regarding the Jews of his day. Indeed, everything rests on self-control. To impose the intellect as a control over fervent passion at the moment of greatest intensity and to say like Joseph: "Never must I commit this abomination for I would sin thereby against God"—this achievement is worth the highest price. When with typical Roman arrogance Tacitus defames the Jews by adding, "among themselves nothing is forbidden," it means very little. How could he know anything about the domestic life of the Jewish people? The criticism suited far better the Roman licentiousness which followed their great conquests. Under Roman rule, as the patriotism of the Jews intensified, their sexual modesty was exemplary. This is why they were able to confront the colossal might of the Roman legions with hundreds of thousands of healthy, tenacious fighters, who lost only because of their numerical weakness. During the Middle Ages, when the Jews were constantly threatened with persecution and violent death, sexual crimes among them were of course impossible. For the modern period the statistical evidence is favorable. In the five large German states of Prussia, Bavaria, Württemberg, Saxony, and Hanover, in the year 1851, the number of illegitimate births reached the frightening figure of more than 100,000. In Prussia alone the annual rate from 1851 to 1870 jumped from 53,000 to 70,000. In contrast, the number of illegitimate births among the Jews is inconspicuously small. My resource man, von Oettingen, observes in a footnote: "In many sectors (of Germany, which in comparison to the Romance-speaking nations is still cool and sober) sexual experience before marriage in order to find a husband and capture 'the goods' is domestic policy." He also records the experience of a pastor from the district of Kurmark who confirms how domestic immorality leads thousands almost unknowingly into the pitfall of premarital intercourse.[43] Thus the palm branch for sexual restraint belongs from antiquity to the present solely to the people of Israel. This behavior pattern and its attendant self-preservation prove sufficiently that the cell is not the tyrannical mistress of man. On the contrary, it is the will, supported and strengthened by diligent training, which tames and governs the inclinations and passions of matter. Thus the spirit if it be energetic and tenacious enough can be master of the organism. The argument against materialism which derives from this data is by no means insignificant. Of course the proof is only fully valid vis-à-vis the past. Whether there are Josephs among the idle rich Jewish youth or even in the adult world is doubtful. Also in this regard they are affected by European culture. But the distaff side of Jewry still holds the palm branch of chastity aloft. The words of Scripture have been confirmed: a nation that sinks to the level of animals will be spewed forth. That means that as a result of internal weakening it will be conquered, expelled, and pulverized. This was the fate of all the nations of antiquity from the Egyptians and Assyrians to the Greeks and Romans. The Jewish people alone has survived antiquity to remain on the stage of history.

Can one really deny that the Jews have an apostolic mission, even if it were only to offer the proof that a nation need not succumb to death, even under the most unfavorable and dangerous conditions, as long as it maintains its health and thereby retains its vitality? If the critically sick civilized nations can be cured at all it is only possible by means of the hunger treatment prescribed by the teachings of Judaism. That is the mission of Israel of which the prophet Isaiah sings, namely to bring light to the nations.

I think this is not an insignificant task. And how much greatness and nobility are connected with it? Virtues and vices respectively hang together like the links of a chain. Just as wickedness produces a coarse character and crude egotism with all its ugly ramifications, so self-control and self-limitation give rise to a mild disposition, respect and love for others, a sense of justice, and a willingness to sacrifice—virtues which Judaism was the first to teach and to which it obligated its adherents.

This mission is formulated somewhat differently elsewhere in the Bible: "You shall be for Me a kingdom of priests and a holy nation" [Exodus 19:6], a statement designed to make us both proud and humble. That apostolic and priestly nation which is to bring light and holiness to the nations must itself manifest light and holiness, must itself be a holy nation. But are we? Self-examination must humble and sadden us. How distant are we from this ideal! But the ideal must and will be reached. How much of what the prophets foretold regarding us has not come true? Therefore, this too shall be fulfilled, that we will discard our unclean garments and put on clothes of light to be worthy of our exalted task. The real guarantee for this is our miraculous stubborn survival, our no less miraculous rise in recent years from the most humiliating oppression, and finally our apparent health which we preserved through rigorous self-control.

Think about this.

Your friend,
Caspi

THIRTEENTH LETTER

Wow! Dear friend,

That was not a letter but an essay which demanded all my powers of concentration and thought. My head is still reeling. In short, then, this is supposed to be the great task of the sons of Jacob: to offer the nations balsam to heal their mortal wounds. That reminds me vividly of the words of that prophet whose prophecies about Israel's destiny, its humiliation and elevation you have quoted several times in your letters. "Who had believed this report, . . . through the wounds of God's servant the nations were to be healed" [Isaiah 53:1, 5]. That agrees literally with your explanation. Either you have infected me, dear friend, with your quotations from Scripture or you have exalted me with your vision. I am almost ready to say that you have convinced me that every Jew and every Jewess ought to be filled with ecstasy about being a part of this apostolic nation which is to prescribe to both individuals and nations how to achieve health and longevity.

Indeed to be aware that one's petty life entails an important task is uplifting and inspiring. But as a woman, I must be allowed to voice a few objections. If you find them unwarranted, you won't hesitate politely to say, "What stupidity!"

First of all, you yourself appear to account for the point of departure which you have taken for Israel's vocation in physical or physiological terms, namely to show by analysis that it came about wholly naturally. You depict the tenacious survival of this collective Jewish body, though covered with wounds and bleeding from the forehead with its crown of thorns, as a miracle, for according to the laws of nature it should have been crushed long ago. And then you show that this collective body preserved its health through sexual restraint and thereby outlasted the world empires and mighty nations which arose in rapid succession. Where then is the miracle? The healthy naturally outlive the sick.

Furthermore, you appear to stress the admonishments of Judaism regarding modesty and restraint as a significant factor. They penetrated into the very flesh and blood of its adherents and effected wonders. Accordingly, chastity would be for Judaism a cardinal virtue and the commandment thereto a basic law (and not monotheism). I don't really have anything against this, but then all the other commandments of Judaism, namely those of a religious or a ritual nature, would seem to be superfluous? Or do they have some inner connection with this basic law, which escapes my feminine mind? Then, indeed, Judaism would refute the contention that morality originally had no connection with religion and was injected only later, a view you seem to share in your letters, for Judaism, you say, postulates the moral law of chastity as the highest principle and articulates it in religious terms. Aren't you contradicting yourself?

Finally—be patient with my questions—something personal is troubling me. You have imbued me with a certain respect for Judaism and the Jews. I am impressed with myself as something phenomenal. I seriously intend to live strictly as a Jew and to raise and instruct my children in such a way that they will be able to reject the abandoning of Judaism as a form of suicide. But how can I or you profess Judaism as it is now constituted with its thousands of injunctions and—don't be angry at me—with all its nonsense which, as they say, was contrived by the perverse talmudic or rabbinic mind and which renders us laughable not only in the eyes of non-Jews but also strike us as laughable? Should I tell my daughters: "You may not play the piano on the Sabbath and festivals, for it's a sin," as is done in the home of Sir Moses Montefiore and other highly respectable religious families in England? On trips, should I not enjoy the table d'hôte because this is stamped as a sin by Judaism? Must I compel my somewhat sickly son to languish for twenty-four hours on the Day of Atonement and to spend the day confessing sins which we don't even know and which would never enter our heads in a language we don't understand and which, if translated into the vernacular, would sound silly? Precisely when we wish to hold Judaism aloft as a powerful, world-historical force and as a source of intense ferment, the question imposes itself on us: are the demands which it makes on us, the sacrifices it calls for justified? Does this network of laws, prescriptions, and prohibitions, which are so numerous and so detailed that with every move you are liable to violate one of them, constitute an integral part of or a necessary supplement to Judaism from which it cannot be freed? That's bad enough, if this be the case! Now let me ask as a mother, whose children's future lies closest to her heart. It would be a painful prospect for me if my children or grandchildren would convert to Catholicism or Protestantism, as long as they are what they are. I would turn in my grave if my descendants would swell the ranks of those who must officially hate the Jews as the murderers of God, or wish to see them humiliated as Semites, or for whom the word Jew has long evoked a repulsive image. In any event they would learn to repeat from the Gospels the terrifying curse against them and their ancestors: "His blood be upon us and our descendants." Or should they join the liberal religion which in America constantly attracts more followers? That's all right for the Yankees. Pfui! How dull, tasteless, and insipid! Its apostles, Hinkley, Potter, and their followers, sacrifice not only God's son, redemption, including resurrection and immortality, and even God, but what's still more unpardonable, all poetry and every uplifting, emotional appeal that allows one to forget for the moment the prosaic routine of daily life. Despite its motto: "Freedom, character, and fellowship in religion," this stripped and glamorless universal religion or irreligious religion is to a great extent utilitarian. Just as love is called "selfishness for two" we might term this "selfishness for all." Its thrust is: I would like to domesticate my neighbor morally, as a wild animal is tamed, so that he will no longer bite.[44] I would be less offended if my grandchildren would profess the religion of the Quakers or Mormons, for they still manifest momentum and youth. But I would be entirely at peace only if I were sure that they would remain loyal to the religion of their heroic ancestors. I would energetically raise them in this direction, if I could only free myself from my own lingering doubts. At birth and during its first period, its days of betrothal, Judaism was so magnificent, colorful, and gorgeous, while at present it is petty, delapidated, and without poetry. Many of its commandments are so attractive, so rational, so morally uplifting—this you have already shown me—but then again others are so silly and petty. If you would only help me over this obstacle I would be most grateful to you.

Your friend,
Edith

FOURTEENTH LETTER

Dear friend,

I much prefer to see the impish manner with which you lightly and impersonally handle current events and intellectual developments than your present pensive, worried look. Had I suspected how seriously and scrupulously you would consider this subject, I would have avoided it. Since I am already involved let me try to smooth the wrinkles on your brow.

But first I must try to resolve the contradictions in which you think you caught me.

Take for example the case of seafarers on a ship which a

storm threatens to sink and a fire threatens to demolish, whose crew has been ravaged by a plague and whose survivors are confronted with starvation. Now if these seafarers, imperiled by a variety of mortal dangers, should suddenly find some unexpected relief, will they not be able to recover from their ordeal and deprivation and go on living, provided they are physically healthy? But doesn't their rescue still remain a kind of miracle, even if they enjoy sound health? Now apply this analogy to the Jewish people surrounded by thousands of mortal dangers. Had it been enervated by depravity and self-defilement like all the nations of antiquity, then it would have been unable to survive under any circumstances. But you would certainly admit that its preserved state of health did not bring about the miracle of its survival, but only enabled it, after enduring the danger of death, to recover and to continue living anew.

And now to my second alleged contradiction. Indeed, Judaism did once constitute an exception, namely that it entered the world as ethics, that this, so to say, represented the primary and cardinal aspect of its teaching, that religion, in contrast, was a secondary matter. Renan once proposed the apparently paradoxical but not untrue idea that the Jewish people have the simplest religion. "The Jewish people is both the most religious as well as the one which has the simplest religion." Do you recall the biblical verse that I once quoted to you that justifies God's selection of Abraham by the fact that he will obligate his descendants to practice righteousness? His selection "to become the father of a multitude of nations" was not made so that he might spread the belief in Jehovah, but rather that he would preserve the idea of morality among his progeny. Judaism, which can rightly complain about being so often misunderstood, is also badly misrepresented on this point. People believe they are paying it a really important compliment when they concede that it paved the way for monotheism. Lessing made this assumption as the point of departure for his *Erziehung des Menschengeschlechtes* (The Education of Mankind)—a divine system of pedagogy which is thoroughly fragile. Lessing, along with many, many others including Buckle, failed to understand that the monotheism of Judaism has only a negative import, namely an attitude of horror and abhorrence for polytheism, for the gods who served as models of depravity, for the cult of Baal and Astarte with its orgiastic worship, for the Babylonian-Assyrian Mylitta with its outrageous sexual rites, for Zeus, the kidnapper of girls, and Aphrodite, whom even Homer called the patron of lust. The passionate fire of the Bible against idols is not due so much to their being irrational nonentities or to their being regarded as demonic forces, which is why Christianity raged against Jupiter and Wotan, but rather solely because of the moral degeneracy which accompanied their cult. Please read Deuteronomy 12:31. "For all the abominations which God detests have they (the nations) performed for their idols; they even burn their sons and daughters for their gods." The human sacrifice of young women was by no means as outrageous as another religious rite practiced by the classical Greeks.

Let me repeat. The monotheism of Judaism has first and foremost a negative, that is an ethical import. The contention of Émile Burnouf that morality is a late religious development is correct in regard to the various Aryan and Semitic religions. Other races didn't even get that far. In contrast, Judaism, insofar as it comes to light in the oldest documents, most vigorously accentuates a higher ethic, especially sexual restraint.

Döllinger is partially right in his book *Heidenthum und Judenthum* (Paganism and Judaism) when he defines Judaism as sexual restraint codified by law. "Holiness was designated as the highest goal of the Law. Israel was to be holy because and in the manner in which God is holy; it ought to be able to discover the model for its own life in the holiness of Jehovah." So far so good. But the validity of his next sentence is doubtful. "It [Israel] must therefore be careful that all its actions within the state and the family should be a mirror for foreign nations, in which they can perceive the loftiness and holiness of Israel's revered God." The holiness which the Law of Judaism imposes on Israel as its highest duty is not a means to acquire the correct knowledge of God, but is an end in itself.

Let me add to this one other observation. On January 27 of this year, Ernest Renan delivered a lecture on Judaism before the Saint Simonians: "Judaism as Race and as Religion." On May 27 he delivered a second lecture before the Société des Études Juives: "Judaism and Christianity."[45] Both attracted a certain amount of attention, perhaps more among Jews. Practically speaking, we have good reason to be thankful to this masterful stylist for his friendly attitude. I don't want to prove to him that present-day Jews are not pure Semites but are mixed with Aryan or European blood. An infusion of Aryan blood entered their veins through marriage with those Greeks, Romans, and Galileans who during the period of Roman rule were attracted to Judaism and became proselytes. His contention is not new. It was raised earlier by Emile Burnouf, Karl Vogt, and others and we can ignore it. This theory of infusion would not disarm the anti-Semites even if it could be proven more convincingly. In fact their rage is also directed against those partial Jews born of mixed marriages. But this is *en passant*. Instead, let's take note of Renan's publicly delivered testimony at the last conference.

> The spirit of Isaiah, the spirit of the prophets prevails more and more (within the Jewish people). This is the spirit of Israel after the return from captivity and this spirit is summed up in the longing for a cult which would suit all of mankind, which rests on the ideal of the moral and the good. The reign of justice on earth, there is the fundamental idea of the ancient prophets.[46]

And elsewhere:

> The founders of such a movement were the First Isaiah, then the Second Isaiah at the time of the captivity, an extraordinary genius. They were the Essenes, those poets who proclaimed a

vision of peace, justice and fraternity. Christianity has also contributed mightily to the progress of civilization. . . . Early Christianity was merely the continuation of your prophets; the glory of Christianity is the glory of Judaism. Indeed the world has become Jewish by converting to the laws of justice, equality and liberty.[47]

Renan, a passionate Frenchman and supporter of the Republic, naturally glorifies the French Revolution which proclaimed justice and equality. Then he continues:

And who better than the Jewish people was able to accept a similar solution? It had itself prepared the way with its entire history, with its great prophets, the great creators of Israel who had proclaimed the future unity of the human species in law and justice.[48]

You will be still more amazed at the testimony which Renan, out of the goodness of his heart, submitted on our behalf, and if you spoke earlier in a somewhat sarcastic vein about our mission, you may now beseech Judaism for forgiveness. Listen to what Renan had to say on this subject.

And now that these great things have been accomplished, we can confidently say: Judaism which has served so well in the past will serve also in the future. . . . In short, the pure religion which we regard as capable of binding all humanity together will be the Jewish religion, freed from the dross which presently encumbers it.[49]

Thus Judaism can, should, and perhaps will someday become the religion of the world. That certainly would be the complete fulfillment of the prophecy of Second Isaiah whose precious words I have repeatedly recommended to your attention: that the servant of God, the despised and reviled people of Israel will bring light and salvation to the nations. But even this is intended only tangentially.

Nevertheless, I must challenge Renan's other assertion, which he stressed in both lectures with triumphant self-assurance, so that you are not taken in by his brilliant rhetoric. He propounded the view that only after the passage of many centuries did Judaism develop into a universal religion, that only after it had stripped itself of its narrow national traits did it acquire an ethical dimension. For this development he fixed the year 725 or at the earliest 800, namely the period of the great Prophets. This claim is by no means new. It is the favorite hypothesis of the critical-theological school and has been attractively propounded by the profound Dutch theologian Kuenen. But despite its respected spokesmen this theory is untenable. Is it really true that the prophets, and especially the First Isaiah, were the first to elevate Judaism to a pure, ethical religion? And Moses, who is admired by these Prophets as the greatest, contributed nothing? Is he to go away empty-handed? He did not reveal, teach or conceive the loftiness and ethical import of his *Ehyeh-Asher-Ehyeh* (I think I can assume that you understand this exalted man of God)? Did Jehovah mean no more for Moses than Kemash for the Moabites, a simple local deity, as Renan contends? And the two stone tablets with their ethical principles in which there isn't the slightest trace of a sacrificial cult, are they before or after Isaiah? Regarding this developmental theory, a German critic writing in the Munich *Allgemeine Zeitung* correctly observed the following:

> Any hypothesis which seeks to explain the development of biblical Judaism while passing over Moses or assigning him merely a minor role is bound to produce pangs of conscience. Whoever does not wish to consider Moses, the man of God about whom it is said no prophet was ever like him, as the instrument of divine revelation must still acknowledge him as the founder of the ethical system which has permeated the human race. It is quite possible that in the wild years of the Judges and during the political struggles of the Kings, the masses did forget the sublime teachings of Moses replacing them with a sacrificial and ritual system, but they continued to survive in the circles of the elite. The great prophets only revived them and brought them to the people.[50]

I must again risk exposing myself to your wit, dear friend,

by sending you once more a theological treatise instead of a letter. However, to respond to your questions and objections, I must fully expound the thoughts which you've provoked in me. Furthermore, in view of a long journey which will probably take me overseas, I will have to forgo the pleasure of corresponding with you for some time.

So that I will not owe you anything, let me return from this digression to our main theme. The biblical documents from the Pentateuch down to the last prophets emphasize ethics, the higher ethics, as being central. However, they cast the commandments of morality and holiness in a religious form as the will and command of God. And rightly so. Because for the actual practice and effectiveness of ethics it is by no means unimportant whether it be only a postulate of the categorical imperative, or, according to Haeckel, a sublimate of the brain's phosphorescence, or the dictate of the highest being. For the individual it may be more virtuous if he would realize the ideal of morality without a compelling religious or secular law. But no community could survive if it were left up to every single member to first construct the ethical life by his own thought process and, if he should fail, to forget about it. What kind of public life existed in the Christian communities during the period of the Apostles with their "evangelical freedom," which misconstrued the ethical obligations of Judaism as compulsion? The first Apostles themselves had to vigorously reprimand the rise of immoral behavior in the nascent communities, because the limitations of an inviolable law had been torn down. Therefore, the Church Fathers, pragmatic and free of evangelical exuberance, were compelled to seek refuge for the Christian communities in the law of Judaism as the word of God and to circumscribe the "evangelical freedom" which had led to such abominable excesses. Once Christianity gained political power the Church Fathers were instrumental in bringing the moral law of Judaism to penetrate secular law, and the former now constitutes a part of the general legal system—and this is what is called Christian culture. Since Judaism, from the very outset, intended to build a society, a *civitas Dei,* a state which "should rest on law, in which justice should find a place to dwell," it had to project ethics as a divine emanation.

But please do not misunderstand me, dear friend. While I am designating ethics as the diamond core of Judaism, I do not wish to deny its purely religious aspect or to conceal it from the unbelievers. No, no! Despite the fact that quite a few churchmen and political scientists do not regard Judaism as a religion or confession, it is still in the true sense of the word a religion, for it relates everything back to the supreme being. Judaism is not, however, a religion of devotional prescriptions and mystical ecstasy for it has a decidedly this-worldly orientation. I have already explained to you once that a religion which should attract adherents must rely on miracles and can survive only if the miracles continue. Which religion can show more conspicuous, striking miracles than Judaism? It does not have to squeeze them out of obscure texts or exhibit them in shrines laden with miraculous relics for they are visible in the flesh wherever Jews wander. You and I are likewise parts of this miracle.

If a supreme being should exist who cares about the fate of mankind and who providentially guides mankind toward a goal by stirring it to independent action, and if world history should turn out not to be a wild conglomerate of chaotic events, acts of violent aggression, and groveling submission in which successive nations alternately play the part of wolf and sheep, but, if, on the contrary, it constitutes a logical, multilinked chain of causes and effects leading to some final purpose, then certainly Israel, like all historically significant nations, belongs to this architectonic plan. It plays too great a role in the service of world history, as Renan himself was forced to admit in his first lecture when he said that "the Jewish race has rendered the greatest service to the world," for its existence to be without meaning. Consequently its survival or immortality is a providential work. Without such higher guidance this miracle would be even less comprehensible than under the assumption of divine providence.

Therefore, the prophets and psalmists related the survival of the people of Israel back to the omnipotent power of God. The Isaiah of the Exile, whom Renan greatly admires, has God say of His servant Israel: "When you pass through floods, I will be with you and rivers will not sweep you away; when you go through fire, you will not be singed, flames will not burn you, for I am your God, the Holy One of Israel" [Isaiah, 43:2-3]. Water and fire! They were not exactly figurative torments for the Jews. Let me just add the strikingly picturesque as well as literally true description of a psalm which more than two thousand years ago was dedicated to the miracle of Israel's survival. "'Were God not for us,' Israel may now say, 'Were God not for us, when men rose up against us, they would have swallowed us alive, when their wrath was kindled against us the flood waters would have swept us away'" [Psalms 124:1-4]. In the course of its long and troubled history, Israel has experienced the protection of a mighty and merciful God and in no way needs the recitation of a catechism to arouse belief in Him. In a noteworthy way, my favorite prophet expresses the idea that Israel's miraculous continuity proves the existence of God: "You are my witnesses that there is no God besides Me" [Isaiah 43:10, 11]. In any event this proof is more cogent than proofs like the ontological one which are concocted out of syllogisms. I don't want to deal here with the case of a Jewish philosopher of the twelfth century who was also a poet and who used this factual proof as the starting point of his own intellectual system. When the normative documents of Judaism admonish and impose obligations, they always have recourse to miracles which God has performed, and not those miracles which an unbeliever could doubt and ridicule, but those which render the continuity of the tribe of Israel believable. Judaism can tie its ethical tasks to the central proposition of religion, because the latter has become a fundamental conviction through the personal experience produced by Jewish history.

But enough for now, dear friend, of this highly interesting but unpopular subject. You are responsible. You struck the chord and I had to let it vibrate. But I can also not let pass your sarcastic comments regarding the practices of Judaism and the Talmud, especially since you asked me with the anxious concern of a mother for guidelines for the religious education of your children. First of all, let's not talk about the Talmud in terms of a cheap trump for ignorant and malicious men. In contrast to them, knowledgeable students find therein rich, untapped ethical treasures. In any case, its bright side far outweighs its dark side. Only the form and method of its analysis is baroque and not according to everyone's taste. The Talmud was, to a certain extent, the winter coat for the organism of Judaism during the period of freezing cold, the thorny protective covering of the four-o'clock. Such a cloak certainly disfigures the man who needs protection rendering him nearly unrecognizable, but in a situation where death threatens one can scarcely be concerned about attractive clothing. With the coming of spring the disfiguring cloak comes off by itself. How much of the Talmud has already crumbled since Moses Mendelssohn and the dawn of emancipation brought a fresh breeze to blow in Judaism! Not even the talmudic obscurantists can deny this; they see it in their own midst. But has spring fully arrived for the Jewish race? On this question opinions differ. The sad events of recent years have vindicated those who insist that for Israel the medieval winter is far from over.

Moreover, the Talmud is merely the most extreme result of the ritualism which the Pentateuch (the Torah), the main document of Judaism, peremptorily commands, though not as cardinal dogma—a position enjoyed by ethics and the idea of God—but rather as a means to realize the basic principles.

Although to a certain extent completed and full-grown since birth, Judaism has still elaborated, expanded, and unfolded itself, thereby outfitting itself for life. The ethical ideals were in some measure to become incarnate in a single tribal nation which was destined to accept the accompanying mission and martyrdom, at first glance a fantastic and unrealizable assignment. This tribe spent many generations in slavery, acquiring the primitive thought patterns of slaves or simply robbed of all ideas. It had to battle for a long time for the conquest of its own land and became barbaric. To be sure, the majority of the people did not worship and relate to their Jehovah any differently than did the Moabites to Kemash. To this extent Renan is right, except that we must always exclude a minority, no matter how small, who held aloft the Ark of the Covenant, not in pagan style as a victorious Palladium in time of war, but because of the ethical content of the two stone tablets inside. The proximity of the Canaanites and Phoenicians, who were by no means wiped out, corrupted the tribes with raw paganism, with the worship of Adonis and Astarte alongside that of Jehovah as the equally legitimate gods of the country. And this cult simply gratified the senses too much for it not to attract adherents. You, my biblically knowledgeable friend, know that Athaliah the queen, the daughter of the infamous Phoenician Jezebel, introduced the cult of Baal and Astarte into the Temple in Jerusalem. She supported this innovation with such force that those who abhorred these deities were compelled to conceal their opinions. At last a healthy reaction erupted with the High Priest Jehoiada cleverly leading the way. But it was easier to banish the pagan cult from the Temple than the pagan disposition from the hearts of the people. The same pattern of abandoning the pure worship of Jehovah and the subsequent reaction, as you well know, occurred often in the history of ancient Israel.

The ritualism of Judaism is the product of these events. It was to serve as a means of banishing pagan sentiments from the hearts of an intellectually lazy people. In fact it presents itself as such a means: "That you do not go astray after your heart and your eyes," or: "That you might remember." An overtly stated reason in one of the pentanteuchal laws reveals that the entire sacrificial system was adopted so that the inclination for offering sacrifices would not mislead the people to sacrifice at the orgiastic cults of the pagans: "So that you won't offer your sacrifices to the he-goats (symbol of lewdness) which you crave" [Leviticus 17:7]. The talmudic sages designate the ritual injunctions which they have introduced as a fence. The fence serves to prevent clumsy feet from trampling the delicate flowers of the garden. To be sure, the sages of the Talmud often overdid it, building one fence after another until their very number prevented the eye from seeeing the lovely garden with its gorgeous flowers. The ritual laws which take up so much of the second and third books of Moses are due to the same caution and apprehension; they are likewise fences. They represent, you might say, a kind of talmudic system before the Talmud. But the sages of the Talmud themselves teach and announce that in the messianic era—when the ethical ideal will have triumphed universally—this ritualism will cease to have any meaning. Are we that far yet?

Don't ridicule the rituals in toto for there are many whose purpose ought to be readily apparent. The dietary laws, which are part of the ritual system of Judaism, you find distateful. But ask the physiologists whether our food intake does not influence our temperament and character. The consumption of blood or the flesh of wild animals, if continued for several generations, certainly leads to a savage and licentious style of life. Who knows, maybe the refusal to eat certain foods calmed the Jews' soul and curbed their demonic passions.

One of the main arguments to prove the intolerance of the Jews rests on their separation from their non-Jewish environment. From Haman to Tacitus down to well-intentioned political scientists and professors, the accusation has been constantly repeated: *separati epulis, discreti cubilibus*.[51] (Your son probably knows enough Latin to translate this for you.) Those intent on harming us call this separateness "a state within a state." But what would have become of Judaism and its ethical mission if it had not taken over some dingy corner? You must always remember that the entire lot of pagan cults were orgiastic, that the entire lot under different names worshiped Aphrodite—and this worship led directly to the demise of these pagan nations. Ancient Israel was often enough seduced by this type of cult, and these relapses constitute the darkest pages in its history. It required all the persuasive power of those imbued by the ethical ideal of Judaism, especially the divinely inspired prophets, to overcome this tendency, for otherwise the ideal would have evaporated before it had begun to unfold. Therefore, Judaism could be preserved and perfected only through the most rigorous system of separation. It is for this reason that the ancient law invokes the necessity of a separating wall: "You shall be holy to Me because I, Jehovah, am holy and therefore I am separating you from the nations to be Mine" [Leviticus 20:26]. How many of the rituals have precisely this separatistic purpose? The national-historical meaning of these joyous festivals is given in the Law itself. They may well originally have been nature festivals, but then the assimilatory power of our religion is all the more evident because it succeeded in tying them to the very beginning of our nation's history. And at least official Christianity will also always be tied to the recollection of this fact. Do you seriously want to discard the Day of Atonement? If it didn't exist, it would have to be created. To deny the body for twenty-four hours, to attune oneself again to God, that is, to one's own conscience, and to precede this reconciliation with God by a reconciliation with other persons whom we have offended by word or deed, as dictated by that much maligned Talmud, all this is definitely not material for ridicule. Don't even the prosaic-looking Jews who observe this day with reverence betray a spark of idealism?

However, in the course of time the relationship and order of priorities changed. The prophets who spoke for Judaism in the biblical period accented the ethical side of Judaism with all their might. With fire and brimstone they censured the moral deficiencies of the people and their rulers, and they passed over in silence the problem of ritual or, at most, intoned the holiness of the Sabbath. In contrast, the sages who followed the prophets and spoke for Judaism in the post-biblical period emphasized ritual. Jeremiah, for example, deprecates the sacrificial system: "Consume your sacrificial animals as meat for I did not make sacrifices obligatory for your ancestors when I took them out of Egypt. . . . To practice justice and righteousness, to adopt the poor and suffering, that is the knowledge of God" [Jeremiah 7:21–22; 22:15–16]. In contrast, the first of the sages of the post-biblical or post-prophetic period whose words we have, Simon the Righteous, speaks an entirely different language. Jewish communal existence depends on three things: "On knowledge of the Torah, on sacrificial worship and on charity."[52] The ethical component is listed last. This reversal of priorities can be explained historically.

You ask further about how the cultured Jew should personally relate to ritual. Should he observe it? First of all, these elite Jews must consider their internal role. If they are convinced of the ethical mission of Judaism and wish to see it succeed, they must also win some influence over the lower echelons of Jewry, and consequently they must avoid withdrawing from the Jewish community. Precisely because they bemoan the fact that the masses misunderstand and violate the fundamentals of Judaism and because they earnestly wish to elevate them, they cannot treat ritual deprecatingly. Even if ritual were only a sign of unity, order and distinctiveness, it would still retain a relative and temporary value. Furthermore, life itself has demolished many of these rituals and the process goes steadily on. But those impatient people who are unable to allow this process of dissolution to occur naturally and wish forcibly to rip off this coat of ritual, violate the spirit of Judaism and destroy Jewish unity. Don't the most recent events show that the sense of unity and togetherness, which preserved us in our darkest days, is still needed? Those who precipitate a schism, whether from the left or the right, bear a heavy responsibility.

Now let me come back to you. If you, as an enlightened lady adorned with all the proper virtues, lead a comfortable life in London, own a charming villa in the country, and betray no trace of Jewishness, then you are simply an eminent lady like a hundred others. But should you also lead some kind of

Jewish life, then you would have some impact on the Jews lower than you and would be respected as a model. Of course if you eat out often the heavens won't fall. But your heroism would be greater if you would deny yourself this pleasure quietly to fulfill a mission. You don't have to sacrifice your intellect. Teach your children this example of moderation and the value of moderation in general, this fundamental virtue of Judaism by which the Jewish race preserved its health in the midst of universal degeneration. They will not abandon their faith nor intermarry, for intermarriage is only a delayed form of apostasy. You must especially impress upon your children that they will have to undertake a holy mission and that they must prepare themselves through self-restraint and sacrifice. George Eliot in her novel *Daniel Deronda* has one of her characters, the enlightened and religious Charizi, the model of a faithful and passionate Jew, say: "Every Jew should rear his family as if he hoped that a deliverer might spring from it." No, that is too proud and too dangerous a role. Israel has not had much luck with its messiahs. More modest but more praiseworthy is the role of a committed emissary, who without shouting, without ranting, without raising his voice announces by his actions: "I cannot abandon the ship. Granted that I am not bearing the gods of the future, but I am carrying a balm which could guarantee recovery to an ailing mankind." If your children are not abnormal, they will heed a serious word. The future of Judaism lies in the hands of the mothers. If they imbue their children with this easily understood and pride-instilling thought, then they will merely snicker at the seductive voice of that German professor of ancient history who advised the Jews: "If you wish to be accepted in our society as equals, then you must merge yourselves with or submerge yourselves in Christianity. You don't have to believe in Christ and his redemptive power, for we too have dropped this belief. What remains is only a kind of conventional Christianity. But this includes the majority of Germans and the minority must consider it an honor to be absorbed by the majority."[53] They will be able to answer this historian calmly: "What indeed did the oft-praised Julius Caesar, a man who represents the epitome of Roman power and whom you deeply admire, along with his dissipated followers actually contribute to the world? He brought into the world men like Caligula, Nero, Domitian, and Commodus. He paired depravity with insanity. The world was already grateful that it was at least freed by Constantine and his descendants from these monsters. And if the Roman world did not end up as a complete swamp, this is due to our prophets and psalmists who brought some fresh air back into European history. At the beginning of the sixteenth century a general stagnation would have set in were it not for the Renaissance of the classical world and the "Hebraic truth" which set off the Reformation. Perhaps we'll talk about this further some other time.

For now and for some time to come, "adieu, adieu."

Your
Caspi

FIFTEENTH LETTER

My dear, dear friend,

As a woman you must allow me to have the last word and I don't want to obligate you in any way thereby to answer me. I must thank you for your last letter precisely because it grew into an essay. I am now fully oriented and I am grateful for your direction. I realize now that every Jew must take care that the link which binds him to a chain of ancestors spreading over several thousand years must not be broken, not out of defiance, or false pride, or aristocratic arrogance, but rather out of an overwhelming sense of duty to preserve and secure the miracle of our people's continued existence. A gaping hole would exist in the world if Jews and Judaism would disappear from the scene. I am really indebted to that pretty lady who was so eager to convert for giving me the occasion to correspond with you on the subject of Judaism and Semitism. But you will not be rid of me so easily; when you will have returned from your long trip abroad I will bother and pester you again for futher instruction. I still have much on my mind that you must help me with.

Thus you gave me no hint as to your thinking on the Palestine question which at present preoccupies many Jews in Russia and Rumania as well as many English Christians. Many fled in the wake of the *katzap* pogroms in Russia. Some found refuge in America; others were driven back to their so-called homeland. In either case they did not exactly find a bed of roses and many began to look longingly toward the promised land. The pseudo-Romans in Bucharest, who snap their fingers at the agreement of the Berlin Congress granting full equality to the Jews in Rumania, force the Jews to emigrate.[54] From the latter a few settled in Palestine. Are the words of the prophets about to come true? "If your dispersion reaches the end of heaven, then I will bring you back from there to the land of your fathers." What is your opinion? Recently in England a committee met to consider building a new canal to open the way from the Mediterranean Sea to the India Ocean or from England to the colonies in India and Australia, namely to build alongside the Suez Canal an Aqaba canal from a point on the Palestinian coast through the Dead Sea down to the Gulf of Aqaba and the Red Sea. Were this project to be completed what a change would take place in the holy land! It would become a bridge between Europe and the best part of Asia. The wastelands would become again fertile, green, and productive. In the vicinity of the Dead Sea beautiful villas and cities would be built, as in the former land of Goshen through which the Suez Canal now passes, Port-Said and Ismailia have arisen. Tourists would frequent Ein Gedi at the shore of the Dead Sea as much as the valley of Engadin in Switzerland. The words of your favorite prophet would then literally come true. "I will open rivers in barren places and fountains in valleys; I will make the wilderness a body of water and the dry land springs of water. I will plant in the wilderness cedars, accacia-trees, myrtles and oil trees" [Isaiah 41:18–19].Even the powers of fantasy do not extend to the point where they could paint the transformation that this innovation would produce. The holy spirit which has inspired so many in this stretch of land to great deeds and thoughts may perhaps again hover over a fortunate and grateful generation. In any event, Daniel Deronda, who set out on a wedding trip to Palestine with his wife, will find not a few followers.

Later you must expound how you feel about this.

Your friend,
Edith,

who wishes you a pleasant trip.

8

Historical Parallels in
Jewish History[1]

Every one knows the myth of the Wandering Jew who
wanders wearily through the world without sleep or rest,
waiting with yearning for the Last Judgment that will give
him salvation and the repose of the grave. The myth has
spread through all the lands of civilization and has produced
a whole literature. Equally well-known is the envenomed
application of the myth to the Jewish people who are
represented as foredoomed to wander weary and aimless over
the whole earth till the end of time. It is not so well known
that it was no stroke of poetic imagination that created the
figure of the Wandering Jew with all its untruth and unreality.
The legend has not the slightest claim to the authority of great
age, but first came into existence in the epoch after the
Reformation, as the offspring of a downright mystification or
of crass superstition.

The Wandering Jew was first put forth as an apology for
Christianity. The Reformation had not alone produced an
incurable split in the hitherto unbroken unity of Christianity;
it had also called into existence doubt and scepticism. The
cries of war and battle resounded in all directions. The Pope
as Anti-Christ and Rome as the sinful Babylon, on the one
side, were opposed by Luther as the child of Satan and
Wittenberg as the throne of Hell, on the other. These cries of
opposite import shattered faith and brought forth sceptical
rationalism. Day by day, throughout the centuries, men had

expected the reappearance of Jesus in the heavens, and the coming of the Last Day, when quick and dead should be judged, and eternal peace should be established. Instead of this, hatred and despair entered Christendom with the warfare of every man against his brother. Faith and hope and love seemed to have fled from the earth. In the midst of all this, the bodily presence of the Wandering Jew was to be a solace and a help. He had seen the crucifixion with his own eyes, and had wandered about ever since. He could bear witness to the New Testament legends, not alone against blind heathens and obstinate Jews, but also against Christians filled with skepticism.

Bishop Paul of Eitzen is said to have met the Wandering Jew living in a wretched plight under the name of Ahasuerus, near Wittenberg or Hamburg, about the time of Luther's death, and to have learnt from him his well-deserved punishment for a harsh word spoken to Jesus. If this Wandering Jew existed, and proved the truth of Jesus' death on the cross, then faith stood fixed and unassailable. Thus Ahasuerus could disperse the clouds of doubt and save Christianity. A publisher's hack in Basle got hold of the story, and distributed it in book from through all Germany in 1602, and it soon went the round of Europe in translations and adaptations. Such is the origin of the legend of the wandering Ahasuerus, or whatever else he may be called.

While in Germany the Wandering Jew was put forth as a caricature of the picture presented by the persecuted and oppressed German Jews, a talented writer in France gave another and more appropriate account of him. The "Turkish spy," who was supposed to have been commissioned to report on the political events of Europe in the time of Louis XIV, also professes to have met him in the flesh and to have conversed with him. This supposed Turkish spy depicts him in far different colors from the coarse anonymous German writer. He appeared before him without any marks of degradation and as a man made wise by experience, to whom a thousand years were as yesterday. You might call him the youngest brother of Time. This Wandering Jew understood all languages, knew all Christian and Moslem dynasties, their rise and fall, their follies, and their aimless actions. He had seen from a lofty hill the flames of Rome when Nero set it alight. He had been at the Court of Vespasian, and spoke of the catastrophe that brought about the destruction of the Temple of Jerusalem. This Wandering Jew had passed through the tortures and horrors of the Inquisition in Spain, Portugal, and Rome, and at this his auditor is astounded, as at a miracle.

This portrait of the Wandering Jew seems to have been painted by a Marrano (he is called Sieur Paule Marana), and was intended as a contrast to the mystification of the German legend. The author was nevertheless a scoffer and scorner, and wished to press home the application of his allegory.

The Wandering Jew is wandering Judaism, that stands on a lofty turret, and from this position surveys the rising and falling billows of the world's history. It speaks all tongues, for it has been in all lands. It escapes, in a manner that must be regarded as a miracle, all dangers and terrors. It is the youngest brother of Time. It has a mighty memory of all the events of the thousands of years which have passed before it.

This mighty memory is enshrined in the historic tablets of the Jewish people. No other people on earth can compare with this in the duration of its historical memory. It has seen the lofty forms of antiquity rise and pass away. It has lived through the wild chaos of the Middle Ages, which pressed on it like a mountain, and it has helped to cause this chaos to vanish like the visions of a dream. It has seen the dawn of modern times arise, and this same people, almost unchanged, has a hold upon the present, bound into a community by holy memories and religious institutions, even though without a common land.

The history of this community runs parallel with that of the world on which it has often actively worked, and by which it has been passively influenced. The history of Israel is a miniature history of the world. They bear the same relation to one another as the microcosm to the macrocosm. Israel has received light or shade from all the important events of the world's history, and has, too, cast them back upon the world.

Nevertheless, the glory of being a historic people from the time of hoary antiquity, of having lasted on into the present, and of playing no unimportant part in it, this glory would not be so enviable were it not accompanied by an effulgence which stamps it as a marvellous phenomenon.

Your great countryman, Charles Darwin, has discovered a terrible law of nature, and won universal acceptance for it. A shudder is produced by the mere name of the law, as given in the formula which sums it up:—*The struggle for existence*, that rules among the infinite bodies of the universe, as much as among the lowest organisms. The stronger assails and destroys the weaker without mercy in longer or shorter time. Weak peoples are conquered by strong ones, and are eaten up and destroyed, even in the historical sphere. Such is the will of this merciless law of nature, and no one can rescue himself from its influence. This inexorable law reaches its final expression in the formula *might before right*.

But is there really no exception to this fatality? Yes, the Jewish people, or Jewish race, offers a remarkable and imposing anomaly. Can there be anything weaker among peoples than this one, especially since it was enslaved by the Romans, scattered to all the ends of the earth, chased like a wild beast, and hunted to death in the Dark Ages, and despised and avoided, hated and downtrodden even to the verge of this century? Is there anything weaker? Such a people might say with patient Job, "Is then my power of stone and my body of brass?" According to the ruthless laws of nature, this little people should have long ago been broken, destroyed, and have disappeared from the earth. And yet it is still in existence.

This ineradicable persistence of the Jewish people was observed and mentioned more than two thousand years ago. A psalmist even made it the subject of his song, "Israel may say: Many a time have they afflicted me from my youth: yet they have not prevailed against me." Does it not seem as if this fatal law of nature, and even death itself, had no power over the individuality of this people? This small and weak people still lives and has survived all the mighty powers of the past who could easily have shattered it, and who often desired to shatter it. It survived the swarms of barbaric inroads, the bloody crusades and the Holy Roman Empire, to which it provided *servi camerae*. It survived the Inquisition with its autos-da-fé. And it has lived through the dawn of the Renaissance, which it has, in part, forwarded. Who can deny that such a people form an anomaly?

Further, it was from its greatest weakness and most debasing inferiority that it raised itself, to its own astonishment, to power and influence. Thrice was it released from the most disgraceful slavery, and became not alone free, but powerful, with all the strength of youth. The Exodus from Egypt, the return from the Babylonian Exile, we know; but the third release and rise, when was that? That, we have ourselves lived through; we ourselves belong to the rejuvenated, released from the fetters of a spiritual death.

A century ago Israel stood with downcast eyes and bowed back all over the earth, despised like an outcast. And to-day? This brilliant assembly, the elite of Judaism, that has established a Jewish Historical Exhibition to display to our eyes the antiquities of our past, the outward signs of our former condition—this assembly speaks more clearly and efficaciously of our marvelous metamorphosis, or our rise and phenomenal position, than any picture in words, however dramatic it might be.

The heart is rejoiced at such an exhibition, and at the eagerness of all the world to make it as interesting and complete as possible. For a Jewish visitor from the Continent, it is especially surprising and praiseworthy to see such an exhibition. From the Continent, I say, for there such a thing would be an impossibility. The importance and influence of this exhibition consist in large measure in the sentiment which it expresses. For, after all, of what importance are these relics and records, even though they may run into thousands, compared with the brilliant trophies of other nations, the documents and memorials of their heroic deeds, their triumphs and their actions? Any such comparison would be ridiculous.

But it was no idle vanity or thirst for glory that influenced the exhibitors and those who took such a warm interest in the work. If I interpret your motives aright, you desired rather to give evidence of your true Jewish convictions. You wished to display the inner connection of your past and your present. You wished to show that while you, as English patriots, are attached to this happy isle with every beat of your hearts, you wished to preserve your connection and continuity with the long series of generations of Israel. And without exactly wishing it, you have thereby raised a practical protest on the one side against thoughtless indifference, and on the other against unprincipled apostasy, two hateful types within the ranks of Judaism which—to your honour be it said—are rarer here than on the Continent.

I have no wish to pay you mere compliments. I desire only, on the scene of this exhibition, to establish the fact that a new birth, full of brilliant hope, has again come to despised and powerless Israel, and to give ocular demonstration that our people, with all its seeming want of strength, has renewed its youth for a third time.

It will be worth our while to consider how it has come about that such weakness has been able to withstand the attacks of the mightiest powers of the world's history. Does not this persistence of a single small people in the midst of an inimical world, hunted to death for more than a thousand years—does not this contradict the iron law of nature, the survival of the strongest? Not entirely. It depends on what one means by strength and weakness. An ancient Greek maxim expresses pointedly the relation between strength and weakness. Nature has given to each creature different means of defense: the lion his jaws, the ox his horns, the bee its sting, and woman her beauty. An artistic picture of early date represents, in a striking manner, how weakness conquers strength, Venus riding on the lion's back, and taming it. The human spirit, which seems but a breath compared with the mighty powers of nature, yet rules them, and makes them subservient to its interests. Thus the essential property of the superiority of spirit is its invincible force. Now the spirit of a nation is its *ideal,* and this alone can produce such energy as to overcome opposing material forces. Of course it depends on the character of the ideal and the capacity of the idealist. Among the known peoples of antiquity there were, besides Israel, only two nations that showed a capacity for the ideal, the Greeks and Romans. The ideals of the Greeks were beauty and science; but these ideals only served them for comfort, pleasure, and enjoyment. Did they ever show any self-sacrifice or produce any martyrs for these ideals? Did they ever consciously attempt to spread a love for beauty or the thoughts of their philosophers as the elements of general culture? By no means. It was for this reason, because they were without this earnestness and energy, that they and their ideals have fallen, and only grateful memories and a few memorials of them remain.

Still less could the old Romans preserve their ideals for themselves; their tendency to expansion and conquest, and above all, their practical political organization, were in themselves of a material nature. They fell before the superior power of nations, strong in the vigour of their youth. Not so Israel. For it clung to its ideal with marvelous tenancity, despising death itself; it clung to it and treasured it till this ideal became the palladium of the people. Its ideal was, and in another fashion still is, higher and purer. Its characteristic cannot be mistaken. The revelation on Mount Sinai taught it to the world, the prophets formed its commentary and interpretation, the poets have sung it, the martyrs have sealed it with their blood. From the beginning we have been predestined to establish and to spread this ideal of a purer knowledge of God on the one hand, and of a higher morality on the other; to carry light to the peoples; to be a kingdom of

266   STRUCTURE OF JEWISH HISTORY

priests, a holy people, a messianic nation. And in order to
reach this lofty aim, the holders of this ideal have had to
traverse the sad path of dispersion and wandering. The tragic
prospect of being scattered through all the quarters of the
globe was prophesied over the cradle of their race. The sages
of the Talmud have expressed the deep symbolism of this
fateful dispersion in the form of an interpretation of a verse of
the Bible, "God has been good unto Israel in ordaining that he
should be scattered through all the earth." The dispersion was
so far a blessing that the weapons of destruction that were so
often directed against Israel, now in one part of the earth and
now in another, could never reach the whole body, but only
separate members. And the dispersion was a blessing in the
development of the world's history, for Israel could, by means
of its wanderings, fulfill its mission to bring light to the
nations. It scattered some sparks at Alexandria, Antioch and
Rome, and thus gave rise to Christianity. It scattered some
seeds in Mecca and Medina, and thus gave rise to Islam. From
a few traces of light left by it, was derived the scholastic
philosophy in the second half of the Middle Ages, and the
Protestantism of the Continent in the sixteenth century, and
more definitely the Independents in your island, influenced
so strongly by the spirit of the Old Testament.

Not in vain, then, has this people dragged its weary feet
round the world, and thus, to some degree, accomplished one
of its tasks. And this steadfast belief that it has preserved a
miraculous power from hoary antiquity—this consciousness
has sustained it and given it power to suffer and persist. Its
apparent weakness was, in truth, its strength. It could with
justice say, "The Lord is my strength: He has given to my feet
the speed of the hind."

The dispersion and wanderings of the Jewish people have *a
third* favorable side to them. When anyone desires to be a
teacher of the peoples in the two cardinal points of human
destiny, clear knowledge of God and clear recognition of
morality, he must not only bury himself among the treasures
of human thought, but must come in contact with the outer

world and compare himself with it so as to appraise his own possessions better. He must coordinate his experiences, and thus reach the maturity of manhood which cannot be reached in the confined area of his original home. He must move in the midst of the peoples, so that his eyes may be opened and his intelligence sharpened.

It is easy for a nation to declare itself to be a kingdom of priests and a holy people, but hardest of all to realize this claim and transform the world. Thousands of years are needed for the work, and Israel must wander in order to be better fitted for his task.

But the wandering Jew does not wander without a goal, driven by chance hither and thither, but follows a path pointed out to him by Providence. The emigration of the Jews began long before the rise of Christianity, and was, at first, carried out voluntarily, and without any compulsion from others, for expulsion only became the fashion in the twelfth century. Emigration followed the course of civilization from East to West. The most fruitful emigration, or rather colonization, occurred in the tenth century, from the Jewish universities on the Euphrates and Tigris, from Pumpedita, Sura, and Bagdad to Cordova, Toledo, and other Spanish towns already peopled by Jews.

It was the crowning epoch of Mohammedan culture. The elite of Judaism was at that time collected in Spain, and there produced another classical period of scientific research into the word of God, of philosophy, and of Hebrew poetry. A galaxy of stars of the first order shone for two centuries on the peninsula: Jonah ibn Ganach, the first thoroughgoing Biblical exegetist; Samuel Nagid, minister and author; Solomon ibn Gabirol, and Jehuda Halevy Abulhassan, both poets and thinkers; Abraham ibn Daud, historian and philosopher; Abraham ibn Ezra, exegete and wit; and last, not least, Moses Maimonides, a beacon and authority for many centuries, besides a crowd of workers in Jewish science and Hebrew poetry, of the second and third rank.

In this land, and at this epoch, Judaism was deeply studied

and philosophically explained, and its import, task, and aim settled. The elite of Judaism here reached a high state of maturity. They held the leadership for the whole of Judaism, just as the Prophets did earlier in the Holy Land, and the talmudic teachers in Mesopotamia in later times.

And when the bigoted rulers of the peninsula began the suicidal policy of expelling nearly half a million Jews and forcing the remainder to a hypocritical change of faith, this terrible and tearful expulsion and the consequent conversions, turned out to be in a marvelous way a blessing for Judaism. New centers were created in lands hitherto closed to the sons of Israel. The largest stream of wanderers and refugees fled eastwards to Turkey and Palestine. But there it was impossible to form a center of gravity, and raise Judaism to a higher stage, or even to keep it at the one already reached. In these lands the insane theories of the Kabbala had spread their snares and disturbed the minds, and produced psuedo-messianic orgies that cast shame upon Judaism even to the end of the last century.

A small remnant of the refugees lucky enough to escape the Moloch of the Inquisition, established itself in lands where civil freedom and religious toleration were political principles—in Holland and England. It was a remarkable class of Jews who wandered there. They were born and bred in Christianity, the third or fourth generation of those who had received baptism from motives of fear and despair. They could not of course be satisfied with a religion that preached the doctrine of love by means of human holocausts. On the contrary, their love of Judaism increased in proportion to their horror against the inhumanity of the Church. In their almost fanatical love for Judaism, these pseudo-Christians—Marranos, they were called—risked all the dangers of death which flight caused to hang over them. They formed a brilliant body, these brands plucked from the burning, men of the cultured professions, doctors, lawyers, soldiers, poets, monks and nuns, unfrocked Dominicans and Jesuits, among them the confessor of a Spanish Infanta.

It was a wonderful occurrence. They formed a series of
brilliant names, with the proud bearing of Spanish hidalgos,
the men who first created the Dutch-Jewish colony, and then
its offspring, the London community. The Jewish colony in
London and in other English towns (which gradually
received accessions from Germany and Poland) produced, it
is true, no movement of consequence for nearly 200 years
after its slight beginnings, but it preserved in its midst the
germs of a maturer development. In the first place, its moral
conduct earned for it respect and consideration even in the
highest circles of the English people. It is worth mentioning
in this connection that already in the middle of the last
century the House of Lords introduced the bill for naturalizing the Jews dwelling in England, and for not treating them
any longer as aliens. This bill after a time passed by the three
estates of the realm, and granting citizenship, though of
somewhat conditional nature, was passed at the time when
Maria Theresa, the Empress of Austria, drove the Jews from
out her kingdom, and even the philosophic King of Prussia
treated those dwelling in his territories as pariahs and
Gypsies.[2]

But you need not fear that I shall attempt to unroll your own
annals before you in detail. I should be plagiarizing from Mr.
James Picciotto, who has written them from the sources. You
will, however, permit me to select a few facts of eminently
historical importance, especially since they belong to the
development of my theme. One of these interesting facts is the
way in which your community, in a single hour, sprung from
a state of passiveness into energetic action, like the
miraculous tree in the legend which brought forth leaves,
blossoms and fruit in one night. A tragic event roused it to
determined action—the blood accusation brought against the
Jews of Damascus in 1840 at the disappearance of a monk,
and resulting in inhuman tortures for the victims. The whole
body of Jews, as adherents of the Talmud, was then for the
first time involved in this charge of ritual murder of
Christians by the malevolence and credulity on the Conti-

nent. Many still living can remember that year so full of anxiety for Judaism. Bitter grief assailed the hearts of all the descendants of Israel when this specter of the Middle Ages was raised again in the clear daylight of modern times.

All felt the bitter grief, but only the English community roused itself eagerly to action to save the accused and bring the truth to light. Ever memorable in the history of Israel will be the meetings of the Board of Deputies, and equally memorable the meeting of distinguished Christians at the Mansion House to protest against the horrors of Damascus, and to give a brilliant testimonial to their Jewish fellow-citizens. And never to be forgotten that journey to Alexandria of Sir Moses Montefiore, in company with Adolphe Crémieux, filled with the same fiery zeal, and their triumphant success. That was an historic deed, a glorious act. The horrors of Damascus and the raising of the cry of "hep-hep" had important consequences. They aroused and accentuated the feeling of solidarity in Jews all over the world. One result of this revival of Jewish feeling took place in your midst, the cordial reunion of your two divisions, the Sephardim and Ashkenazim, who had previously been separated by so deep a gulf that intermarriage was prevented.

Another event of the highest interest to you, and of considerable importance to Jewish history deserves to be mentioned—not the mere fact that you gained complete emancipation, but *how* you gained it. At first sight it seems very perplexing that the Jews of England gained their emancipation considerably later than those in the remaining lands of civilized Europe, although the English people are ahead of all others in liberality and humanity. Neither the French Revolution of 1789, which freed the Jews of France and Holland, nor the stormy period of 1848, which gave equal rights even to the Jewish pariahs of Galicia, induced the English legislature to grant the same to the Jews of their country. Where they less worthy of the rights of men and citizens? No; just because they were, generally speaking, even more worthy, arose this hesitation against full emancipation.

On the Continent, especially in Germany and Austria, emancipation was forced upon the rulers in a moment of despair, and was granted by them with a mental reservation to restrict or even to revoke it. In England, on the contrary, your freedom was to be granted fully, and with all its consequences. These consequences would deeply influence existing laws and religious relations. The legislature had to make heavy sacrifices for your sakes, and accordingly scruples were long entertained, and freedom, though often brought near, was often withdrawn. But when public opinion stood firm, after due consideration, and regarded it as a shame that full rights should be withheld from a highly respected class of citizens merely on account of their religious belief, they were at last—it is scarcely thirty years ago—granted to you without the slightest reservation.

You had not to give solemn assurance that you are good patriots, that you love your native country as much as your fellow-citizens. Nor had you on this account to give up a jot of your religious convictions, as the French Sanhedrin had to do at the demand of the Corsican despot. The honors you have received have been granted you *sans phrase* as the descendants of Jacob, as the guardians of your ancient birthright.

Recently another event of historical importance to Jews has occurred in your midst, the foundation of the Anglo-Jewish Association, which has already in its short term of existence done much, and given rise to great expectations. It may appear to be merely a branch of the *Alliance Israélite Universelle* with which it goes hand in hand. But important as is this latter institution founded by Adolphe Crémieux and Charles Netter, yet it has one fault, even though this be regarded in its program as a special claim. It excludes all consideration of religion, and especially fails to give sufficient attention to desolate Zion. But the Anglo-Jewish Association takes thought for our mother Zion, afflicted, tossed with tempest and disconsolate. In this you follow the example which Providence gave you in Sir Moses Montefiore, of whom one can say without exaggeration, "The memory of the just brings a blessing with it." Just as he, notwithstanding his glowing patriotism for England, notwithstanding his wide philanthropy, yet kept heart and eye steadily fixed on Jerusalem, so do you in your thoughts. You have attempted to remove the disgrace that for thousands of years has lingered over the Holy Land, and bring back the glories of old. But before Jerusalem can rise from the dust it must shake off the fetters of the spirit. Or, to put it more clearly, if Israel is to think of realizing its ideal task of bringing light to the nations, it must first and above all have light within itself. It must recognize clearly its past and its future, what it means and what it implies. It must consider the road by which Providence has hitherto guided it, and the goal which it must reach at the end of days.

But for this it needs guidance, and this post you, more than any other community of Israel, seem called upon to fill. God has blessed you with special blessings. You dwell in a land blessed by God where the Holy Scriptures, the study of our lives, our alpha and omega, are highly honored, and the study of our glorious antiquity greatly encouraged. You live with your Christian fellow-citizens in full accord, so that they fully recognize that your love for your fatherland need not exclude love for the land of your fathers.

Let me, in conclusion, connect with this fact the expression of an earnest desire of mine. *Noblesse oblige.* Establish your claims to this leadership which would be granted you without envy, by founding a Jewish academy. I need not dilate on the fact that Judaism in its nature and development is a science, an object of research. "Thou shalt reflect thereon day and night." This science, or to give it its name, Jewish theology, has spread over an astonishingly wide field. There is, first, biblical exegesis, which by itself needs a whole lifetime. We, who used to be the teachers of Christian exegetes, are nowadays almost entirely surpassed by them, and many cast in our teeth that we have fallen behind in this branch of study. A new method of biblical inquiry has been introduced recently that clears up most doubts, and makes many commentaries superfluous: this method is only slightly utilized by us. For the study of the Bible is further needed the geography of the Holy Land, and biblical archaeology, which again embraces a wide field of study. This field can only be rightly cultivated by a Jewish academy.

Next there is the Talmud, which has been represented as a well of poison by ignorant and malevolent men; and we are all made responsible for this, even the great mass of Jews who have no notion of the Talmud, and even believe that it contains monstrous doctrines. We cannot deny or shake off the Talmud: it is ours. We do not wish to deny it, for it was our manna through the years of wandering, and is full of light, though it may have its less bright side. But the Talmud is a labyrinth for which no Ariadne has yet found a clue, a chaos that can be illuminated, but only by a number of workers working with united forces. A translation of the Talmud, with its many subsidiaries, would be an insane undertaking; but an encyclopaedia of the Talmud both can and must be prepared, so as to show the world what it contains, and especially what it does not contain. But such an encyclopaedia could only be called into existence by a Jewish academy.

Then comes the subject matter and the history of Jewish philosophy and ethics, with their widespread contents. Here we have also to repel charlatans who wish to make this subject a pedestal for their own pretentious importance. A satisfactory performance of this difficult task would be a desirable object for a Jewish academy.

And, finally, the almost inexhaustible field of Jewish history, the sources of which spread over centuries and are as scattered as the Jewish people themselves. The sources speak in various tongues, ancient, mediaeval, and modern. We have to collect these polyglot sources, to sift, explain, arrange, and criticize them. A Jewish academy would have, as one of the most important of its tasks, to form a *corpus historicorum Judaicorum*.

You will recognize from this sketch that a Jewish academy would have enough to do, and that in order to master Jewish science it must be separated into various sections, dealing with (i.) Biblical Exegesis, (ii.) Talmud, (iii.) Philosophy and Ethics, (iv.) History and Archaeology. There are, at present, thank God, seminaries for Jewish Theology, in which these studies are pursued, in London, Paris, Berlin, Breslau, Amsterdam, Budapest, and recently also in Rome. But for various reasons, the teachers at these institutions cannot deal with these studies with that thoroughness that modern science demands. Even the teachers would be glad to have the results worked out for the purposes of their own teaching. Only such scientific workers as are entirely free from every yoke can produce really academic results. You have, within a short time, performed worthy service, and added one more golden leaf to the annals of Jewish history. You have offered the world this spectacle of the Anglo-Jewish Historical Exhibition, on which the curtain has not yet fallen. Set now the crown to your work and establish a Jewish academy, or at least make a beginning with one of its four sections.

9

The Significance of Judaism for the Present and the Future[1]

I

It is, perhaps, not inopportune to discuss the question as to the significance of Judaism at the present time. Certainly it is a problem that must engage the attention of Jewish thinkers, who cannot live spiritually from hand to mouth, but must desire to account to themselves why they are Jews, and why they remain within the pale of Judaism. When merely regarding it as one of the religious beliefs which are, significantly enough, called the ruling creeds—quite apart from its rights of primogeniture—the question as to its right to further existence is not a superfluous one. We live in an age of criticism, a fact which some deplore, others praise, and thus every branch of knowledge which claims any rank in the hierarchy of science must justify itself by showing whether it takes a part in general culture or is an indispensable factor in the intellectual and moral development of humanity, or contributes somewhat to the totality of human effort; or, on the other hand, whether it forms only an isolated, and perhaps moribund, member in the social organism, with an existence only permitted as a matter of custom. Theology itself is required to prove its right to live. Divinity, which in earlier times stood at the summit of all the sciences, held them under control and defined their place, holds that lofty position no longer; and even if it still takes the first rank in some academic

275

circles, it owes that apparent advantage only to the past, and to a regard for seniority. It must itself recognize that it has no longer any right to the title of queen of sciences. Even philosophy, that claimed precedence in the last century, must now lay aside ròyal privilege in favor of the exact sciences. The more cultivated classes who have tasted of the tree of knowledge live no longer in a state of naive faith, ready to accept all that theology teaches as truth, that requires no proof and brings certain salvation. Criticism, which once only whispered its doubts or was forced to keep silent if it spoke too loud, has nowadays become bold and arrogant. It has usurped the throne, and summoned all the sciences to its court; it tests all means of ascertaining truth, and allows nothing to pass approved which cannot be rigorously tried or ascertained by facts, or numbers, or undoubted records.

It is true that the ruling religion is not much affected by the attacks of criticism. Although some cultured persons stand in a critical or sceptical attitude towards it and turn their back on it, it does not find its position very precarious so long as a numerous following, above and below, remain true. Among the upper classes, religion is carefully preserved as a means of power even more than ever, at least among the empires of the Continent. Religion has become the close ally of the state, and therefore finds in the state an unassailable support. Among the lower classes, whose powers of thought are poorly developed and entirely directed to the satisfaction of their present needs, it has still the majority on its side. The ruling religion, whether Catholic or Protestant, United or Orthodox Greek, does not trouble itself about its continued existence, and does not find it necessary to establish scientifically its right to live. This is not even necessary in America, where rationalism or atheism has founded a kind of opposition church of incredulity. The ruling religion has an overwhelming majority, and can rest satisfied with that. Possession gives it nine points of the law.

But how about Judaism? It has no outward means of maintaining itself. It has no hold on the political powers. No minority is so weak as one whose members are scattered through all parts of the world, and live disconnected from one another. Besides this, Judaism has numerous enemies both within and without its ranks. The external opponents who contest its right to existence are by no means its most dangerous enemies.

In consequence of the tragic fate that befell its adherents who, for centuries, had to wander here and there in degrading slavery, Judaism has itself adopted a garb which is by no means especially attractive, but which, as a whole, unlike some of its entirely emancipated followers, it has scarcely the power or desire to remove. And yet, notwithstanding this in nowise brilliant exterior, it demands from its adherents more earnest and serious sacrifices than any other religion, though these duties appear to many as externalities—obsolete survivals of a sad past which should be rather laid aside than preserved. The modern finery which the Reforming party in Judaism has introduced into the synagogue and public life has had no influence on that side of Jewish life which has not a synagogal or a ritual character, viz.: on married life, on the family, and on the home; these because they are matters of conscience and find their strength in the affections, cannot so easily be transformed. Rigid conservatives say of ritual matters: "*Sint ut sunt aut non sint.*" And it is just on this side of Judaism, in its ritual, that skepticism, not to say scorn, makes its appearance among those who have lost their respect for the past, for criticism is much sharper and incisive among Jews than elsewhere. Now criticism in Judaism is confined to the cultured, and makes them indifferent to the heritage of many thousand years, if it does not make them despise it. These inner enemies of Judaism are, so far, more dangerous than the others, because the latter, except for the rabid anti-Semitic *Judenfresser* who cast scorn on Moses and the prophets, at any rate show their respect for Jewish antiquities. The opponents of Judaism among its own sons banish all reverence for the long roll of their ancestral heroes of intellect and martyrs of faith. How can Judaism maintain itself if its

most distinguished sons, the cultured classes, turn their backs
on it? Or shall the word of the prophet find fulfillment: "a
poor and lowly people shall be left in the midst of thee?" And
the fidelity of these lowly ones is not quite assured. They as a
rule urge their children to adopt the culture of the time, and
these in their turn strive to obtain equality and social position
by means of scientific ability. This is the case where Jews
exist in large numbers, as in Germany, Austria, Russia and its
dependencies, Romania and the Balkan principalities; this
striving after European forms of culture, in its way so
praiseworthy, has spread even to the Turkish Orient, and has
crossed over into Africa. It is encouraged by the *Alliance
Israélite Universelle* and by the Anglo-Jewish Association. In
two generations there must be a relative increase in the
numbers, if not of apostates, at least of indifferents. How shall
the existence of Judaism continue?

Or will it have no further existence? Has it already fulfilled
its mission, and is it no longer anything but a ghost longing
for the rest of the grave? Must it withdraw from the scene of
practical influence because the civilizing element in it has
passed over into the general atmosphere of culture, and its
principles have become an integral part of public law and
justice? Has it done its duty, and may it now retire from the
stage?

The question of the function of Judaism in the present and
the future has become a burning and vital question for
cultivated Jews. Is the ancestral heritage so valuable that for
its sake one should put up with a despised position in life, and
forever submit to the ban which the intolerance of Central
and Eastern Europe has imposed on the adherents of
Judaism? Is it worthwhile to take up a martyrdom not alone
for oneself but for one's children? It is true the Jews in the
most civilized lands, in which the principles of liberty have
been carried out to their full consequences—*i.e.*, in England,
France, and also in Italy—are more fortunate; they do not
suffer any loss through their religion, whether political or

social. But Judaism requires sacrifices even from them, if not of a material nature, still sacrifices of blissful sentiments and yearnings.

Readiness to sacrifice for an ideal can only be inspired by the most strenuous conviction of its truth and excellence. But how shall the present generation become possessed of such a conviction? It has grown skeptical under the influence of the exact sciences, and only lays weight on figures and facts.

Perhaps it may be possible to gain such a conviction of the importance of Judaism even at the present day without forsaking the firm ground of actuality. It may be possible to produce proofs that Judaism has preeminent value, just because it rests on the solid basis of actual phenomena, and can therefore look forward to the future with equanimity, and needs no material power. It may, perhaps, be demonstrated that its ideal mission, its capacity of fruitfulness, which is even more or less allowed by its external opponents, and its power of transformation, still continue and must continue. This necessity is easy to recognize if one clearly understands, on the one hand, the essence of Judaism and its characteristic qualities by which it is distinguished from other forms of religion; and if, on the other hand, one compares with these the prevailing ethical and religious tone, as manifested in society and in the life of the individual.

In order not to mistake the essential characteristics of Judaism, one must not regard it as a *faith*, or speak of it as "the Jewish faith." The application of a word is by no means unimportant. The word often becomes a net in which thought gets tangled unawares. From an ecclesiastical standpoint, the word "faith" implies the acceptance of an inconceivable miraculous fact, insufficiently established by historical evidence, and with the audacious addition, *credo quia absurdum*. Judaism has never required such a belief from its adherents. When it is said that religion stands in fierce conflict with science or with reason, that only applies to forms of religion whose dogmas and the foundation of whose institutions rest on unprovable facts, which faith alone has raised to certainty. Such a faith must naturally be engaged in an internecine struggle with science.

But Judaism is not a mere doctrine of faith. What is it then? The celebrated and original French historian Renan, who often gives expression to striking *aperçus,* though he has never entirely freed himself from the memories of priestcraft, has said of Judaism that it is "a minimum of religion." This *aperçu* sounds rather curious when one thinks of the huge folios which contain the Jewish religious codices, the Talmud and its addenda, Maimonides' *Mishneh Torah* or Caro's *Shulḥan Arukh,* with their commentaries and supercommentaries, which offer a boundless extent of religious duties. And yet Renan's utterance is true, as true in reality as it is concisely expressed. It hits the mark not only in the sense that Judaism demands few or no articles of faith, but also in the sense that its center of gravity is not to be found in the religious sphere. What then is its essence? It has been characterized often enough and yet misconceived by friend and foe, as much misconceived as if it were an esoteric mystery or a coarse superstition. When the king of Judah and his people were carried away by such a misconception that they even brought human sacrifices in imitation of foreigners, the prophet Micah said: "Thou askest what the Lord requireth of thee? Only to do justly, and to love mercy, and to walk humbly with thy God." That is a minimum of religion, is it not? Similarly, 700 years later, the great Hillel characterized it to a heathen who had asked him what was the quintessence of Júdaism: "'Love thy neighbour as thyself.' That is the whole of the law; all the rest is but commentary on this text." So, too, 150 years later, an authoritative council also reduced the fundamental duties of Judaism to a minimum. The Emperor Hadrian, who in his own lifetime ordered his own worship as a God, had decreed a terrible religious persecution on all the Jews of the Roman Empire as a punishment for the way in which the Jews of Palestine had fought for liberty and still higher possessions against the Roman legions. The least display of a religious symbol or the slightest sign of religion was to be met by corporal punishment, or even by death. By this means, Judaism was to be driven from the hearts of its adherents, and uprooted from the memory of men. Under these sad circumstances, the rabbis of the time came together in council in order to provide the people with a rule of conduct. Though they were themselves prepared to undergo a martyr's death for every single precept, yet they did not require the same degree of self-sacrifice from the whole of Israel. In this mournful condition of affairs, the Council of Lydda made a well-weighed distinction between the fundamental provisions of Judaism and those that merely applied to the ritual. The latter might, under certain circumstances, be transgressed, in order to avoid punishment; but the former, on the other hand, must not be denied even for fear of death in its most horrible shape. The council reduced the fundamental principles of Judaism to three: avoidance of idolatry, avoidance of unchastity, and, finally, avoidance of an attack on human life.

It is easy enough to perceive from all this that prophets and talmudists did not regard sacrifice or ritual as the fundamental and determining thing in Judaism, but another and higher element, or, more rightly speaking, two elements which apparently do not belong to one another but are in reality radically interdependent. We must, to a certain extent, analyze these elements, in order to recognize and to formulate their fundamental constituents. Both elements have a positive and a negative side; the one element is ethical, the higher ethics, including in its positive aspects love of mankind, benevolence, humility, justice, and in its negative aspects, respect for human life, care against unchastity, subdual of selfishness and the beast in man, holiness in deed and thought. The second element is religious, and in it the negative side is predominant, to worship no transient being as God, whether belonging to the animal kingdom, the race of men, or the heavenly world, and, in general, to consider all idolatry as vain and to reject it entirely. The positive side is to regard the highest Being as one and unique and as the essence of all ethical perfections and to worship it as the Godhead—in a single word, monotheism in the widest acceptation of the term. The ethical is so far intimately connected with the religious element, because the divine perfection gives the ideal for the moral life. "Be ye holy even as I am holy," is the perpetually recurring refrain in the oldest records of Judaism. On the other hand, idolatry leads to debased acts and feelings, as the history of the world has conclusively proven in the coarsest fashion. The worship of paganism was for the most part orgiastic. If Zeus is a god, licentiousness is no sin. If Aphrodite is a goddess, chastity cannot be a virtue.

To biblical critics it would be superfluous to prove that these two elements, the ethical in its richness and the religious in its purity, are the fundamental principles of Judaism. The Law, the prophets, and the other books of the Canon, are full of them. They force themselves on the notice of every reader of the Bible, and the verses which speak of them require no interpretation. The prophets directed their burning eloquence essentially against transgression of either element, against vice and against idolatrous worship. They rarely touch on ritual problems. Even in the Decalogue, the foundation of Judaism, the commandments apply to the two elements, and only a single one, the sanctification of the Sabbath, has a ritual character. In Deuteronomy even the Sabbath is based on an ethical principle, viz., that the man-servant and maid-servant may also enjoy rest. The prophet Jeremiah positively depreciated sacrifice, for he makes God say: "I did not enjoin sacrifice at the Exodus from Egypt." The prophets Amos and Hosea establish the same principle, that sacrifice—the chief element in the culture of ancient peoples—and, therefore, that ritual, was of subordinate importance.

The foundation of Judaism has accordingly rested on these two elements since its first revelation. This truth cannot be repeated too often or made known too widely, for it has often been misunderstood and is still misunderstood at the present day. It is the characteristic of Judaism and is its essential difference from all other forms of religion. A profound French thinker and historian, Eugène Burnouf, has demonstrated that no religion, not even Christianity, in its initial stages lays stress on ethics or the theory of morals as being involved in religion. Only gradually does religion become humanized, so to speak, i.e., bring morality within its fold.[2] Classic paganism at first failed to recognize the ethical element and when Marcus Aurelius and Julian the Apostate realized its worth and desired to introduce it into the Roman religious world, it was too late. Christianity was originally only faith and only made ethics its aim after a long development, and then simply because it was a child of Judaism. To the sharp eye of criticism, the ethical element which was added later, is easily distinguishable from the original dogmatism. The mechanical mixture of the two elements shows its artificial nature. What has the belief that Jesus is the Christ to do with "Christian charity"? They belong to different orders of thought.

It is not so in Judaism. In it, the ethical element and the pure worship of God are clearly the earliest data. Abraham is selected by God as the father of many nations so that he might teach his house and his descendants to keep God's way, to exercise kindness and justice. Thus it is written in the very first book of Holy Writ. The "way of God," or "knowledge of God," is nothing more nor less than what we term "humanity," or morality in the widest extent of the word. That is the essence of Judaism, and does not stand in any conflict with reason or with science. It does not affect this foundation in the slightest whether criticism explains the stories and miracles of the Scriptures as legends and poetic ornaments or not.

Can this doctrine—Judaism describes itself by this name rather than as faith or as religion, i.e., cultus composed of sacrifice and ritual—can this doctrine, which has worked as an elevating, sanctifying, and enfranchising element for thousands of years, have lost its influence? The religions which have been born in its bosom have only taken a part of the blessings with which this original teaching is gifted. I will only refer to one. The inequality of property threatens to subvert the very foundations of society, and the difficulties cannot be removed from the world by means of force. Judaism suggests a means of avoiding this precipice, a means deduced from its ethical principles. It does not despise mammon, and does not imagine that the rich man cannot enter the kingdom of heaven. It recognizes that individual possession is justified, but it sanctifies it by demanding that it should be used and applied in a moral way, and thus overcomes the egoism of possession. It is true that the statutes of the law relating to the sabbatical and jubilee years, in which debts were released in a fixed cycle, and the ordinance that the products of the earth should be accessible to all, even to the penniless—these enactments are not applicable to the economic circumstances of the present day in the same form. But if the ethical principle underlying these laws were always borne in mind and were properly carried out, so that, e.g., the soil of the United Kingdom should not be monopolized by 200,000 owners, but the remaining 35,000,000 inhabitants should also have some small rights in it, this recognition would, at any rate, do something to soften the ever-increasing bitterness of the indigent against the accumulation of riches. On this principle institutions might be established which might avert the chaos with which the European states are threatened. The tender care for the poor which the laws of the Torah, that is, of Judaism, display in regard to the harvests and the tithes, which were only to the narrowest extent adopted by Christianity, might also be applied to modern circumstances. If Judaism disappeared, the ethical postulates which it includes, and on which the continuance of society and civilization depend, would disappear also.

More urgently necessary still is the continued existence of Judaism at present and in the future for the preservation of the religious principle. In the strictest sense, absolute monotheism, as Judaism has revealed it, is rationalism; it is the negation of all the absurdities by which the religious views and the cults of the ancient nations were dominated. But it

required a high stage of cultivated intelligence to arrive at the
conviction that the gross fetishes, the deities of wood and
stone, that Baal and even Zeus, who stood under the power of
Atè, that Jupiter, whose grave was shown in Crete, that Thor
with his hammer, that all these gods, and even the luminaries
of day and night, were not divine beings, that the goddess of
love, under the names Astaroth, Mylitta, Beltis, Aphrodite,
Venus, and the worship of Priapus were abominations
(תועבה), as Judaism called them. Idolatry, which sanctified
immorality, only appears absurd and abominable to the
present generation because Jewish rationalism has for
centuries arrayed itself against it; because the prophets, with
their burning language, struggled against it, because the
Jewish Sibyl and the Book of Wisdom, Philo and Josephus
and other Jewish thinkers made this offspring of mad fancy
food for laughter. The worship of the emperors lasted on even
into Christian times, i.e., the emperors, even the most vicious
of them, were *divi*, and had to have sacrifices brought to them.
The ruling creed is likewise anthropolatry; cathedrals,
cloisters, and pilgrims' shrines are dedicated to it. The only
defenders of true monotheism, in other words, of rationalism
in religion, are still the adherents of Judaism. From Zion went
forth this rationalistic teaching.

How stands the matter at the present time? Rationalism,
which seeks to distinguish the ethical from the mystical in
religion, which was all-powerful in the last century, and in
Germany had no less a patron than the philosophical King
Frederick and the king of poets, Lessing, this rationalism has
altogether lost its potency in that country and has become
powerless there. The leading spirits in religion scorn rational
thought with such audacity that any opposition is despised as
heresy. In France the upper classes are either intensely
bigoted, or they become atheists in order to avoid becoming
clericalists. In England there has arisen a tendency towards
ritualism with a Roman Catholic tinge, because no place is
allowed to rationalism in the sphere of religion.

Thus Judaism, which is throughout rationalistic, is the sole stronghold of free thought in the religious sphere. Its mission, to overcome erroneous belief, is far from being fulfilled. There are still enough phantoms in the temples of the nations and in the hearts of men which are by no means innocuous. Millions of men still recognize a representative vicar of God on earth, whose words they credulously accept as an infallible oracle. Such phantoms, to which even the most civilized peoples on earth continue to pray, can only be banished by Judaism just as it destroyed the altars of Baal and Astarti, of Zeus and Aphrodite, and hewed down the trees of Woden and Friga—for the inspiration came from Judaism, though the agents were Christian iconoclasts. The visionary images which becloud thousands of minds and produce the maddest enthusiasms can only be dispersed by that pure idea of God formulated by Judaism. Rationalism has no other representative but Judaism.

Regarded from this point of view, Judaism has still the same importance for the present and for the future, as it had in the past. Its mission is, on this side, by no means superfluous. We Jews are the representatives of Judaism and its mission; its ideas and principles pulsate in our veins. If the apostles of the pure monotheistic idea had been destroyed in their conflicts with Assyrians, Chaldaeans, Greeks, and Romans, the madness of idolatry with its orgiastic forms of worship would still exist today, and the civilization of Europe would itself not have been developed.

But even on the ethical side Judaism still gives example and thrust. There has been a certain phrase formulated about carrying out practical Christianity. If this phrase is to have any sense, it can only mean that morality should penetrate the institutions of the state; Judaism preached this doctrine thousands of years ago. The ethical principles which it lays to heart were not alone to be carried out by individuals, but were to become the leading principles of government. They had not only to be written on the doors of houses, but at the gates of cities. The king was always to carry with him the Book of the Law, which put the essence of Judaism in the short sentences,

"Thou shalt love one God with all thy heart," and "There shall be no poor in thy cities." Methods were also indicated in this Book by which the ethico-religious ideals might be realized.

Thus Judaism is the source alike of humanity, of monotheism, and of religious rationalism. It has still its function to play, its mission to fulfill, in bringing these ideals to reality. If it vanished from the world, if its adherents, one and all, deserted it, a mighty factor for the progress of ethical and religious civilization would be wanting; it would be wanting now, just as much as it would have been wanting of old, if Judaism had disappeared before the rise of Christianity.

Of course, Judaism contains an elaborate ritual besides these ideal principles, which, unfortunately, owing to the tragic course of history, has developed into a fungoid growth which overlays the ideals. But originally the ritual in its pure form had its justification, and was intended to surround and protect ideals in themselves of an ethereal nature. It must be reserved for a later article to explain the manner in which the ritual was adapted to the ideal.

II.

The inquiry whether fixed articles of faith form the essential kernel of Judaism, learnedly discussed in this Review by Mr. Schechter,[3] and the accuracy of the classification of the differences in religious opinion among English Jews, so cleverly elaborated by Mr. Israel Zangwill,[4] are both internal questions which have only a very incidental relation to the real subject-matter of my former article.

I had not then, nor have I now, to deal with what may be considered as orthodox or heterodox in Judaism, whether touching the importance of the ritual or even the apparently fundamental dogma of revelation, of which the denial in rabbinic language is expressed by האומר אין תורה מן השמים or in modern phraseology, by doubt in the supernatural. According to Mr. Zangwill's classification, there is among English Jews a group of persons "professing natural Judaism." This might, indeed, occasion a practical question within the Jewish community itself. For the question might arise whether holding such heterodox opinions would unfit a man for giving evidence in a matter of ritual, as e.g., in a marriage or a divorce *"more Judaico."* In such a case, a rabbi would be not a little puzzled to decide whether the marriage or the divorce would be ritually valid. For the code book he would have to consult would not enlighten him on matters of dogma. It would, for instance, give him no information, how to act in the case of a witness who had never violated the Sabbath in his actions, but who was not thoroughly imbued with a belief in the supernatural command to obey it. Moses Mendelssohn's dictum that Judaism only judges actions and not religious opinions remains unshaken. Whether an intelligent Jew finds more happiness, assurance, and solace from his convinced belief in the ideal principle of Judaism and its ethical consequences than a Russian or Polish Hasid from the mechanical performance of some ritual ceremony, and from a vague messianic hope is purely a matter of sentiment. It could only become practically important if the externalities of the synagogue were undergoing transformation. We might then have to determine whether more consideration were to be shown to Moses Mendelssohn, who rejoiced in the thought that the essentials of Judaism were in perfect harmony with deistic philosophy, or to Steinheim, who was filled with joy at the conviction that the truths of revealed Judaism were at variance with the dogmas of philosophy. Translating these differences of theory into practice, we might then have to decide whether the repulsive abuses commonly regarded as Jewish and religious should be abandoned, or whether the feelings of a naive believer should rather be spared who finds his spiritual bliss in the noisy shaking of the willow branches upon the Feast of Tabernacles.

But, as aforesaid, these reflections are foreign to my subject.

I would only like to consider whether Judaism still has a real significance and value in the critically minded present, and in that future which may be yet more estranged from all religious forms, only to show that those who are deeply convinced of its fundamental principle and historical influence, may joyfully make it their vocation to hold by Judaism steadfastly, and so transmit it to posterity. Taking as my guides the Bible, the Talmud, and the intelligent rabbis, I have endeavored to prove that this fundamental principle must be sought for in ethical idealism (humanity in the highest sense of the word), and in pure rational monotheism, adverse to all mysticism and disfigurement. I have also attempted to show that for the future of mankind these qualities have not yet become superfluous for the education and regeneration of society.

The immense influence, which these two most closely connected sides of the law of Moses, "the heritage of the congregation of Israel," have exercised on the development of human civilization, has indeed been freely admitted even by Christian thinkers. No matter how much Mr. Zangwill may doubt the validity of this statement and oppose to it the argument that Confucius, and Sophocles, and Aryan celebrities in general, were equally impressed with the categorical imperative of the moral law, he cannot maintain that these individuals caused a worldwide and historic change in the thoughts and actions of the whole civilized portion of mankind, or that they looked upon their own convictions as material for what we may call an ethical circulation of the blood. Socrates may have had a more accurate conception of the Deity than his countrymen and the Sophists, but only a paradoxical disputatiousness could assert that he was fully penetrated with the conviction that this conception of the Deity postulated the sanctity of life and the purest morality. Plato and Aristotle might indeed have learned "practical reason" from the Jews, for their ethical doctrine compares most disadvantageously with that of Judaism, as was already known to Philo.

Christianity was perfectly justified in priding itself on having vanquished the essential corruption of paganism, but it ought not to have ignored the fact that it was only the organ and interpreter of an original inspiration behind it, and that it had not itself remained free from some heathen contamination. As long as Judaism was gagged and silent, Bossuet[5] could attribute the whole progress of civilization to Christianity, a view in which Ranke, undisturbed by Buckle's[6] conclusions, has partly followed him. But at the present day, the ban which suffered no dispute to the assertion that salvation came forth from Golgotha and not from Zion is gradually being broken through. For it is now admitted as an undeniable historical fact by many earnest Christian thinkers, such as Kuenen and Renan, and even hesitantly by German historians, despite a touch of anti-Semitism, that ethical consciousness is the property of the people of Israel, that it was called into the world by the three great prophets, Amos, Hosea, and Isaiah, and that they may be said to have been evangelists eight hundred years before the rise of Christianity although without the mystic by-taste of a kingdom of heaven. To this admission we must cling fast, without at present examining closely whether this ethical revelation was first proclaimed from Mount Sinai, or from the wilderness of Tekoa. A part, I might say the flower, of this pure ethical system, has become the common property of the world, through the medium of Christianity—justice, charity even towards the stranger, care for the poor, the sanctity of life, conscientiousness. But the world has not yet fully appreciated the root of this rich development, that pure monotheism which teaches that God is the father of the fatherless and the protector of the widow, and that, as holiness is the essence of His nature, all unholiness, unchastity, and self-pollution[7] are an abomination to Him. Neither has the world always adequately realized that this lofty conception of Deity is the true teaching of Judaism.

What relation, then, exists between the ceremonial system and this fundamental principle or essence of Judaism? It cannot be denied that in its constitutive document, the Pentateuch, in which ethical laws fill a considerable space, we find also prescribed a whole series of ritual enactments, though the prophets treat these ordinances almost with contempt. Through talmudism and rabbinism they have been so improperly exaggerated, and received so enormous an extention in the various codes, that the ethical element seems to have been almost entirely crowded out, and Judaism has consequently appeared to consist of nothing but outward ceremonies, and to place the highest value on the mechanical performance of an infinite series of ritual acts. Let us now inquire whether this ritualism in its original form was related to the ethical element, or whether it is to be considered as something foreign to its purpose, an interpolation from without. From the earliest times, both Jewish and non-Jewish circles have been in the habit of considering Judaism as composed of two distinct parts—articles of faith and moral laws on the one side, ceremonies and ritual observances on the other. It was reckoned as one of the merits of the founder of Christianity, that he aided the progress of religious consciousness by eliminating the ceremonial law. On this view he becomes, in a sense, the founder of a reformed Judaism. The reform party of modern times sought to justify the transformation of Judaism by means of another line of argument. They held that the national character, which Jewish law has always retained, was unessential as compared with its religious and ethical features, and, as much of the former had necessarily been given up with the destruction of national independence, all that had any tinge of nationality might now also be eradicated. Judaism was thus to adopt a universal or cosmopolitan character, and be able, as it were, to compete with Christianity, at any rate with Unitarianism. This is the point of view of a large number of Jews in America.

The value or worthlessness of the ceremonial element in Judaism and its original signification are well worth considering. That it has some deeper meaning is sufficiently

proved by the testimony of the Book of Deuteronomy, which
was found in the temple by the high priest Hilkiah. Although
it places the ethical laws in the foreground, it also enforces
ritual observances, though on a far less extensive scale than in
the other books of the Pentateuch. The ceremonies must
therefore possess at least a certain value and some definite
relation to the ethical elements. It is worthwhile to investigate
what this relation is.

When the prophets gave frequent utterance to the prediction, "The earth shall be full of the knowledge of the Lord, as
the waters cover the seas"—full, that is, according to our
interpretation, of ethical idealism and submission to God
—they did not delude themselves with the belief that this
"kingdom of heaven" was near at hand. They relegated the
realization of the ideal to "the end of days." The two
prophets, Isaiah and Micah, who predicted eternal peace on
earth in connection with Israel's mission, that "nation shall
not draw the sword against nation, and that they shall not
learn war again," preface this statement with the words, "and
it shall come to pass in the last days." They were gifted with
the prevision that the teaching which goes forth from Zion
would have power to effect a great moral transformation over
the whole world—in some distant age.

But how is this teaching to endure to the end of days? How
is it to be taught and to spread its influence abroad? A doctrine
must possess its teachers. It must therefore have created for
itself an organ, an interpreter, who should proclaim it and
preserve it, and lead it to victory. Not an association pledged
by contract to carry on the work, not an order which has to be
constantly recruited lest it should die out was chosen to be the
bearer of this teaching, but a *tribe*, which, united in itself even
after apparent extermination is ever again renewed. The
oldest record, the Scriptures, tells of the selection of a race of
guardians for the regenerating doctrine. Abraham was chosen,
so that he might command his sons and their descendants
after them to keep the way of the Lord and to practice justice
and righteousness. The promise to Abraham was that he

would thus become the father of many nations, because his tribe, the people of Israel, was entrusted with the mission and the task of guarding the teaching of salvation until the end of days. Such is the language of Scripture. Or did this tribe become the guardian and preserver of the teaching because in it the ethical consciousness, though but in feeble outline, had been awakened and developed very early, and it was therefore more fitted than other nations for this ethical office?

In whichever way the fact be expressed, Israel, the descendant of Abraham, has played its part in the history of the world as guardian and propagator of a peculiar regenerative teaching. The Hebrew language has created a special name for the ideal import of this tribe. It is called Yeshurun (ישורון), of which word the etymological meaning is, "The perfection of uprightness, or integrity." In this one term is comprehended what is elsewhere described as, "Thy people shall be all righteous, the work of my hands that I may be glorified"; or again: "a kingdom of priests and a holy people." As such an ideal, Israel, the servant of God, is destined to be a light to the nations and to bring them righteousness or salvation. If Israel possesses this lofty destiny and historic mission "for the latter days," its existence has an *exceptional* significance. Its beginnings are therefore represented in a peculiar light, and certainly were of an extraordinary character. It is an undoubted fact that the Israelites were slaves in Egypt, an undoubted fact that they left the land of their captivity, and equally certain that in order to reach the land in which they undeniably lived for seven hundred years, they had to pass through a terrible wilderness. These events, together with the passage of the Red Sea and the revelation of the Decalogue, which the older poetry glorified and in so doing confirmed, were looked upon as the gracious proofs of a special Divine guidance. The prophet Jeremiah calls those days the bridal state of Israel. These first chapters of Israel's national history were to be all the more zealously remembered, inasmuch as they were to serve as an encouragement to remain steadfast through thousands of years of inward and outward trials and temptations. Israel's servitude and misfortunes at the beginning of its history, and its subsequent deliverance through a wonderful providence, were therefore immortalized by special ritual observances. The Law itself does not enforce these observances as ends in themselves, but designates them as *means* for a higher end, "so that thou mayest remember all the days of thy life." In these words the connection between the spiritual essence of Judaism and a considerable part of its ritual observances is clearly designated: they are the means to an end, and that end is the memory of the past. National memories are dear to every nation; they urge it on to activity, to the maintenance of what it has already achieved, and to the increase of its fame. But the people of Israel was to pride itself not on the great deeds of its ancestors, but on the Divine guidance, which had shaped its destiny; and its national memories were intended to keep alive and unforgotten its own exceptional position and significance.

Another consideration is the following. This tribe was to be the bearer and guardian of what, in modern language, we should call moral and religious truth. But it lived among nations who despised these truths, or rather it lived in the midst of a polytheistic and orgiastic world. Contagion from this world was inevitable and did not fail to come. Polytheistic error had so entirely undermined morality, that the law had to threaten with severe punishment fathers who sacrificed their children to Moloch, or who sacrificed their daughters' purity to other shameful divinities. It had to forbid the price of prostitution being brought into the Temple. Sins which we now regard as impossible, and upon which we cannot reflect without a shudder, must therefore have become domiciled amongst the Israelites just as they were in Babylon, Tyre, Corinth, and throughout the ancient world. Hence the continual relapse of the people to the abominations of polytheism and apostasy, which recurred even after the reigns of Hezekiah and Josiah, until, at the return from the Babylonian captivity, the apparently inexhaustible tendency to idolatry was finally overcome.[8]

The Law, the "Torah," had therefore to take measures by which to wean the people from its polytheistic aberrations. Just as the Great Synagogue in the post-exilic period introduced "hedges" forbidding certain things that had been hitherto permitted, in order to prevent some essential law from being transgressed, so the Torah prescribed a series of ritual observances which were intended to counteract polytheism and its worship. We may call them anti-polytheistic observances. Separatism followed as necessarily as B follows upon A. In the Pentateuch, stress is even laid upon separatism. The preservation of national memories and the necessity of exclusiveness made ceremonialism indispensable. The observances have thus either a mnemonic or a prophylactic character. Those that were to remind the people of their early history have necessarily a national character. First comes the institution of the festivals. The rationalists at the end of the last and beginning of the present century thought they were attaching an ineradicable stigma to Judaism by proving that the two great festivals of Passover and Tabernacles were originally nature festivals, commemorating the beginning and end of the harvest. No doubt they were so, originally, but they were converted into national festivals. In this assimilation, or metamorphosis, is shown the spiritual energy that stamped its mark on all it found. The new ethical and religious conceptions had no *tabula rasa* before them; it was a people already accustomed to certain habits and institutions which had to receive, preserve, and develop them. Thus the festival of the spring was converted into a national festival, to remind the people of their deliverance from slavery; and the harvest festival, the grape and fig harvest, which was spent in the open air and in booths, became a reminder of the many years spent in the wilderness. The exodus from Egypt was further to be called to mind by the redemption and sanctification of the first-born, by the removal of leavened bread, by the wearing of certain visible signs (phylacteries and tefillin) on forehead and hands, and possibly also by the blue fringes on the edges of the garment. If it should be proved that the nobles of Egypt wore fringes

either for ornament or in compliance with some religious
custom, we should here again have an example of the
transformation of an old custom into a symbol of a loftier
conception of life. It has not yet been made quite clear in what
the so-called phylacteries (טוטפות, זכרון) and tefillin (אות)
originally consisted. As they are enforced in Deuteronomy,
they must have been of considerable importance inasmuch as
the fifth book of Moses frequently modifies the injunctions of
the central three.

As the Book of Deuteronomy accentuates more sharply than
the others the fundamental monotheistic doctrine, it uses the
law of tefillin and phylacteries, as well as that of the mezuzot,
to impress and to sharpen the monotheistic idea. The special
significance of this commandment lay, no doubt, in the
words, "Hear, O Israel, the Lord our God, the Lord is one,"
which were to be fastened to every door post, so that
everybody at every moment of the day might be exhorted to
conceive the God of Israel as a perfect Unity.

As I have already explained in my first article, this
confession, or more accurately, this consciousness of monotheism, was not intended to be an article of faith, but an
antithetical protest against polytheism; and polytheism was
abhorred, not so much on account of its logical error, but first
and foremost because of its incitement to ethical corruption.
Hence the prophylactic ceremonials. Paganism laid special
stress upon sacrifices to the dead, which originated in
hero-worship. The departed kings, national leaders and
heroes, were represented as continuing to exist in Hades or
elsewhere, transfigured into divinities (manes divi). This was
the foundation of the superstition respecting evil spirits and
demons. In Egypt especially, the deceased kings entombed in
their pyramids, were made the objects of an elaborate system
of worship. The mummies were considered sacred. The
Israelite conception of God had to protest energetically
against adoration of the dead, and it consequently pronounced the state of death to be unclean and a source of
pollution. To touch a corpse, even that of a parent or a king,

made a man unclean. Whoever had come in contact with a corpse, a skeleton, or a funeral feast, was not permitted to enter the sanctuary of the holy God until he had submitted himself to a seven days' purification, which purification had also a symbolical meaning. This is the probable origin of the Levitical laws of purification, against which so many objections have been raised. Perhaps it is only a natural sequence that dead animals were also pronounced unclean, with reference to the Egyptian custom of holding sacred the dead bodies of animals that were worshipped as divine.

It is possible that the command not to eat the flesh of certain quadrupeds, birds, fishes, and reptiles also had its origin in the reaction against the Egyptian worship of animals, which even included reptiles (רמש). This explanation is further suggested by the warning to avoid uncleanness by touching the carcasses of such animals, and also by the motive given for the institution of these laws: "Ye shall sanctify yourselves and be holy, for I, the Lord your God, am holy, therefore you shall not defile yourselves."

Two of the sacrificial rites were certainly introduced as a counterblast against Egyptian animal worship. The laws respecting the *red heifer* are extremely remarkable. A red heifer that had never borne a yoke was to be taken outside the camp and burnt to ashes. The person who accomplished the process was thereby rendered unclean, and yet the ashes were to be used for purification in cases of Levitical pollution. Even to the Talmudists, who were not apt to be taken aback by irrationalities, this ceremony appeared exceedingly strange. But when we remember that the bull (Mnevis), worshipped in certain districts by the Egyptians, had always to be red in color and never to have borne the yoke, the Pentateuchal ritual of the *red heifer* becomes intelligible. The god-ox or god-heifer was to be destroyed, and the *parah adumah* represents the climax of pollution. The ceremony of mixing the ashes with water and sprinkling it with a bunch of hyssop, as a means of purification had, no doubt, also a symbolical meaning.

The rite of the scapegoat which has so often served in the
past as well as in the present for the slandering of Judaism,
finds a complete explanation by reference to Egyptian
worship. In that country the goat was worshipped on account
of its lasciviousness, as is related by two eyewitnesses,
Herodotus and Diodorus Siculus. One could not possibly
repeat in a living language the horrible details given by the
latter historian concerning this worship. A Latin translation
may be quoted here.[9] Women openly used to practice
bestiality with goats; this was part of the religious ceremonial.
The Israelites were wont to imitate even this abominable goat
worship; therefore the Law (Leviticus 17:7) admonishes them
"to sacrifice no more unto *goats*, after whom they have gone a
whoring." For this reason the scapegoat, i.e., the symbol or
essence of unchastity, was to be sent away into the
wilderness, to "a land cut off" (ארץ גזרה), which was called
Azaz-El, and there, according to the traditional interpretation
of the passage, it was to be flung over a precipice. But before
the conclusion of the ceremony, the high priest was to lay his
hands upon the scapegoat and confess and renounce all the
sins and transgressions of the people of Israel, that is to say,
all idolatrous and obscene worship. With all this the
celebration of the Day of Atonement is also closely connected,
and certainly the Israelites could not do sufficient penance for
having yielded to the debasing and disgusting worship of
Astarte and the goats.

It is thus evident that the ceremonial system in its origin
stood in close relation to the fundamental idea or essence of
Judaism; that its office was to promote and combine with that
essence, and that it was not by any means invested with a
magical character (as was the case with the cult of ancient
religions generally) in order to check the interference of
demoniacal powers (ἀποτροπιασμός) or to conciliate the
gods and appease their anger. Now the sacrificial ritual in the
Pentateuch accords so little with the essence of Judaism that
some prophets openly proclaimed its inappropriateness. The
combination of these heterogeneous elements into one

uniform teaching positively invites criticism. The explanation given by Maimonides was that the sacrificial ritual was a concession to the customs of the Israelites, who were used to heathen ideas, and that the commands concerning it were only a pedagogical means for setting bounds to the craving for sacrifice (*Moreh Nebukhim*, 3, 32). But this explanation leaves the contradiction unsolved. If it was really a pedagogic means, it failed to attain its end, for the multitude considered the sacrificial worship so essentially important, and the ethical laws of so little value in comparison to it, that the Prophet Isaiah was compelled to declare: "To what purpose is the multitude of your sacrifices unto me? saith the Lord. . . . Bring no more vain oblations; incense is an abomination unto me. . . . Make you clean, put away the evil of your doings" [Isaiah 1:11, 13, 16].

This part of Leviticus, however, shows itself externally as well as internally to be a foreign element. A fortunate chance led, in the reign of Josiah, to the discovery of the beautiful Book of Deuteronomy, which has an obvious tendency to modify the sacrificial worship, and reduce it to a minimum. One of its most noticeable injunctions is: "If thou shalt forbear to vow, it shall be no sin in thee" [Deuteronomy 23:22]. Next, there is not a word about sin offerings or guilt offerings, but only about peace and thank offerings, which were to be sacrificed, and eaten in the family circle. The ethical side of the ceremony is, moreover, strongly insisted on. The Levites, who had "no part or possession" of their own, the poor, the widow, the orphan, and the stranger, were to be invited to share the feast. Unlike the older code, the Book of Deuteronomy attaches no sacred character to the firstlings of the cattle; and, instead of assigning them to the priesthood, ordains that they are to be eaten (like the festive offerings) in the family circle, while the poor must be allowed to have their share. Only on one ceremonial point does Deuteronomy lay special stress, and that is that no sacrifices were to be offered except in the one central and chosen locality.

Deuteronomy sought to deprive the priesthood of the greater portion of the tribute assigned to it in Leviticus; only a small part of the sacrifices together with the first fruits of corn, wine, oil, and wool were to be allotted for its support. The tithes were to be the property of the owners of the cattle and the ground, on condition that they shared them with the poor.

The Book of Deuteronomy breathes an atmosphere different from that of Leviticus. Ceremonialism occupies only a small portion of it, while the ethical precepts are treated at length and enforced with heart-moving earnestness. It is one of the fatalities that hindered the development of Judaism that the line laid down by Deuteronomy was not followed up. On the contrary, one excess caused another. Because the Torah was known and valued but little and by few during the centuries of the First Temple, while the tendency to polytheism remained persistent till the time of the Babylonian captivity, and because during that period the conviction became vivid and strong that the chastisements threatened by the prophets had come to pass in consequence of obstinate transgression of the Law, the general post-exilic view was, that all its commands and precepts must be minutely and conscientiously obeyed or else a new judgment would overtake the guilty community. As there was then more opportunity for carrying out the ceremonial than the moral laws, these came to the front, and post-exilic Judaism received a ceremonial character. In addition to this there came the advice of the Great Synagogue to make a fence round the law, without considering the injunction not to set the fence above the plantation.[10] Thus, in order to prevent some remotely possible infringement of a law, the previously permitted now became forbidden. The rigorousness of the talmudists was grafted onto the hedge of the soferim, and onto that of the talmudists, the scrupulousness of rabbinism and the superstitions of the Kabbala. During the long years of persecution and suffering, the few voices that were raised in warning against this excess of ceremonialism passed unheard; Judaism gradually assumed a repellent aspect. As a consequence, there followed (and there follows still) apostasy. The pure wellspring of Judaism, the Bible, was so buried under all this accumulation that it almost seemed to have disappeared altogether. The system of instruction was as erroneous as the habitual method of thought. The natural consequence was that as soon as the first ray of enlightenment penetrated the ghetto, throwing upon the outward aspect of Judaism a sudden and glaring light, indifference and apostasy followed close upon each other. Nothing but the strong sense of family union, deepened and fortified by centuries of suffering, offered resistance. Now that at the present day the outward appearance of Judaism has assumed a more attractive form, and the uncultivated Polish customs have been nearly banished from the public ceremonial (while Christianity, on the other hand, has lost something of its ancient halo), the apostates from Judaism are less numerous than those who are merely indifferent; indifference is chiefly caused by ignorance. For Judaism, which does not rest upon the broad basis of state institutions, indifference is far more deadly than apostasy. If this indifference is to be shaken into life, Judaism must more lavishly display and make use of its civilizing riches; it must seek to engrain the conviction that its apostolic mission is not yet ended. Long ago it lifted the ancient world out of the slough of moral corruption into which it had sunk, and although its right of original priority is ignored or denied, a part of its moral principles has been crystallized in State institutions, and has passed into the consciousness of all civilized humanity. Whereas the Latin race is more permeated with the spirit of Hellenism, the Anglo-Saxon race is penetrated with the Biblico-Judaic spirit because its mind is more directed to truth than to beauty. Now what has not been crushed by the mailed footsteps of history must be indestructible and of lasting value. Not in vain has the Jewish people continued to exist for more than three thousand years; not in vain has it survived all catastrophes, caused by a succession of hostile forces, and even the immense disadvantage through the past eighteen hundred years of struggling as a small and a feeble minority against a powerful and hostile majority. Its continued existence—in itself a wonderful fact—is an irrefutable proof of its historical necessity, and what would the Jews be without Judaism, the body without the soul, the Levitical bearers without the Ark of the Covenant?

Notes

Chapter 1: The Structure of Jewish History

1. Published originally in Zacharias Frankel's *Zeitschrift für die religiösen Interessen des Judenthums*, III (1846), pp. 81–97, 121–132, 361–368, 413–421.

2. Rabbi in Luxembourg from 1843 to 1866, Samuel Hirsch became an important spokesman for religious reform. His *Religionsphilosophie der Juden* (1842) was a masterful defense of Judaism in light of the challenge posed by Hegel's philosophy of religion. (See Emil Fackenheim, "Samuel Hirsch and Hegel," in *Studies in Nineteenth-Century Jewish Intellectual History*, ed. by Alexander Altmann [Cambridge, 1964], pp. 171–201). In 1866 Hirsch followed David Einhorn in the pulpit of Kenesseth Israel in Philadelphia and quickly became a recognized leader in the American Reform movement. (See Gershon Greenberg, "Samuel Hirsch's American Judaism," *American Jewish Historical Quarterly*, LXII [1973], pp. 362–382.)

3. A man of many talents and interests, who earned his living as a physician, Salomon Ludwig Steinheim remained intellectually and organizationally a solitary figure in German Jewry of the mid-nineteenth century. His four-volume *Die Offenbarung nach dem Lehrbegriffe der Synagoge* (1835–1865) mounted an original and vigorous defense of the validity of revealed religion against the prevailing rationalism of the age. (See Joshua Haberman, "Salomon Ludwig Steinheim's Doctrine of Revelation," *Judaism* XVII [1968], pp. 22–41).

4. With the publication of *Nineteen Letters on Judaism* in 1836 and *Horeb* in 1837, Samson Raphael Hirsch (Ben Uziel) became the leading proponent of a revamped religious orthodoxy which confidently welcomed the opportunities and challenges of emancipation. The two long Hebrew essays by Isaac Heinemann in *Sinai*, XXIV (1948–1949), pp. 249–271 and in *Zion*, XVI (1951), pp. 44–90 as well as his English essay in *Historia Judaica*, XIII (1951), pp. 29–54 still constitute the best available introduction to the sources and nature of Hirsch's interpretation of Judaism.

5. In 1845 Isaak Mises published an 80-page pamphlet, *Beitrag zur Würdigung der Wirren im Judenthume,* which received a favorable though not uncritical review in Frankel's *Zeitschrift für die religiösen Interessen des Judenthums,* II, pp. 400–407. Though not entirely opposed to individual reforms, Mises came down hard on the Reform movement. He contended that the basic tendency of Judaism was eudaemonistic, striving to realize a legal system in which every human need, drive, and faculty would receive its due.

6. In order to avoid misunderstandings, the undersigned feels obliged to reveal the editorial policy governing this journal. The public is certainly justified in expecting that a journal should have a point of view, a character, especially when it intends to represent religious interests. But it must not pursue this point of view one-sidedly and accept only those essays whose opinions fully concur with its own and constitute only an echo of its point of view. Also that which diverges, as long as it does not directly contradict the stance of these pages, must find its place here. Nevertheless, the editor must be allowed to add a note to those passages which contain a direct or indirect attack against the preferred point of view. This is an act of self-defense which is certainly permitted to everyone and we hope that no contributor will be offended thereby. This principle must also be abided by when we are of the opinion that the basic truths of religion appear to be impugned; likewise, in scholarly matters we hope it will not be taken amiss if we point out an inaccurate quotation or an incorrect interpretation. But the editor cannot be held responsible for everything nor answer for every word or sentence; he must not assume the role of fault finder and exercise a kind of belated censorship over his contributors. He must be sparing with his observations and articulate them only where an assertion is made which constitutes the basis for a larger structure.

Although the author in his vivid history of ideas labels the assertion that the monotheistic idea is the primary principle of Judaism as erroneous and chooses to regard it only as a secondary consequence of the transcendent God-idea, still much of the sketch, which can be drawn only in bare outline, may be viewed favorably. That monotheism is the primary principle of Judaism, we believe, is enunciated clearly enough by the first of the Ten Commandments and by the equally important sentence "Hear, O Israel! the Eternal, our God, is a single God!" A subjective view and interpretation must never be hypostatized in such a way that what was regarded for thousands of years by the most pious and wisest men as the foundation of Judaism, now is called an error, a hypostasis first made by Steinheim and which, all the more, should not be imitated because, as this coryphaeus shows, under the guise of the most enthusiastic allegiance to revelation it actually undermines it fully and exposes it to caprice. Our author has erred in speaking of primary and secondary levels when, fundamentally, there is only a single indivisible concept. Where the deity is not immanent, does not appear as a refined personification of the forces of nature, oneness is inseparable from God's essence, just as in the concept of a single God the notion of an extramundane God is already clearly implied. The sublimeness of the idea, however, presents itself first in the "oneness of God," which, as the antithesis of multiplicity, appears more directly to the intellectual faculty than the antithesis between the extramudane divine substance and pantheism. Moreover, the pagan world eventually moved beyond this and forgot that its cult originally served the deified forces of nature. Upon its entry, Judaism did not have to proclaim that there was a God, but that there was only one God, this was its particular principle; and the loftiest and noblest knowledge stemmed from it.

Granted that the controversy over the above passage is actually only a semantic one, still the claim which the author makes here that Judaism without the firm soil of material life resembles an inwardly hollowed-out and half-uprooted tree seems to be a very questionable generalization and leads to a result which, to judge from the author's own intention, he least of all intended. If the revealed Law—the Torah—is essentially bound to the soil, then it is not at all clear whether it would remain obligatory for those uprooted from this soil. The hope for the restoration of the state and for the Messiah would provide a weak reason for such a duty; and if the author had in mind here the view of Ramban at the end of מות יאחרי, then it still would require more precise reasons, just as Ramban himself avoided such general terms. (Cf. *ibid.*)

But the Mosaic constitution points to an idea different from the one which the author wishes to attribute to it. He sees in it only a political constitution and therefore leaves no place for the individual, pays no attention whatsoever to men as such. How far removed the Mosaic legislation actually is from this view is readily discernible in its two fundamental concerns: justice and virtue. These are its principal components; the former it shares with every political constitution, the latter it bears as the seal of the Divine Lawgiver. For this reason, the Mosaic legislation handles, not only the areas of action, but also the realm of the will. It is not limited only to questions of individual rights with negative commandments—the prohibition against infringing on the rights of another, the defense against injustice—but manifests as well a positive side as a goal, a partial surrender of our rights for the welfare of another. It commands virtue no less than justice. Thus, in the final analysis, the sentence: "Hear, O Israel: God is a single God," which expresses the basic principle of Judaism, is immediately followed by the commandment: "You should love the Eternal, your God," a pronouncement which could be addressed only to the individual who recognizes himself as independent, who in his immediacy feels close to the One who demands love and whose love he has experienced. The Mosaic legislation belongs in some respects to the state, but to a much greater extent to the individual, just as the divine lawgiver is not only the God of the land, but of the entire earth. (Zacharias Frankel)

7. In 1874, when volume one of Graetz's *Geschichte der Juden* eventually

appeared, it's point of departure, despite lengthy flashbacks, was the
period of the conquest.

8. A cryptic reference to the work of Isaac Jost. See Graetz, *Geschichte*, XI,
2nd ed., p. 414.

9. Particularly striking is the poetic formulation in the Talmud, according
to which the inclination toward idolatry יצרא דעבודה זרה was
exorcised by the prophets. (Yoma 69b, Sanhedrin 64a) [G].

10. An allusion to Daniel 7:6.

11. My colleague Prof. Menahem Schmelzer was kind enough to inform me
that Graetz was referring here to Judah ha-Levi's poem "Teshuvah
le-Mokhiah" in Ḥayim Shirman, *Ha-Shira ha-Ivrit be-Sefarad u-ve-
Provence*, I (Israel, 1959), p. 493, line 27.

12. A typical example is Josephus' report that the richest support
Sadduceeism; also the following remark attributed by *Megillat Taanit*
to the Sadducees:, משה רבינו אוהב ישראל היה, תקן להם עצרת לאחר שבת [G].

13. ארבעה דברים יצר הרע משיב עליהם, דכתיב בהן חוקה: אשת אח וכלאים ושעיר
המשתלח ופרה אדומה (*Num. Rab.* 19, 3). [G].

14. אפילו דברים שאתה רואה אותן יתרון למתן תורה כגון הלכות ציצית , תפילין ומזוזה,
אף הן בכלל מתן תורה (*Lev. Rab.* 22, 1) [G].

15. "Then one takes the books and reads aloud and another of especial
proficiency comes forward and expounds what is not understood. For
most of their philosophical study takes the form of allegory, and in this
they emulate the tradition of the past." (Philo, *Quod Omnis Probus
Liber*, Mangey, II, p. 458; Leob, IX, p. 57) [Graetz may well have
understood the final, somewhat ambiguous Greek phrase according to
the alternate translation suggested in a note in the Loeb edition: "with
ardour worthy of the men of old."] [G].

16. The following comparisons may serve to show that Philo's method of
exegesis has a distinct aggadic quality: "He says that in six days the
world was created, not that its Maker required a length of time for this
work, for we must think of God as doing all things simultaneously,
remembering that 'all' includes with the commands which He issues
the thought behind them. Six days are mentioned because for the things
coming into existence there was need of order, etc." (*De Opificio
Mundi*, Mangey, I, p. 3; Leob, I, p. 13) This is approximately the same
idea as expressed by the Aggada בעשרה מאמרות נברא העולם, והלא במאמר
אחד יוכל להבראות, אלא להיפרע מן הרשעים וכו'   where the number ten
implies merely a certain order. Well-known is Philo's aggadic
interpretation of מקום, referring to God, which is typically midrashic.
"God Himself is called a place by reason of His containing things, and
being contained by nothing whatever. . . . I, mark you, am not a place,
but in a place . . . the Diety, being contained by nothing, is of
necessity Itself Its own place." (*De Somniis*, Mangey, I, p. 630; Leob, V,
p. 329. Cf. also *De Fuga*, Mangey, I, p. 557; Leob, V, p. 51.) The same
concept is found in the Aggada מפני מה מכנין שמו של הקב"ה וקוראין
אותו מקום מפני שהוא מקומו של עולם ואין עולמו מקומו (*Gen. Rab.* 68, 10).
This particular comparison of Philo with the Aggada is still more

striking if we consider that he allegorizes the verse ויפגע במקום as "he met a Divine Logos," so that "Logos" is also called "place" (ibid.) The same seems to underlie the aggadic interpretation of ויפגע במקום as באת השכינה (Yalqut 117); for מימרא דה' = שכינה = Divine Logos. The peculiarity of Philo to allegorize biblical names by reference to their etymological roots is also to be found in the Aggada. For example, to choose one name from the many interpreted by Philo: בצלאל "Bezalel means, then, 'in the shadow of God'; but God's shadow in His word." (*Legum Allegoria*, Mangey, I, p. 106; Loeb, I, p. 365). Compare this with the Aggada ר' מאיר היה דורש שמות, ר' יהושע בן קרחה היה דורש שמות. ושם האיש אלימלך שהיה אומר אלי תבוא מלכות, ושם אשתו נעמי שהיו מעשיח נאים (*Rut Rab.* 2,5) On the basis of this material the assumption that Philo was entirely ignorant of Hebrew is still open to question. We certainly would not try to argue that the students of Aggada knew no Hebrew simply because they occasionally were guilty of some wild interpretations. [G].

17. *De Vita Mosis*, Mangey, II, p. 137; Loeb, VI, p. 457. [G].

18. "Nay, we should look on all these outward observances (the Sabbath, festivals, circumcision, sanctity of the Temple) as resembling the body, and their inner meanings as resembling the soul." (*De Migratione Abrahami*, Mangey, I, p. 450; Loeb, IV, p. 185). [G]

19. The four methods of interpreting Scripture signified by the acronym פרד"ס are well known. They were also used by the scholastics. Their names and functions are specified by the following two hexameters:
    Litera gesta docet, quid credas allegoria
    Moralis quid agas, quid speres anagogia.
    Thus *litera* is the equivalent of פשט (the plain sense), *allegoria* of רמז (an allusion), *moralis* of (a homily), דרוש and finally *anagogia* is the equivalent of סוד (the esoteric meaning). [G]

20. *Emunot ve-Deot*, introduction and VIII, 3. [G]

21. Cf. *Moreh Nebukhim* I, 71. Schmölders, *Essay sur les écoles philosophiques chez les arabes*, pp. 185ff. [G]

22. וחכמת הבורא ברעתה למעלה מכל מה שישינוהו המדברים (*Emunot ve-Deot*, II, 2) The same humble admission is found in Philo. After he expounded the views regarding the fact that the Torah was given in the desert, far removed from all human contact, he concludes: "These are the reasons suggested to answer the question under discussion; they are but probable surmises; the true reasons are known to God alone." (*De Decalogo*, Mangey, II, p. 183; Loeb, VII, p. 15) [G]

23. עשרת הדברים הם אמות התורה ושרשיה . Similarly Philo: "The Decalogue is a summary (or outline) of the particular laws." (*De Decalogo*, Mangey, II, p. 183; Loeb, VII, p. 15). [G]

24. Similarly Philo: "Circumcision is a symbol of the excision of pleasures." (*De Decalogo*, Mangey, II, p. 211; Loeb, VII, p. 105) [G]

25. לא תחשוב כי החכמה האלהית לבד היא הנמנעת מן ההמון אבל רוב חכמת הטבע וכבר נכפל לה אסרנו ולא במרכבה ביחיד ולא במעשה בראשית בשנים (*Moreh Nebukhim*, I, 17 and introduction). [G]

מבני אדם אנשים שיכבד עליהם נתינת סבה למצוה מן המצוות והטוב אצלם שלא יושכל למצוה ולא 26.
לאזהרה ענין כלל ואשר יביאם אל זה הוא חלי . . . שהם יחשבו שאם יהיו אלו התורות מועילות בזה
המציאות ומפני כך נצטוינו בהם יהיו כאלו באו מסחשבות והשכלות בעל שכל
(*Moreh Nebukhim*, III, 31; Cf. also p. 26). [G]

27. Permit me here to refute an attack made by Dr. Beer in Frankel's
Zeitschrift (1846 p. 120) against my assertion that Maimonides' view of
the sacrificial laws was very superficial, an assertion which I repeat here
without, however, intending in any way to tarnish Maimonides'
greatness or to diminish the great respect he enjoys. I had contended
that "Maimonides interpreted paganism only according to its outward
appearances in an entirely external manner and that in an equally
external fashion he juxtaposed Judaism to paganism, particularly to its
obscene cultic practices," and here I would like to add the proof. In
light of the fact that the Egyptians revered the ramlike constellation
Aries, and the Sabians worshiped demons in the form of goats, and
other idolators such as the Indians feared slaughtering cows, so that in
the pagan world these three species were forbidden for pleasure,
Maimonides insisted that Judaism commanded specifically these three
species as sacrificial animals (*Moreh Nebukhim* III, 46). In the same
manner Maimonides treats other commandments, such as the prohibition against bringing leaven or honey onto the alter. The entire
sacrificial system in fact was merely a concession to a weak people still
firmly attached to paganism. It is for this reason that I call this
exegetical method rationalistic, because it does not derive from the
inner nature of the substance, but rather is brought from the outside and
thereby amounts to little more than a nice insight. Or can Dr. Beer really
feel comfortable with the Maimonidean explanation that incense was
prescribed only to dispel the foul odors from the Temple courtyard left
by the sacrifices (ibid., 45)? Or with the view that the laws of
purity— דיני טומאה וטהרה —were intended only to make visits to the
Temple truly rare, because as a result of frequent visits the sense of
grandeur and awe, which the Temple should evoke, might be lost (ibid.,
47)? I have not characterized Maimonides' theory in the way that I have
because "it contradicts" my own, but because this is its basic character,
and "great teachers" of Judaism have long recognized and refuted this
weakness of the Maimonidean system, as is well-known to Dr. Beer.
Since when has it become the practice in Judaism to swear by the
teachings of the master in scientific studies? [G]

28. On Hegel's conflicting views of Judaism, see Nathan Rotenstreich,
"Hegel's Image of Judaism," *Jewish Social Studies*, XV (1953), pp.
33–52.

29. At the University of Breslau, Graetz had studied with Christian Julius
Braniss, a professor of philosophy and a noted Hegelian. Hans
Liebeschutz has suggested that Graetz's emphasis on transcendence
rather than monotheism as the theological essence of Judaism may well
have been inspired by Braniss. (See his *Das Judentum im deutschen
Geschichtsbild von Hegel bis Max Weber* [Tübingen, 1967], pp.
139–140).

30. The product of a mixed marriage and an assimilated home in Montpellier, Joseph Salvador turned to a study of ancient Judaism under the impact of the anti-Jewish riots in Germany in 1819. In a series of major works in French, he treated fully the nature of the Mosaic state, the Jewish origins of Christianity, and the rebellions against Rome, which he presented as heroic national movements. In his final work in 1860, he propounded a universal religious transformation which would realize the principles of pure Mosaism. (See now Paula Hyman, "Joseph Salvador: Proto-Zionist or Apologist for Assimilation?" *Jewish Social Studies*, XXXIV [1972], pp. 1–22.)

31. The author has offered a further discussion of his views on pp. 69–77 in a postscript in which he deals with the strictures made by us. We are pleased that the author agrees with our view and we regret that due to lack of space we are unable to print this postscript here. (Zacharias Frankel)

Chapter 2: Introduction to Volume Four of the *History of the Jews*

1. Translated by Rev. James K. Gutheim in his translation of Heinrich Graetz, *History of the Jews*, IV (New York, 1873). The translation has been slightly revised.

Chapter 3: Introduction to Volume Five of the *History of the Jews*

1. This is a veiled reference to Graetz's belief that the Pfefferkorn-Reuchlin controversy paved the way for Luther's Reformation. See our introduction pp. 53–55.

2. *Tana di Be Eliyahu Rabba*, Chapter 5. [G]

Chapter 4: The Rejuvenation of the Jewish Race (1864)

1. Published originally in the *Jahrbuch für Israeliten 5624*, edited by Josef Wertheimer and Leopold Kompert, X (1863–1864).

2. Cryptic reference to First Isaiah. See Isaiah 1:1.

3. Cf. Graetz, *Geschichte*, II, Part Two, 3rd ed., p. 68; also Ezra 2:64.

4. Graetz's essay with its interpretation of the Suffering Servant of Second Isaiah as referring to Israel and its messianic role quickly led to litigation. Following an attack on the essay by the well-known anti-Semitic *Wiener Kirchenzeitung*, the Viennese public prosecutor deferred charges against Leopold Kompert, the editor, since Graetz as a foreigner was beyond reach. Graetz's interpretation was accused of contradicting the teachings of Judaism, a religion officially recognized by the Austrian state, and violating the sensibilities of the Catholic

majority. The prosecutor singled out as particularly offensive Graetz's claim that to interpret the prophecy "as a single personality makes it a caricature and leads to romantic excesses." In the ensuing trial, Kompert was convicted on the second count, fined forty gulden, and forbidden to distribute his *Jahrbuch*. The copies which remained were to be destroyed. Never one to suffer an attack supinely, Graetz returned to the offensive in 1864 with his lengthy survey of the evolution of Jewish messianism. (See *AZJ*, 1864, pp. 29–36).

Chapter 5: The Stages in the Evolution of the Messianic Belief (1865)

1. Published originally in the *Jahrbuch für Israeliten 5625*, edited by Josef Wertheimer and Leopold Kompert, XI (1864–1865).

2. 'Ερήολαος the destroyer of the nation, a successful Greek copy of the biblical paradigm of animosity toward Israel, בלעם Balaam. A much better version appears in the Apocalypse of John as ‏ ‎, obviously also a translation for Balaam, and Nikolaiten stands for Balaamiten—תלמידיו של בלעם הרשע. The anti-messiah Eremolaos is already found in the Aramaic translation to Isaiah and to other biblical verses and constitutes a permanent figure in the messianic apocalyptic literature of the geonic period. In this apocalyptic literature a לופינוס קיסר is also mentioned as an anti-messianic figure, but this is a corruption of לטינוס קיסר. Also in the Apocalypse of John, Latinus is hidden behind the number 666 as anti-Christ, that is the numerical value of the Greek word Λατεινος: 30 + 1 + 300 + 5 + 10 + 70 + 200. Recent New Testament exegetes have tried to equate the number 666 with the two Hebrew words נרון קסר (Caesar Nero). But the Jews always wrote these two words *plene*, indicating the vowels, נירון קיסר, which adds up to 686. [G]

Chapter 6: Introduction to Volume One of the *History of the Jews* (1874)

1. Since the uninitiated so often accuse the people of Israel of arrogance because of its chosenness, a few passages are collected here in which the prophets deny Israel any inherent superiority. Deut. 9:4—5 "Not by virtue of your merit and the uprightness of your heart are you to possess the land." Amos 9:7 "You are the same to me as the Ethiopians." Amos 6:1–2 is to be taken in the same sense. Isaiah 42:19 "Who is as blind as My servant, as deaf as My messenger whom I am sending?" [G]

2. Reference to Ezekiel 16

3. Reference to Jeremiah 31:14ff.

Chapter 7: The Correspondence of an English Lady on Judaism and Semitism (1883)

1. Published anonymously as *Briefwechsel einer englischen Dame über Judenthum und Semitismus* (Stuttgart, 1883).
2. A light that does not shine.
3. The nickname for Great Russians in Little Russia.
4. The reference is to Heine's *Die Bäder von Lucca*, especially chapter nine. Hyacinth was the Germanized form of the all too Jewish Hirsch. Heine's deft satire of Hyacinth is a telling portrait of an alienated, ambitious, and thoroughly practical emancipated Jew.
5. In 1835–1836 young David Friedrich Strauss published a massive and radical historical study of Jesus, which treated the stories of the Gospels as myths and their discources as the composites of a later age. In the final work of his controversial career, entitled *The Old Faith and the New* and published in 1872, he fully repudiated the validity of traditional Christianity in the present scientific age. It is to this book which Graetz refers.
6. Oettingen was professor of theology at the University of Dorpat from 1856 to 1891. In 1868 he published a massive volume entitled *Die Moral Statistik und die christliche Sittenlehre*, which attempted to assess the level of contemporary European morality. This pioneering sociological work was revised and republished in 1874 and again in 1882 under the title *Die Moralstatistik in ihrer Bedeutung für eine Socialethik*. Graetz misspelled the author's name throughout his essay (Oettinger).
7. Maxime du Camp, *Paris, ses organes, ses fonctions et sa vie dans la 2. moitié du XIX siecle* (Paris, 1872). Graetz is quoting the passage as cited by Oettingen, 3rd ed., p. 196n.
8. In 1840, three years after Carlyle had introduced the English public to the French Revolution through his historical *tour de force*, he fully expounded his great-man theory of history in a series of biographical essays entitled *On Heroes and Hero-Worship*.
9. Peregrinus, nicknamed Proteus, was a second-century convert to Christianity of somewhat dubious character. After a career as a wandering preacher, he committed suicide in 165 by throwing himself on the flames at the Olympic games.
10. Apollonius of Tyana was a first-century Neo-Pythagorean sage who pursued a career as an ascetic, wandering preacher, miracle worker, and anti-Christian polemicist.
11. Alessandro Cagliostro was a Sicilian imposter, alchemist, medical quack, and self-styled founder of a new branch of Masonry, whose séances were the rage of Parisian society in the 1780s. After being expelled from France in 1786, he was convicted by the Inquisition in Rome and died in prison six years later.

12. John William Colenso was an Agnlican theologian who became Bishop of Natal in 1853. He translated the New Testament into Zulu and authored a six-volume work on *The Pentateuch and the Book of Joshua* in which he expressed doubts about the authenticity and historicity of the Pentateuch.

13. Bishop of Benevento who was martyred during the persecutions under Diocletian. A relic, preserved in a glass phial at the cathedral of Naples, often turned to liquid upon exposure.

14. Proving to you once again that against the spirit, matter can do nothing.

15. Henri Dominique Lacordaire (1802–1861) became a follower of Lamennais and a well-known preacher, who delivered his sermons in Notre Dame since 1835. After joining the Dominicans, he succeeded in gaining readmission into France for the order.

16. George Eliot began her literary career as the translator of Strauss and Feuerbach into English. As a talented novelist, she turned her attention to the Jewish question in 1876 in *Daniel Deronda*. (Penguin Books, 1967). In a desire to improve the image of Jews in England and disturbed by the prevailing ignorance of the Jewish component in Christianity, she delivered a powerful affirmation of Jewish nationhood and of the longing for national redemption in Palestine. The novel had a resounding impact in Jewish circles. See David Kaufmann, "George Eliot und das Judentum," *Gesammelte Schriften*, I (Frankfurt a. M., 1908), pp. 39–79. Graetz's reference is probably to the long speech on pp. 590–591.

17. Particularly *Coningsby* (1844) and *Tancred* (1847). Graetz added a paragraph on these two novels in the second edition of volume eleven of his *Geschichte* (1900), pp. 530–531. On Disraeli's Jewish consciousness, see the recent suggestive analysis by Isaiah Berlin, "Benjamin Disraeli, Karl Marx and the Search for Jewish Identity," *Midstream*, Aug.–Sept. 1970, pp. 29–49.

18. See Josephus, *Against Apion*, Leob ed., I, pp. 329–331.

19. The Broglies were an important French aristocratic family that had immigrated from Piedmont in the mid-seventeenth century. Charles Louis Victor, Prince de Broglie, served as a deputy to the Constituent Assembly from Alsace during the Revolution. He opposed Jewish emancipation. The eventual requirement of a special oath of citizenship for Jews wishing to gain emancipation was his proposal. In the 1830s his son served as a member of the board of directors of the Union Générale, a Catholic, monarchist-backed bank designed to break the alleged financial monopoly exercised by Jews and Protestants.

20. In September 1882, in the wake of the Tisza-Eszlár ritual murder case, Alexander Pinkert, the leader of the radical anti-Semites in Saxony, had convened the First International Anti-Jewish Congress in Dresden. The standing committee which was elected converted itself into the Alliance Anti juive Universelle, obviously to combat the Alliance Israélite Universelle. In 1883 a second congress convened in Chemnitz with delegates from Austria, Hungary, Russia, Rumania, Serbia, and France.

(See Nathaniel Katzburg, *Antisemitism in Hungary 1867–1914,* [Hebrew] [Tel Aviv, 1969], pp. 208–211.

21. Graetz's analysis of the motivations behind the readmission of the Jews to England in the mid-1650s in his *Geschichte,* X. 3rd. ed., pp. 85–87, 106, is not quite so moralistic.

22. Apion headed the anti-Jewish delegation sent from Alexandria to the Roman emperor, Caligula, after the riots of 38 C.E. He accused the Jews of failing to honor the emperor properly. Apion also authored a five-volume *History of Egypt* whose anti-Jewish tendency provoked Josephus to write his brilliant defense of Judaism, *Against Apion.*

23. Johannes Capistrano was a Franciscan monk who since 1451 had been traversing Austria and Germany to preach against the Hussites. In 1453, as Papal legate, Capistrano came to Poland to assist the local clergy with his incendiary public speeches in their campaign against Casimir IV's liberal Jewish policy.

24. Thomas de Torquemada, prior of the Dominican monastery of Santa Cruz in Segovia and confessor to Queen Isabella, was appointed in 1483 as inquisitor general for all territories under the Spanish monarchs. Under his efficient leadership, the Inquisition became the major instrument for the liquidation of Spanish Jewry.

25. Victor von Istoczy and Géza von Onody were both members of the Hungarian parliament and leaders of contemporary political anti-Semitism in Hungary. Together they effectively incited public opinion over the alleged ritual murder at Tisza-Eszlár in 1882. Both men also attended the international congress of anti-Semites in Dresden in September 1882.

26. George Heinrich August Ewald was one of the "Göttingen Seven" who refused to recognize the abolition of the Hanoverian Constitution in 1837 and were immediately deposed. A major semitic and biblical scholar, Ewald's multivolume *Geschichte des Volkes Israel* (3rd ed., 1864–1868) was a pioneering work much admired by Graetz.

27. The pogroms of 1881 in southern Russia erupted in the middle of April and lasted through the summer, effecting more than 100 Jewish communities, including the centers of Kiev and Odessa.

28. The actual German word is "Halbasien" and was taken by Graetz from the title of the enormously popular essays on eastern Europe, *Aus Halb-Asien,* published in two volumes in 1876 by Karl Emil Franzos, a Jewish writer born in Galicia of a German father and a Russian mother. (See Ludwig Geiger, *Deutsche Literatur und die Juden* [Berlin, 1910], pp. 250–304).

29. *Heinrich Heine über Ludwig Börne,* in *Heinrich Heines Sämtliche Werke,* edited by Ludwig Holthof, 9th ed. (Stuttgart, n.d.), pp. 926–927.

30. Since 1868 Alphonse de Rothschild headed the Parisian branch of the family. He was also the director of the important railroad company Chemin de fer du Nord and one of the members of the board of directors of the Banque de France. A member of the Consistoire Central

des Israélites de France since 1851, he became its president in 1869 and served the Jewish community in numerous ways.

31. An allusion to Montesquieu, *The Spirit of the Lqws,* trans. by Thomas Nugent and introd. by Franz Neumann (N.Y., 1966), p. 365.

32. Graetz appears to be quoting from memory, because his awkward French varies considerably from Renan. Cf. "Identité originelle et séparation graduelle du judaïsme et du christianisme," in Ernest Renan, *Discours et Conférences* (Paris, 1887), p. 333. This address was actually given on May 26, 1883 before the Société des Études Juives.

33. Graetz had met Marx and his wife in Karlsbad in the summer of 1876. Later Marx sent Graetz two photographs and a copy of *Das Kapital.* Graetz's warm response is republished by Arthur Prinz, "New Perspectives on Marx as a Jew," *LBIYB,* XV (1970), pp. 121–122.

34. An ambitious and frustrated Roman politician, who, abandoned constitutional methods to lead an unsuccessful rebellion in January 62 B.C.E.

35. *The Fifty-Third Chapter of Isaiah according to the Jewish Interpreters,* translated by S. R. Driver and A. Neubauer with an introduction by E.B. Pusey (Oxford & London, 1877).

36. Berthold Auerbach, an important German Jewish writer of the nineteenth century, is best known for his *Dorfgeschichten.* The eruption of German anti-Semitism in the 1870s depressed him greatly. When Ignaz von Döllinger, the renowned Catholic theologian and historian who had repudiated the recent doctrine of papal infallibility and been duly excommunicated, publicly indicted Christianity for the tragedies of medieval Jewish history, Auerbach felt moved to express his gratitude in a personal letter. (Published in the *AZJ,* 1881, p. 555.)

37. Emilio Castelar (1832–1899), Spanish politician, writer, and historian, whose works enjoyed a wide audience.

38. Ernst Haeckl, professor of zoology at the University of Jena, became the leading apostle of Darwin's theories in Germany. Moving from science to philosophy, Haeckl vigorously propagated a materialistic, monist theory of existence in which all transcendental concepts were abandoned. His quasi-religious views enjoyed enormous popularity and led to the formation in 1906 of a federation of monists for the purpose of disseminating the faith.

39. Émile Burnouf, the author of six long essays on "La Science des Religions: sa Methode et ses Limites," in the *Revue des deux mondes,* LIV (1864), LXXIV (1868), LXXVI (1868), LXXVII (1868), LXXXII (1869). Graetz's quotation appears in volume LXXVI, p. 868 in a somewhat different order.

40. Although in the text Graetz cites p. 461 as the source for this quotation, I have been unable to locate it on that page in any of the three editions of Oettingen's work.

41. Graetz cites p. 583 as his source, but again I have been unable to locate this material on that page in any of the editions.

42. On the nature of and reason for Tacitus's virulent anti-Semitism, see the superb Hebrew essay by Yoḥanan Levi, *'Olamot Nifgashim* (Jerusalem, 1960), pp. 115–196.

43. Again I have been unable to find this material in any of the editions on the page (310) cited by Graetz.

44. Graetz seems to be referring to the Free Religious Association founded by James William Potter, a former Unitarian minister, in Boston in 1867. F.A. Hinkley served as its secretary. According to its constitution, the association was "to promote the interests of pure religion, to encourage the scientific study of theology, and to increase fellowship in the spirit." The mid-1870s proved to be the association's most active period. From 1879 to 1882 Felix Adler served as its president. He left to found the Society for Ethical Culture. (See Stow Persons, *Free Religion* [Boston, 1963]).

45. Ernest Renan, professor of Semitic languages at the Collège de France, was the first Catholic to write a life of Jesus in the nineteenth century. In a series of other studies, he tried to give a complete account of the history and dogma of the early Church. His interest in the origins of Christianity brought him to write a five-volume *Histoire du peuple d'Israël des origins à l'époque romaine* (1887–1893). (See S. Almog, "The Racial Motif in Renan's Attitude towards Judaism and Jews," Hebrew, *Zion*, XXXII, 1967, pp. 175–200.) The two lectures on Judaism referred to by Graetz were printed in Renan, *Discours et Conférences* (Paris, 1887).

46. Ibid., pp. 320–321. Graetz is quoting a bit loosely.

47. Ibid., p. 336.

48. Ibid., pp. 335–336.

49. Ibid., pp. 336–337.

50. Graetz rejected the documentary hypothesis unequivocally. See his *Geschichte*, II, part one, 2nd ed., pp. 408–439.

51. Separate in food and apart in bed.

52. *The Ethics of the Fathers* 1:2.

53. The reference is to Theodor Mommsen's famous contribution to the Treitschke debate reprinted in Walter Boehlich, *Der Berliner Antisemitismusstreit*, pp. 212–227. Graetz's paraphrase reflects his interpretation of Mommsen's somewhat ambiguous advice to the Jews. The ambiguity is now fully resolved by the recent publication of a letter which Mommsen wrote to a converted Jew in 1882, in which he spelled out what he meant: German nationality is inseparable from Christianity and eventually the Jews will have to convert. (See Stanley Zucker, "Theodor Mommsen and Antisemitism," *LBIYB*, XVII [1972], pp. 237–241.)

54. At the Congress of Berlin in 1878, which stripped Russia of the spoils she had taken on the battlefield against Turkey, Jewish diplomatic efforts succeeded in making the emancipation of Romanian Jewry a prior condition for the recognition of Romanian independence. But this

noteworthy diplomatic victory brought neither collective emancipation nor an improvement in the living conditions of Romanian Jews. Ignoring the Congress, the government maintained and even increased the Jewish disabilities during the ensuing decades.

Chapter 8: Historical Parallels in Jewish History (1887)

1. Translated by Joseph Jacobs in *Papers Read at the Anglo-Jewish Historical Exhibition 1887* (London, 1888).
2. In the spring of 1753, Parliament passed a naturalization bill which granted individual resident Jews the opportunity to be naturalized without first having to take the Anglican sacrament of Communion. The act aroused such widespread and virulent opposition throughout the country that by December 1753 Parliament had fully repealed it. For a brilliant political interpretation see Thomas W. Perry, *Public Opinion, Propaganda, and Politics in Eighteenth-Century England* (Cambridge, Mass., 1962).

Chapter 9: The Significance of Judaism for the Present and the Future (1889-1900)

1. Published originally in English in *The Jewish Quarterly Review*, I (1889), pp. 4–13; II (1890), pp. 257–269.
2. The thesis is actually that of Émile Burnouf. See *supra*, p. 231.
3. Solomon Schechter, "The Dogmas of Judaism," *JQR*, I (1889), pp. 48–61, 115–127. In this important historical study, Schechter challenged the long prevailing view, shared by Graetz as well, that Judaism is a religion without dogmas.
4. Israel Zangwill, "English Judaism," *JQR*, I (1889), pp. 376–407. In this essay, prompted by the earlier pieces of Schechter and Graetz, Zangwill came down particularly hard on Graetz for what he regarded as an arbitrary, unhistorical, and wholly naturalistic definition of Judaism. Zangwill, who contended like Schechter that Judaism does control belief, saw little to distinguish Graetz's conception from the Liberal Judaism of Claude Joseph G. Montefiore.
5. Jacques Bénigne Bossuet (1627–1704) was a French bishop, historian, and preacher. His *Discours sur l'histoire universelle* (1681) was a learned and celebrated specimen of sacred history.
6. Henry Thomas Buckle, the author of a much heralded unfinished two-volume *History of Civilization in England* (1857–1861) which epitomized the general effort to render history a pure science. Buckle tried to relate progress directly to the amount, nature, and diffusion of knowledge.
7. The talmudists very keenly realised this element in the Jewish

conception of God אלהיהם של אלו שונאי זמה "The God of Israel hates unchastity, bestiality." [G]

8. The views of modern criticism that represent both David and Solomon as polytheists and fix the date when Yahvism developed into monotheism at as late a period as possible, are contradicted by the fact that in Solomon's Temple the Holy of Holies (צבור) lay towards the west, just as in the description of the Tabernacle, the entrance to it was in the east, and the Holy of Holies in the west. As Helios was worshipped by almost all nations, the centre of the temple, the *Adyton*, was turned towards the east. The contrast between the Israelitish and the polytheistic temple arrangements is strikingly given in Ezekiel 8:17. He saw twenty-five Israelites, worshippers of idols, standing at the entrace of the inner temple towards which they turned their backs, while they looked towards the east and prayed to the sun in the east, והמה משתחוים קדמה לשמש. If Solomon had been still a polytheist, he must have placed the Holy of Holies in his temple in the east. [G]

9. "They have deified the goat, just as the Greeks are said to have honoured Priapus, because of the generative member, for this animal has a very great propensity for copulation, and it is fitting that honor be shown to that member of the body which is the cause of generation, being, as it were, the primal author of all animal life. And, in general, not only the Egyptians but not a few other peoples as well have in the rites they observe treated the male member as sacred, on the ground that it is the cause of the generation of all creatures. . . ." (Diodorus of Sicily in Loeb, I, p. 299.) [G]

10. *Aboth di R. Nathan*, ed. Schechter, Version II., page 2. [G]

Selected Bibliography
on Graetz's Work

Abrahams, Israel. "H. Graetz, the Jewish Historian." *JQR*, IV (1892), 165–194.

Baron, Salo W. "Heinrich (Hirsch) Graetz, 1817–1891." *History and Jewish Historians*. Philadelphia, 1964, 263–275.

Bernfeld, Simon. "Dorshe Reshumot." *Ha-Shiloah*, II (1897), 396–407.

Bloch, Philip. "Memoir of Heinrich Graetz." Graetz, *History of the Jews*. Vol. VI. Philadelphia, 1956, 1–86.

Brann, M., ed. *Heinrich Graetz: Abhandlungen zu seinem 100. Geburtstage*. Vienna and Berlin, 1917.

Ettinger, Shmuel. "Mifalo ha-Historiografi shel Graetz." *Historionim ve-Askolot Historiot*. Jerusalem, 1963, 84–92.

————. "Yahadut ve-Toldot ha-Yehudim b-Tefisato shel Graetz." Ettinger, ed. *Heinrich Graetz: Darkhe ha-Historiah ha-Yehudit*. Jerusalem, 1969, 7–36.

Feuchtwanger, Ludwig. "Zur Geschichtstheorie des jungen Graetz von 1846." *Die Konstruktion der jüdischen Geschichte*. Berlin, 1936, 97–107.

Herlitz, Georg. "Three Jewish Historians: Isaak Markus Jost—Heinrich Graetz—Eugen Täubler." *LBIYB*, IX (1964), 69–90.

Kaufmann, David. "H. Graetz." *Gesammelte Schriften*. Vol. I. Frankfurt a. M., 1908, 272–282.

Lewkowitz, Albert. *Das Judentum und die geistigen Strömungen des 19. Jahrhunderts*. Breslau, 1935, 375–382.

Liebeschütz, Hans. *Das Judentum im deutschen Geschichtsbild von Hegel bis Max Weber*. Tübingen, 1967, 132–156.

Meisl, Josef. *Heinrich Graetz*. Berlin, 1917.

Michael, Reuwen. "Graetz und Hess." *LBIYB*, IX (1964), 91–121.

319

_____ "Zavi Graetz—Toldot Hayav." Ettinger, ed., *Heinrich Graetz: Darkhe ha-Historiah ha-Yehudit.* Jerusalem, 1969, 37–51.

Rippner, Benjamin. *Zum siebzigsten Geburtstage des Prof. Dr. Heinrich Graetz.* Magdeburg, 1887.

Rotenstreich, Nathan. *Ha-Mahshaba ha-Yehudit ba'Eit ha-Hadasha.* Vol. I. Tel Aviv, 1966, 71–84.

_____. "Nisyono shel Graetz be-Pilosofia shel ha-Historia." *Zion,* VIII (1943), 51–59.

_____. *Tradition and Reality.* New York, 1972, 49–61.

Wiener, Max. *Jüdische Religion im Zeitalter der Emanzipation.* Berlin, 1933, 217–227.

Index